THE
COMPLETE
IDIOT'S
GUIDE® TO

Success as a Teacher

by Anthony D. Fredericks, Ed.D.

ALPHA

A member of Penguin Group (USA) Inc.

To Mike McGough— for his steadfast camaraderie, sincere friendship, and bounteous humor …
may they always be constants!

ALPHA BOOKS

Published by the Penguin Group

Penguin Group (USA) Inc., 375 Hudson Street, New York, New York 10014, U.S.A.

Penguin Group (Canada), 10 Alcorn Avenue, Toronto, Ontario, Canada M4V 3B2 (a division of Pearson Penguin Canada Inc.)

Penguin Books Ltd, 80 Strand, London WC2R 0RL, England

Penguin Ireland, 25 St Stephen's Green, Dublin 2, Ireland (a division of Penguin Books Ltd)

Penguin Group (Australia), 250 Camberwell Road, Camberwell, Victoria 3124, Australia (a division of Pearson Australia Group Pty Ltd)

Penguin Books India Pvt Ltd, 11 Community Centre, Panchsheel Park, New Delhi—110 017, India

Penguin Group (NZ), cnr Airborne and Rosedale Roads, Albany, Auckland 1310, New Zealand (a division of Pearson New Zealand Ltd)

Penguin Books (South Africa) (Pty) Ltd, 24 Sturdee Avenue, Rosebank, Johannesburg 2196, South Africa

Penguin Books Ltd, Registered Offices: 80 Strand, London WC2R 0RL, England

International Standard Book Number: 1-59257-380-0
Library of Congress Catalog Card Number: 2005925418

07 06 05   8 7 6 5 4 3 2 1

Interpretation of the printing code: The rightmost number of the first series of numbers is the year of the book's printing; the rightmost number of the second series of numbers is the number of the book's printing. For example, a printing code of 05-1 shows that the first printing occurred in 2005.

Printed in the United States of America

Note: This publication contains the opinions and ideas of its author. It is intended to provide helpful and informative material on the subject matter covered. It is sold with the understanding that the author and publisher are not engaged in rendering professional services in the book. If the reader requires personal assistance or advice, a competent professional should be consulted.

The author and publisher specifically disclaim any responsibility for any liability, loss, or risk, personal or otherwise, which is incurred as a consequence, directly or indirectly, of the use and application of any of the contents of this book.

Most Alpha books are available at special quantity discounts for bulk purchases for sales promotions, premiums, fund-raising, or educational use. Special books, or book excerpts, can also be created to fit specific needs.

For details, write: Special Markets, Alpha Books, 375 Hudson Street, New York, NY 10014.

Publisher: *Marie Butler-Knight*
Product Manager: *Phil Kitchel*
Senior Managing Editor: *Jennifer Bowles*
Senior Acquisitions Editor: *Randy Ladenheim-Gil*
Development Editor: *Christy Wagner*
Production Editor: *Megan Douglass*

Copy Editor: *Nancy Wagner*
Cartoonist: *Shannon Wheeler*
Cover/Book Designer: *Trina Wurst*
Indexer: *Brad Harriman*
Layout: *Becky Harmon*
Proofreading: *Mary Hunt*

Contents at a Glance

Contents

Appendixes

Foreword

I could tell you *The Complete Idiot's Guide to Success as a Teacher* is the most comprehensive classroom management desktop reference for teachers I've seen in dozens of years in education. And it is. I could tell you the book is devoid of educationeze wordiness. And it is. I could tell you it's an enjoyable read that's also super-organized, making it easy to find just what one needs. And it certainly is. But these statements would still not convey the flavor of this extraordinary effort.

From step one on day one in the classroom, teachers using this book know we won't make the journey alone. Tony Fredericks is there, holding our hands, providing both advice and ideas honed through his many years in the classroom. Tony knows well that classroom management skills can make or break a teacher, and he makes sure we're given all the information needed, in depth, to make all teachers successful.

The classroom can be a lonely place, and Tony's book is a comforting presence. This 368-page wonder starts by examining the reasons most of us decided to teach and quickly segues into concrete suggestions on how to be the best teacher one can be. Tony's classroom teacher's voice comes through loud and clear as the book takes us through personal goals for our classrooms, coping with administrative requirements, meeting and greeting parents (as well as making them an integral part of our teaching), and even the physical arrangement of the classroom.

Discipline and homework questions are dealt with head on: How much homework? How often? Special needs children in your classroom? There's an invaluable section on legal terms with which to become familiar and some especially successful practices in the area of special education. Working with the gifted is information for another section. Then there's how-to for field trips, hosting visiting authors, the elements of a balanced literacy program, science processes, steps to process writing, and math tips for teachers.

Whew! Are you envisioning a book that's a mile high? Not on Tony's watch. Remember, he's been there and knows how little time teachers have, whether it's the newbie learning as much as possible as quickly as possible, or the 21-year veteran looking for a refresher. The super-organization referred to earlier has chunked all the content into short, concise paragraphs that provide just the right—and critical—amount of information. The sidebars extend information when necessary, and other format devices make quick reference a breeze.

After spending time with this book, I feel it shouldn't be reserved for teachers. One can only hope lawmakers and critics of teachers will flip through it for enlightenment. In browsing its breadth and depth, they just might become more aware of the enormity of the compendium of skills required of any teacher.

We should all be thankful for Tony Fredericks who, in *The Complete Idiot's Guide to Success as a Teacher*, has given us a step-by-step roadmap to make us all stars at classroom management's best practices.

Patricia M. Broderick
Vice president/editorial director
Teaching K–8 magazine

Ms. Broderick worked as a teacher and an educational book editor before cofounding, with Allen Raymond, *Early Years* magazine in 1970. After selling their company to Highlights for Children in 1985, they changed the magazine's name and scope to *Teaching K–8*. Ms. Broderick directs the course of the magazine and visits schools and classrooms around the country every month except July and August to secure the school story, a monthly feature in every issue. She also writes a monthly review column for the magazine and its website. She lives totally in the teacher's world, keeping up with curricula, management, strategies, and so on. And she still gets excited over her work every day. For the past 18 summers, Ms. Broderick has worked at the Highlights Foundation Writers Workshop at Chautauqua.

Introduction

I travel around the United States as a visiting children's author. I talk to students about my role as an author, how I use the same processes of writing in my work as they do in their classrooms, and some of the discoveries I've made about the natural world as I gather materials for my books. I also have the privilege of working with teachers in a wide range of schools. We talk about teaching strategies and techniques that stimulate, encourage, and energize students. I lead workshops and present keynote addresses at education conferences and conventions every year. Always, I discover people who are interested in the learning/teaching process—how to be better learners and how to be effective teachers.

I wrote this book for many reasons. The most important was because there was a need for one concise, down-to-earth, practical guide on successful teaching. This is not a textbook—you've read too many of those—especially the ones filled with dull theories and long-winded explanations that say little yet take up lots of pages (and lots of your $$$). What you have in your hands is a resource that brings it all together, lays out all the basics, and shows you what you need to know. No long-winded sermons; no excruciatingly complex theories. My focus in writing this book was on three words: *practical, practical, practical!*

For me, teaching is the most exciting profession I know. But after more than three decades as an educator, I also know there's lots to master and lots to learn. I hope this book will be your personal guide to a lifetime of teaching success. Read it often, and refer to it frequently. You're about to begin an exciting journey!

How to Use This Book

Becoming a successful educator is not about theories and hypotheses. It's about the day-to-day practical strategies and no-nonsense techniques that work in real classrooms with real students. I've organized this book into five sections to tell you exactly what you need to know. Teaching is always challenging, but learning to be a good teacher doesn't have to be.

Part 1, **"Teaching and Learning: The Dynamic Duo,"** gives you an inside look into the field of education. You'll discover how the human brain learns and the qualities and attributes of an effective teacher (like you).

Part 2, **"Making It Happen,"** shows you how to make that all-important first day memorable, how to create the best possible lesson plan, how to make use of the incredible variety of teaching resources at your disposal, and how to test your students.

You'll learn the secrets of time management—one of the persistent concerns of teachers everywhere.

Part 3, "Effective Teaching, Effective Learning," is chock full of practical ideas and sensible solutions. You'll discover the secrets of an effective presentation, how to question your students, how to use group work in any subject or any grade, and how to promote thinking skills. And you'll learn motivational techniques that you can use from day one.

Part 4, "Management Tools (or How to Maintain Your Sanity and Keep Your Job)," details the procedures for creating a positive learning environment, preventing discipline problems (or handling the ones that do arise), presenting effective homework assignments, and creating some special projects for any classroom. You'll also discover a wealth of tips for all your special needs students.

Part 5, "Different Folks, Different Strokes," discusses all the people you need to know and need to work with as a teacher. You'll discover how to effectively teach all the elementary subjects, what you need to know as a secondary teacher, which people in a school can help you, and how to reach out and involve parents. You'll also discover ways to reduce the stress in your life and plan for a long-term teaching career.

I've also provided you with lots and lots of practical resources you can use every day. There's a glossary of terms used in the teaching world, a comprehensive listing of valuable websites, a list of some creative teacher resource books, an array of nonfiction children's literature, and valuable information on teacher certification tests. You'll find all these in the appendixes.

More Bang for Your Buck

In addition to all the practical tips, ideas, and strategies throughout this book, I've included several sidebars that provide you with even more stuff to help you succeed.

It's Elementary

These boxes hold interesting or fascinating ideas that have particular application in the elementary classroom.

Secondary Thoughts

Here, you will discover a thought or perspective particularly relevant to secondary teachers.

Fire Alarm _____

Remember fire drills when you were in school? Well, these boxes are similar. Here you'll learn about some of the things you need to watch out for.

 Expert Opinion _____

These are tips, ideas, and stories I've collected from teachers all over the United States and Canada. I've also included some of my own experiences and stories.

 Jabberwocky _____

Just like any other field, teaching has its own set of terminology and vocabulary. I define some of that lingo for you in clear and simple language in these boxes.

Acknowledgments

Teachers are fortunate to work in a fraternity that supports, encourages, and stimulates its members to achieve and succeed. Authors are no different. In fact, any book (this one included) is never really the sole effort of the author whose name appears on the cover. I have been most fortunate to enjoy the contributions and deliberations of a veritable army of advisers, colleagues, and friends—all of whom have made this book far better than I could have ever done on my own.

First of all, I would like to give a standing ovation and thunderous applause to a most incredible "brain trust" of colleagues at York College of Pennsylvania who offered insights, perspectives, and frequent reality checks throughout the creation of this book. They include Pete Piepmeier, Mike McGough, Phil Monteith, Brian Glandon, Mary Louise Hooper, Dave Kochik, Stacey Dammann, Bonnie Blake-Kline, Rick Mauro, and Deb Watkins. I am equally honored to have had the advice and suggestions of two long-time friends and incredibly dynamic teachers—Vicky Lynott and Jane Piepmeier, both of whom know how to "cut to the chase" and provide practical, engaging advice.

To all the teachers who invited me into their classrooms, I extend a warm and gracious "Thank you." I was privileged and honored to observe exciting lessons and dynamic teachers in classrooms scattered throughout the United States. Educators in California, Florida, North Carolina, Oregon, Nevada, Colorado, Illinois, Arizona, Hawaii, Iowa,

Louisiana, Maryland, Maine, Michigan, Wisconsin, New York, New Hampshire, South Carolina, Washington, Virginia, New Jersey, and Delaware opened their classrooms to me and shared their sage advice—allowing me to pick their brains and view the realities of day-to-day teaching. I am forever indebted to their spirit, creativity, and dedication to the highest ideals of teaching excellence.

My sincerest appreciation to my agent, Kim Lionetti, who connected me to this project. She exemplifies the highest ideals of the publishing industry—informative, dedicated to her clients, and personable. Thanks, Kim, you're the greatest!

A tip of the hat (and lots of "warm fuzzies") to Randy Ladenheim-Gil, an editor extraordinaire who brought insight, patience, and support to the initial stages of this project. I am equally indebted to Christy Wagner, who capably shepherded this project through the maze of publication tasks and deadlines. So, too, does the guidance and direction provided by Megan Douglass truly deserve lots of "high fives."

Above all, I am forever indebted to my wife, Phyllis, who not only embraced this project from the very beginning but also took on extra duties ("Sweetheart, would you mind taking out the trash this week?"), endured forgotten "honey do's" ("I promise to clear out the attic in the spring. No, really!") and suffered long, empty weekends ("We'll go to Hawaii after I finish the last chapter. I promise!"). Without her support and encouragement, this project would never have been possible. She is my rock and my love.

Trademarks

All terms mentioned in this book that are known to be or are suspected of being trademarks or service marks have been appropriately capitalized. Alpha Books and Penguin Group (USA) Inc. cannot attest to the accuracy of this information. Use of a term in this book should not be regarded as affecting the validity of any trademark or service mark.

Part 1

Teaching and Learning: The Dynamic Duo

For as long as you can remember, you've always wanted to be a teacher. Or maybe you have decided to make a career change and step into the wild and wonderful world of education. Whatever your reason for becoming an educator, you are beginning to realize that teaching is much more than working with a bunch of kids for nine months each year and having long summer vacations.

Part 1 introduces you to the many hats you will wear as a teacher, the working of the human brain when it is learning something, and the qualities you need to become the most effective teacher possible. This part is like three college semesters all crammed together—an instant collection of basic facts and practical information you need to become an effective and memorable teacher. So fasten your seat belt—you're in for a great ride!

> *Oliver's Law:* Experience is something you don't get until just after you need it.

An Inside Look

In This Chapter

- ◆ Who is this book for?
- ◆ Facts and figures
- ◆ Roles of a teacher
- ◆ Major teaching issues and concerns
- ◆ What they never told you in college
- ◆ What this book can do for you

Individuals become teachers for a variety of reasons: to make a difference in the lives of youngsters, to impart wisdom and an excitement for learning as the result of an influential teacher in their lives, or to follow in the footsteps of a relative (mother, aunt, grandfather) who was a teacher.

Although your reasons for becoming a teacher are personal and unique, know that you're among a select group of individuals—people who make a difference. Not everybody is cut out to be a teacher; teaching takes a special combination of talents, attitude, commitment, and knowledge. It is truly one of the most demanding of professions, yet it is also one of the most satisfying.

First Things First: Who Is This Book For?

So you want to be a teacher. Or maybe you've been teaching for a few years. You might even be in the middle of a teacher education program and need some immediate answers. Or perhaps you've just gotten your first teaching job and are wondering, *What do I do now?* This book is full of practical information, advice, resources, and ideas for teachers—and teachers-to-be—at all levels.

"I'm Thinking About Teaching as a Career"

You may be in high school, preparing to enter college, or already enrolled in college. Perhaps you're unsure of a career path or what you want to be "when you grow up." You might be wondering if teaching is the field for you. I've designed this book to provide you with a complete and thorough overview of effective teaching and what good teachers need to be successful. Use this book as an introduction to the skills and talents necessary for a successful career in education.

"I'm Already in a Teacher Education Program and Need Answers"

Perhaps you've taken some teacher education courses or you might be looking ahead to your student teaching experience. You're wondering if you have everything you need to be successful as a classroom teacher. You might be asking yourself, *What do I really need to know before student teaching? Do I have the necessary skills to be a good teacher? Besides the theories, are there any practical strategies I need to know?* or *I'm scared, can you help?*

These are all important and relevant questions which I'll help you find the answers to so you can and will succeed!

"I've Just Been Hired for My First Teaching Job. What Do I Do Now?"

You've worked long and hard to get to this point—your first job. But now you're probably asking yourself lots of questions. Your anxiety level is building, and your stressors are escalating because now you have to put everything you have learned into practice.

Don't be so hard on yourself! Your feelings at this point are the same as every other beginning teacher's. I had them when I began, and so do thousands of other teachers just prior to that all-important first day. This book will offer you down-to-earth suggestions that will ease your transition into teaching, deal with the challenges you face, and ensure your success from day one.

"I've Been Teaching for a While and Want to Improve"

Congratulations! One of the major signs of a good teacher is the realization that you can never know everything about teaching. One of the reasons why I've been in this profession for more than 30 years is the anticipation that there's always something new to learn.

As a practiced teacher, you, like your students, might be looking for some new perspectives, new information, or new solutions to common challenges. Rest assured, this book will provide you with practical ideas garnered from experienced teachers in urban, suburban, and rural schools—large and small—and in communities just like yours. Tap into their expertise, and take advantage of their insights.

Why Teach? What's in It for You?

Teaching is an incredibly rewarding career! It offers unlimited possibilities to influence generations of students, imparting to them the excitement of learning, the passion of discovery, and the magic of an inquisitive mind. Some would say that teaching is a calling; it's a way of life rather than just a way to make a living.

Expert Opinion

"I touch the future. I teach."
—Christa McAuliffe

In the "old days," teaching was quite different. For example, take a look at these rules for teachers, circa 1915:

You will not marry during the term of your contract.

You are not to keep company with men.

You must be home between the hours of 8 P.M. and 6 A.M. unless attending a school function.

You may not loiter downtown in ice-cream stores.

You may not travel beyond city limits unless you have the permission of the chairman of the board.

You may not ride in a carriage or automobile with any man unless he is your father or brother.

You may not smoke cigarettes.

You may not dress in bright colors.

You may under no circumstances dye your hair.

You must wear at least two petticoats.

Your dresses must not be any shorter than two inches above the ankle.

To keep the school room neat and clean, you must:

> Sweep the floor at least once daily
>
> Scrub the floor at least once a week with hot, soapy water
>
> Clean the blackboards at least once a day
>
> Start the fire at 7 A.M. so the room will be warm by 8 A.M.

Teaching is both a science and an art. It is also a passion, a way of making a difference in the lives of others. It is the shaping of minds and the shaping of futures.

Just the Facts, Ma'am

If you're thinking about a career in education or even if you're just beginning your first year of teaching, consider the following interesting facts and figures about teachers and teaching.

Teacher Demand

Over the course of the next decade, schools will need to hire more than 2 million *elementary* and *secondary teachers*.

According to the American Association for Employment in Education (AAEE), the following teaching fields are in demand:

- ◆ **Fields with considerable shortage:** special education, physics, mathematics education, chemistry

- ◆ **Fields with some shortage:** bilingual education, Spanish, Japanese, earth/physical sciences, English as a second language, general science, computer science education

- ◆ **Fields with balanced supply and demand:** reading, elementary education, French, German, music, English/language arts, middle school, business education, art, driver education, social studies, health education

- **Fields with some surplus:** physical education, dance education
- **Fields with considerable surplus:** none

You can obtain the most current information from the AAEE's website: www.aaee.org.

Jabberwocky

In most states, **elementary teachers** are those who teach preschool up through grade 6. **Secondary teachers** are those who teach in grades 7 through 12.

Average Teacher Salaries

Teacher salaries are geographical; teachers in some states earn more than teachers in other states, and teachers in some regions of the country earn less than teachers in other regions of the country. Even school districts within the same county or parish will have different pay scales.

- In 2003, the average teacher salary (nationally) was $45,771 (up 3.3 percent from the previous year).
- In 2003, the average beginning teacher salary (nationally) was $30,496 (up 3.2 percent from the previous year).
- In 2003, California had the highest average teacher salary at $55,693.
- In 2003, South Dakota had the lowest average teacher salary at $32,414.
- In 2004, Alaska had the highest average beginning teacher salary at $38,597.
- In 2004, Montana had the lowest average beginning teacher salary at $23,790.

Your Many Roles as a Teacher

As a teacher, you will wear many hats. You don't just teach; you are a multiple-personality-type person who satisfies many roles in the lives of your students and the school. Take a look at some of the multi-faceted responsibilities you'll assume as a teacher:

- Doctor/nurse (patching up bruised elbows and knees)
- Counselor (patching up bruised egos and personalities)
- Confidant (patching up bruised friendships and love lives)
- Surrogate parent (explaining the facts of life)

- Traffic cop (keeping the peace with bus duty and hall duty)

- Accountant (handling lunch money, field trip money, book and club money)

- Social worker (understanding family relations)

- Interior decorator (creating posters and decorations)

- Repair person (fixing computers, copy machines, etc.)

- Architect (designing and laying out your classroom)

- Librarian (organizing books and bookshelves)

- Journalist (creating or overseeing class newsletters and bulletin boards)

- Waitress/waiter (working "Meet the Teacher Night" and open houses)

- Secretary (dealing with paperwork, paperwork, paperwork!)

Suffice it to say, the roles and responsibilities of teachers are many. Some seasoned veterans will tell you that teaching is like a circus juggling act—you're trying to keep as many objects in the air as you possibly can without dropping a single one. Sometimes it's demanding; sometimes it's complicated, but it is never, ever dull!

Some Major Teaching Concerns

Whether you're contemplating becoming a teacher, are in the midst of a teacher education program, or just about ready to start your first year of teaching, you probably have some concerns in the forefront of your thinking right now. You're not alone! New teachers everywhere have some major concerns about:

- **Classroom management.** How can I achieve order in a classroom so productive learning can take place?

- **Classroom discipline.** What are the norms for students' general conduct and the behavioral routines or procedures that students follow in specific situations?

- **Assessment and evaluation.** How do I know if students are learning the material?

- **Motivating students.** How do I stimulate and encourage students to want to learn?

- **Relationships.** Will I be able to get along with administrators, parents, and other teachers?

- **Homework.** How much should I give, and how do I make it worthwhile?

- **Individual students.** Will I be able to meet the needs of my individual students?

- **Planning and preparation.** Will I have enough planning time to accomplish all I want to do?

Does this sound like a lot? Don't worry! I discuss each of those concerns in the pages of this book. And I aim to provide you with practical, down-to-earth ideas and suggestions to help you become the best teacher possible.

Fire Alarm _____

Not surprising, the most important issues with most beginning teachers (both elementary and secondary) are classroom management and classroom discipline.

What They Never Told You in College

Let's assume you have made it through four years of college and now maybe you're about to start your first year of teaching. Or maybe you've been teaching for a few years. Let's also assume you took several *methods* and *content courses* in college. You learned *how* to teach as well as *what* to teach.

Unfortunately, your professors might not have told you everything. So here's some practical information passed along by teachers who have been right where you are:

- You'll need to develop new bathroom habits. Suffice it to say, going to the bathroom is both a skill and an art for most teachers. Regular restroom patterns you've followed in your "normal life" are nonexistent when you become a classroom teacher.

- Society will frequently blame you if students aren't learning or if they don't get high scores on district or state tests. It's a fact: teachers get blamed for a lot of stuff—much of which they might have little control over. It's not always easy to hear these things, but it's often part of the job.

Jabberwocky _____

Methods courses are teacher-preparation courses that focus on the methods, ways, procedures, or strategies of teaching (the "how-to's" of teaching a subject). **Content courses** focus on the specific content or factual information about a subject (e.g., chemistry, social studies, algebra). Students in secondary teacher education programs most often take these classes.

- You're now the boss! That might seem evident and very simplistic, but it's true. In the past, you were used to being the student, the observer, the intern, the student teacher, or whatever. In the past, everything was assigned to you. Now, you're the one making the assignments, the decisions, the schedule, the class list(s), and the rules.

- Students will come, and students will go. The students you end the year with may be an entirely different bunch than the ones you started with at the beginning of the year. You will change your class roster many times throughout the school year.

CAUTION   **Fire Alarm** _____

Veteran teacher Mike McGough shares this valuable piece of advice:

Here's something important to remember: you won't save every kid. You will do your best; you will craft dynamic and exciting lessons; you will have a classroom that students love; and you will be incredibly effective, humorous, and personable. But you just won't reach every single student. It's a tough reality, but one you need to acknowledge to maintain your sanity.

- You'll get sick! Kids will share their cold, flu, and a dozen other disease germs with you. You'll live on aspirin and chicken soup for weeks at a time. And you'll go through more boxes of tissues than you can count.

- Students will enter and exit your classroom at various times of the day. Some will come and go from music lessons; others will come and go from gifted programs or remedial reading classes; still others will go and return from dentist and doctor appointments; and some will go and return from the nurse's office, guidance counselor, or principal's office. Also many unannounced visitors will weave their way in and out of your room. You'll often feel like a traffic cop.

- Most important: there is no such thing as an average day or an average student. By the same token, there is no such thing as an average teacher!

What This Book Can Do for You

Teaching is much more than standing in front of a classroom full of students and giving them lots of information. If you are wondering what you need to know to be a successful and effective teacher, keep reading.

Experience Pays

The information in this book is not textbook information. You won't get lots of theories and pages of dull, dry research. What you will get are my own experiences as both a secondary and elementary teacher as well as a teacher educator for more than three decades. You'll also get the experiences of hundreds of other teachers from around the country who have been where you are now. I've interviewed them, visited them, and blatantly stolen their tips and ideas to share with you. Their wisdom and suggestions are liberally sprinkled throughout this book. Most important, this book is a guide based on what actually works in real live classrooms with real live kids.

The emphasis in this book is on practicality. You want information and ideas that work. You want suggestions that can be used *right now!* You want support and encouragement from classroom teachers who know what works and what doesn't. Every idea in this book has been classroom tested and teacher approved by classroom teachers in every section of the country. There are no long, boring theories here, but simply information on what works based on the day-in and day-out experiences of seasoned educators. This is *not* a book written by a gray-haired, doddering old college professor who hasn't been in a classroom in a hundred years or so.

Your Single Source of Information

You could consult thousands and thousands of websites, teacher resource books, government publications, state journals, and other informational resources. You could check them all yourself. To do so, however, would probably take the rest of your life. I've cut through all the resources, checked them out, and provided you with the most useful, relevant, and necessary information. You can consider this book your one-stop shopping guide to effective teaching.

Your Personal Companion

Please use this book as your companion and as your guide. I don't expect you to read it from cover to cover. Pick a chapter, any chapter, read it, and implement its practical ideas into your classroom. Do the same for other chapters—in fact, I would suggest that you dip in and out of this book on a regular basis. Read the chapters in any sequence that makes sense to you and provides you with the immediate answers you need to answer your questions. Keep this book on your desk, and read a section every other day or so. Make this book *your book*, your companion. Use what you need when you need it.

Not a Panacea

Looking for guidance on becoming a successful and effective teacher? I'll give you the basics—the strategies and methods you can use to create a classroom where students are learning with enthusiasm and you're teaching with passion and energy. But every classroom is different, just as every student and every teacher is different. I don't pretend to know every student in your room, the policies of your school or district, or your state's curriculum. I don't have an answer for every single problem, situation, or concern that might pop up in your unique situation. But I can give you a set of practices and procedures that will make your job less stressful and your students more engaged in the real business of the classroom—learning. I can't offer you guarantees, but I can offer you practices that have worked in classrooms like yours and with teachers like you.

Of all the professions in the world, teaching is always dynamic, always changing. For me, even after more than three decades in this profession, teaching is a continual process of learning and discovery—as I hope it always is for my students. Ever since I first stepped into a classroom, I have long held to the following philosophy: "The best teachers are those who have as much to learn as they do to teach."

I sincerely hope you enjoy your journey through this book. This compilation of the best thinking, the latest research, and the finest teachers' advice from around the country will give you lots to learn and lots to think about. I'm here to help you choose the strategies and procedures that will make you an unforgettable teacher— one who inspires students and has a long and productive career.

The Least You Need to Know

- Teaching is a demanding and challenging profession, but one filled with incredible possibilities.

- The demand for new teachers is great—and will continue to be so.

- Teachers assume many different roles in addition to instructional leader.

- New teachers have several understandable concerns about their first year of teaching.

How Students Learn (Ed. Psych. in a Nutshell)

In This Chapter

- ◆ How the brain works (yours, too)
- ◆ The basic laws of learning?
- ◆ Dimensions of learning
- ◆ We're all intelligent (in different ways)

Have you ever thought about your brain? Have you ever wondered how you've learned all the things you've learned in your life? Have you ever thought about how you think? Or do questions like these leave you confused and/or brain-tired?

The human brain is a marvelous piece of body equipment. This 3-pound mass of gray matter is 78 percent water, 10 percent fat, and 8 percent protein. The remainder is a combination of other substances. This organ keeps us alive and keeps us functioning. It also has the capacity to learn a wide variety of new tasks and abilities (like all the stuff in this book).

How Learning Happens

The human brain is incredible simply because it's multidimensional. But the brain's greatest assets are its ability to learn, remember what it learned, and use that learning to survive or solve problems.

To a human brain, only two events are possible: it is doing something new, or it is doing something it already knows how to do. The first is known as a stimulus; the second as exercise. The brain can quickly and efficiently determine the difference. Learning begins when there is a stimulus. The stimulus can be an external event (a book to read, a problem to solve) or an internal event (a brainstorm). The stimulus can be a brand-new experience (learning chess) or an extension of a familiar task (using a new tool to repair a car engine).

When the brain is stimulated, it produces electrical energy. This energy (think of each brain cell as a tiny battery) moves quickly from one brain cell to the next through the release of special chemicals. The release of these chemicals triggers the creation of new electrical energy. The process is repeated over and over again until millions or billions of connections are made. The connections between brain cells are sometimes called *neural forests*. The thicker the forests (the more connections), the more knowledge we have about a specific topic.

If, for example, you have a thicker neural forest about California wines than I do, you've likely learned more about those beverages than I have. If I have a thicker neural forest about writing children's books than you, I've probably learned more about that topic than you. Each of us may have many neural forests, or connections, in our brains that are thicker or thinner than other people's.

Expert Opinion

Memory is the other side of learning. Often, when we learn something we remember it—in whole, in part, or maybe not at all. We know brain cells change their receptivity to messages based on previous stimulation. Brain cells (in a certain neural forest) that have been previously stimulated several times might just require a weaker stimulus to get excited again. They've remembered what to do and how to respond.

Getting Smart(er)

Getting smarter or increasing your intelligence is a process of increasing the number of connections between brain cells. It also involves holding on to the connections you already have. The more connections we grow and the more connections we maintain is the key to increasing or enhancing our intelligence.

Let's look at that idea from another angle. The average human brain has approximately 100 billion neurons (brain cells). Each brain cell normally connects with 1,000 to 10,000 other brain cells. Each brain cell has several thousand *synapses;* thus trillions of possible connections can be made. One researcher has postulated that the total number of connections possible for a single human brain is 10 to the 100 trillionth power! That's more than the total number of known particles in the entire universe.

Medical researchers are continuing to learn more about the human brain and how it learns, but we do know some things to be important. First, the human brain is capable of learning an undetermined number of new tasks. Second, the human brain is amazingly adaptive. It can process information, remember that information, and use it productively. Third, teachers can provide the stimuli necessary for learning to occur, not just in the classroom but also in the world outside the classroom.

Learning can occur at any time and at any place. But the conditions that stimulate learning, as well as utilize that learning productively, can always be facilitated in a classroom environment. Knowing *how* your students learn is just as important as knowing *what* they need to learn.

> **Jabberwocky**
>
> A **synapse** is the place where electrical and chemical connections are made between one brain cell and another.

> **Expert Opinion**
>
> The single best way to grow a better brain is through challenging problem-solving. Kids need complex, challenging problems to solve. It doesn't matter to the brain whether it ever comes up with an answer; it's the frequent, new learning experiences and challenges that are critical to brain growth.

Give Me a Break!

Several researchers say that mental breaks of up to 20 minutes several times a day increase productivity. Workers need 5 to 10 minute breaks every hour and a half.

Genuine academic attention can be sustained at a high and constant level for only a short time, generally 10 minutes or less.

In the classroom, constant attention is counterproductive. Much of what we learn cannot be processed consciously because it happens too fast. We need time to process it. And to create new meaning, we need internal time. Meaning is always generated from within, not externally. Also, after each new learning experience, we need time for the learning to "imprint."

A classroom that's plagued by discipline problems might have many overlapping causes. One of the first places to start to address discipline problems is attention. Try cutting the length of focused attention time expected or required. Remember that the human brain is poor at nonstop attention. Consider these guidelines:

Secondary Thoughts

Cramming more content per minute or moving from one piece of learning to the next virtually guarantees that little will be learned or retained. In fact, many teachers who complain of having to do so much reteaching are the same ones trying to cram too much material into a class period.

- Use 5 to 7 minutes of direct instruction for kindergarten through grade 2 students.

- Use 8 to 12 minutes of direct instruction for students in grades 3 through 6.

- Use 10 to 14 minutes of direct instruction for students in grades 7 through 12.

After learning, the brain needs time for processing and rest. In a typical classroom, this means rotating mini-lectures, group work, reflection, individual work, and team project time (see Chapter 10).

It's Elementary

Strong and positive links exist between movement or motor development and learning. Physical education, movement, and activity-based games directly relate to learning. Positive changes in self-discipline, grades, and sense of purpose are the direct result of regular and systematic physical activities. The last word: Recess is important for positive academic development.

Chunky, Chunky, Chunky

The human brain has "memory limits"; it can only hold or remember a selected amount of data at any one time. A 3-year-old's brain can only hold one chunk (a chunk is a single thought, idea, or group of related ideas). A 5-year-old's brain can hold two chunks; a 7-year-old's holds 3 chunks. By 15 years old, the brain can hold up to 7 chunks. To help your students remember and apply knowledge, try the following memory aids:

- Review frequently.

- Minimize chunks.

- Organize graphically (see the "Acquiring and Integrating Knowledge" section later in this chapter).

- Present the most important material first and last.

- Introduce wholes before parts.

- Use student-created visuals.

- Have peers teach.

- Problem solve.

- Use different learning locations.

- Integrate movement.

- Use storytelling.

Laws of Learning

From my conversations with teachers around the country about how students learn and how teachers teach, I have discovered that certain laws govern the learning process. These laws apply to any student at any grade and in any subject area. Just as important, they are also supportive of what we know about brain growth and development. Although they have direct application for you as a classroom teacher, you'll note they are also applicable to adults who want to learn, too (for example, the person reading this book).

- **Law of readiness.** Students learn more easily when they have a desire to learn. Conversely, students learn with difficulty if they're not interested in the topic.

- **Law of effect**. Learning will always be much more effective when a feeling of satisfaction, pleasantness, or reward is part of the process.

- **Law of relaxation.** Students learn best and remember longest when they are relaxed. Reducing stress increases learning and retention.

- **Law of association.** Learning makes sense (comprehension) when the mind compares a new idea with something already known.

- **Law of involvement.** Students learn best when they take an active part in what is to be learned.

- **Law of exercise.** The more often an act is repeated or information reviewed, the more quickly and more permanently it will become a habit or an easily remembered piece of information.

- **Law of relevance.** Effective learning is relevant to the student's life.

- **Law of intensity.** A vivid, exciting, enthusiastic, enjoyable learning experience is more likely to be remembered than a boring, unpleasant one.

- **Law of challenge.** Students learn best when they're challenged with novelty, a variety of materials, and a range of instructional strategies.

- **Law of feedback.** Effective learning takes place when students receive immediate and specific feedback on their performance.

- **Law of recency.** Practicing a skill or new concept just before using it will ensure a more effective performance.

- **Law of expectations.** Learners' reaction to instruction is shaped by their expectations related to the material (*How successful will I be?*).

- **Law of emotions.** The emotional state (and involvement) of students will shape how well and how much they learn.

- **Law of differences.** Students learn in different ways. One size does not fit all!

Dimensions of Learning

Teaching and learning occur in dynamic environments. In these environments, teachers, students, materials, textbooks, technologies, and social structures are all related and interactive. Learning and teaching occurs across five basic dimensions:

- Confidence and independence

- Knowledge and understanding

- Skills and strategies

- Use of prior and emerging experience

- Critical reflection

These five elements are known as the dimensions of learning. They cannot be treated individually; instead, they are dynamically interwoven. They describe the basic elements that must be part of every classroom learning (and teaching) experience. Students learn best when these five dimensions are addressed and incorporated into every teaching/learning experience.

Positive Attitudes and Perceptions About Learning

Attitudes and perceptions affect students' ability to learn. Learning occurs best when the development of positive attitudes and perceptions is made part of every learning task. Students learn to think positively about themselves, their peers, and the material they are learning.

Here are some suggested classroom behaviors and practices:

- Establish a relationship with each student in the class.

- Practice positive classroom behavior.

- Provide opportunities for students to work together in cooperative groups.

- Establish and communicate classroom rules.

- Use a variety of ways to engage students.

- Provide appropriate feedback.

- Teach students to use positive self-talk.

- Provide clear performance levels for tasks.

Acquiring and Integrating Knowledge

We know that students build new knowledge by relating it to prior learning and experience. Additionally, we know there are different types of knowledge students can learn. This knowledge is best learned by making connections between what is known and what is to be learned.

Here are some suggested classroom behaviors and practices:

- ◆ Help students understand what it means to construct meaning.
- ◆ Have students use *graphic organizers* to organize information.

Jabberwocky _____

A **graphic organizer** is a chart, outline, or web of ideas or concepts organized into groups or categories. For example, a nutrition graphic organizer might have the word *Food* written in the center of a sheet of paper. Around that key term would be categories of food such as *Fruit*, *Vegetables*, *Dairy Products*, and *Grains*. Around each of those categories would be written selected examples. The category of *Fruit* might have *plums*, *cherries*, *apricots*, and *apples* written around it. A graphic organizer illustrates how ideas are related to each other.

- ◆ Have students create pictorial representations of information.
- ◆ Help students construct models.
- ◆ Point out common errors and pitfalls.
- ◆ Help students set up a practice schedule.

Extending and Refining Knowledge

For learning to be effective and meaningful, students should be provided with opportunities to use knowledge in practical situations. Processing knowledge for greater understanding can be done through activities designed to help them apply that knowledge.

Try some of these classroom behaviors and practices:

- ◆ **Compare.** How are these things alike?
- ◆ **Classify.** Into what groups could you organize these things?
- ◆ **Induce.** Based on this information, what is the likely conclusion?
- ◆ **Deduct.** What predictions can you make, or what conclusions can you draw?
- ◆ **Analyze errors.** How is this information misleading?

- ◆ **Construct support.** What is an argument that will support this claim?

- ◆ **Abstract.** What is the general pattern underlying this information?

- ◆ **Analyze perspectives.** What is the reasoning behind this perspective?

Using Knowledge Meaningfully

Students learn best when they need knowledge to accomplish a goal they consider important. Six kinds of thinking processes can be used to encourage students to use knowledge meaningfully:

- ◆ Decision-making

- ◆ Problem-solving

- ◆ Invention

- ◆ Experimental inquiry

- ◆ Investigation

- ◆ *Systems analysis*

Jabberwocky

Analyzing the parts of a system and the manner in which they interact is called **systems analysis.**

Productive Habits of Mind

Teachers can help students develop the mental habits that will enable them to learn on their own. Instruction to foster habits of mind includes both short-term and long-term practices.

Here are some suggested classroom behaviors and practices:

- ◆ **Think critically.** Be and see accurately. Be open-minded.

- ◆ **Think creatively.** Push the limits of one's knowledge. Find new ways of looking at a situation.

- ◆ **Self-regulate.** Be aware of one's own thinking. Evaluate the effectiveness of one's own actions.

We All Learn Differently: The Eight Intelligences

According to Howard Gardner of Harvard University, each individual possesses eight different intelligences in varying degrees, as opposed to a single intelligence quotient as traditionally reported via many standardized intelligence tests. These intelligences help determine how individuals learn and how they fare in their daily lives.

Gardner defines an "intelligence" as consisting of three components:

♦ The ability to create an effective product or offer a service that's valuable in one's culture.

♦ A set of skills that enables an individual to solve problems encountered in life.

♦ The potential for finding or creating solutions for problems, which enables a person to acquire new knowledge.

Individuals differ in the strength (or weakness) of each of the eight intelligences in isolation as well as in combination. For example, whereas some individuals learn best through linguistic means, others are more kinesthetic learners, and still others are spatial learners. No two people learn in the same way, nor should they be taught in the same way.

Verbal-Linguistic Intelligence

This intelligence involves ease in producing language and sensitivity to the nuances, order, and rhythm of words. Individuals who are strong in verbal-linguistic intelligence love to read, write, tell stories, and think in words.

Verbal-linguistic students learn best through writing, reading, storytelling, speaking, debating, and discussing.

Logical-Mathematical Intelligence

This intelligence relates to the ability to reason deductively or inductively and to recognize and manipulate abstract patterns and relationships. Individuals who excel in this intelligence have strong problem-solving and reasoning skills and ask questions in a logical manner.

Logical-mathematical students learn best through problem-solving, outlining, calculating, patterning, and showing relationships.

Musical-Rhythmic Intelligence

This intelligence encompasses sensitivity to the pitch, timbre, and rhythm of sounds as well as responsiveness to the emotional implications of these elements of music. Individuals who remember melodies or recognize pitch and rhythm exhibit musical intelligence.

Musical-rhythmic students learn best through composing, singing, humming, making instrumental sounds, and creating vibrations.

Visual-Spatial Intelligence

This intelligence includes the ability to create visual-spatial representations of the world and to transfer them mentally or concretely. Individuals who exhibit spatial intelligence need a mental or physical picture to best understand new information. They are strong in drawing; designing maps, puzzles, and mazes; and creating things.

Visual-spatial students learn best through painting, drawing, sculpting, pretending, and imagining.

Bodily-Kinesthetic Intelligence

This involves using the body to solve problems, make things, and convey ideas and emotions. Individuals who are strong in this intelligence are good at physical activities; eye-hand coordination; and have a tendency to move around, touch things, and gesture.

Bodily-kinesthetic students learn best through dancing, miming, role playing, exercising, and playing games.

Intrapersonal Intelligence

This entails the ability to understand one's own emotions, goals, and intentions. Individuals strong in intrapersonal intelligence have a strong sense of self, are confident, and can enjoy working alone.

Intrapersonal students learn best through thinking strategies, focusing, metacognitive techniques, silent reflection, and emotional processing.

Interpersonal Intelligence

This intelligence refers to the ability to work effectively with other people and to understand them and recognize their goals and intentions. Individuals who exhibit this intelligence thrive on cooperative work, have strong leadership skills, and are skilled at organizing, communicating, and negotiating.

Interpersonal students learn best through communicating, receiving structured feedback, collaborating, and cooperating.

Naturalist Intelligence

This includes the capacity to recognize flora and fauna, to make distinctions in the natural world, and to use this ability productively in activities such as farming and biological science.

Naturalistic students learn best through planting, raising and tending, nurturing, observing, and experimenting.

Teachers who subscribe to the idea of multiple intelligences observe that teaching aimed at sharpening one kind of intelligence will carry over to others. Also mounting evidence shows that learning opportunities that involve a variety of intelligences allow students to take advantage of their preferred intelligence(s) as well as strengthen weaker intelligences.

Lessons that provide learning opportunities aimed at most or all the intelligences will benefit the greatest number of students in any classroom and in any subject area. An attention to all the multiple intelligences allows you to extend, expand, and take advantage of students' learning preferences to design well-rounded and intellectually stimulating lessons.

The Least You Need to Know

- ◆ The human brain's greatest capacity is its ability to learn.
- ◆ Many classroom conditions and practices affect students' learning.
- ◆ The fourteen laws of learning are applicable to students in any grade or subject area.
- ◆ The five dimensions of learning should be elements of every lesson.
- ◆ Multiple intelligences provide teachers with a wide range of teaching possibilities.

The Effective Teacher—You!

In This Chapter

◆ The qualities of good teachers—according to students

◆ The 10 basic standards of good teaching

◆ The 5 roles of good teachers

◆ Reasons why some teachers fail

Think about the best teacher you had. What did that teacher do that made you enjoy being in her or his classroom? What did that teacher do that made you enjoy her or him as a person? What did he or she do that causes you to have fond and lasting memories of that course, class, classroom, or topic?

That teacher undoubtedly expressed or displayed many features, characteristics, and qualities. In this chapter, we'll consider those attributes. Most important, you will learn how you can make those attributes your own, how to become an effective teacher—a teacher your students will remember long after they leave your classroom.

What Students Think

What is it that makes some teachers good and others slightly less than memorable? That's a question I've been asking for a long time, so I decided to go to some experts—students.

I asked a classroom full of eager and excited second-grade students for the qualities they felt were characteristic of good teachers. Here's a sampling of what they said:

"Teachers should be nice and not yell a lot."

"Teachers should not be mean. They should be respectful."

"I like when teachers are helpful."

"I wish my teacher would always like me."

"Teachers should be trusting, caring, and give lots of hugs."

"A good teacher is kind everyday."

"Teachers should be smart and know everything."

"I want my teacher to be cool."

I then asked a class of freshman college students about their criteria for effective teachers. They completed the following sentence: "Good teachers _____." Here's a sampling of their responses:

"Good teachers ask good questions that make us think."

"Good teachers get along with their students. They aren't 'buddies,' but they foster open lines of communication."

"Good teachers have a discipline policy that is consistent, fair, and impartial."

"Good teachers can explain a topic clearly and without a lot of big words."

"Good teachers admit when they're wrong and are always trying to improve themselves."

"Good teachers respect students; they never put students down or ridicule them."

"Good teachers make learning fun and aren't afraid to laugh or make fun of themselves."

"Good teachers roll with the punches—they don't let little things get the better of them."

"Good teachers know what they are doing; their lessons are planned (rather than off the cuff)."

"Good teachers like to teach; they make learning enjoyable because they are enjoyable people."

When I asked the college freshmen for the number-one quality of a good teacher, they all said that the most important quality was having a passion for teaching. That characteristic held true for their elementary teachers, high school teachers, and even college teachers. For these "experienced" students, excitement about teaching was the single most significant quality of any classroom teacher.

Standards for Good Teaching

You and I and a couple million other people have all been in schools for a number of years, and we all have some pretty good ideas about the qualities we feel are important for good teaching. Not surprising, several agencies and organizations have looked into the characteristics of good teachers. One of those is the Interstate New Teacher Assessment and Support Consortium (INTASC).

The INTASC establishes guidelines for preparing, licensing, and certifying educators. Among other things, they promote 10 standards that should be part of every teacher's classroom practice or personality (after each principle I have listed the chapter or chapters in this book that address the specific topics):

- **Principle 1.** The teacher understands the central concepts, tools of inquiry, and structures of the discipline(s) he or she teaches and can create learning experiences that make these aspects of subject matter meaningful for students (Chapters 20 and 21).

- **Principle 2.** The teacher understands how children learn and develop and can provide learning opportunities that support their intellectual, social, and personal development (Chapter 2).

- **Principle 3.** The teacher understands how students differ in their approaches to learning and creates instructional opportunities that are adapted to diverse learners (Chapters 2 and 18).

- **Principle 4.** The teacher understands and uses a variety of instructional strategies to encourage students' development of critical thinking, problem-solving, and performance skills (Chapters 10 and 13).

- **Principle 5.** The teacher uses an understanding of individual and group motivation and behavior to create a learning environment that encourages positive social interaction, active engagement in learning, and self-motivation (Chapters 12 and 14).

- **Principle 6.** The teacher uses knowledge of effective verbal, nonverbal, and media communication techniques to foster active inquiry, collaboration, and supportive interaction in the classroom (Chapters 10 and 11).

- **Principal 7.** The teacher plans instruction based on knowledge of subject matter, students, the community, and curriculum goals (Chapter 5 and 17).

- **Principle 8.** The teacher understands and uses formal and informal assessment strategies to evaluate and ensure the continuous intellectual, social, and physical development of the learner (Chapter 9).

- **Principle 9.** The teacher is a reflective practitioner who continually evaluates the effects of his or her choices and actions on others (students, parents, and other professionals in the learning community) and who actively seeks out opportunities to grow professionally (Chapters 24 and 25).

- **Principle 10.** The teacher fosters relationships with school colleagues, parents, and agencies in the larger community to support students' learning and well-being (Chapters 19 and 23).

It's important to point out that your effectiveness as a teacher depends on much more than your knowledge of one or more subjects. In fact, your success will be driven by characteristics and dynamics that are as much a part of who you are as they are of your classroom behavior.

Conversations with hundreds of teachers around the country indicate that good teachers are effective because they assume five interrelated roles:

- You as a person
- Student orientation
- Task orientation
- Classroom management
- Lifelong learning

I invite you to consider these roles in terms of your own personality dynamics as well as in terms of your reasons for becoming a teacher.

You as a Person

The reasons you are a teacher are undoubtedly many. Who you are as a person and how you would like to share your personality with students are significant factors in why you choose to be a teacher. So, too, will they be significant in terms of your success in the classroom. My own experience with hundreds of teachers has taught me that the personality of a teacher is a major and predominant factor in the success of students within that teacher's influence.

Joy to the World

Good classroom teachers are joyful. They relish in the thrill of discovery and the natural curiosity of students. They are excited about learning and often transmit that excitement to their students. They are stimulated by the unknown and are amazed at what *can* be learned, not just at what *is* learned.

Students consistently rate teachers high when humor is part of the classroom environment. This humor does not come from telling lots of jokes, but rather from the good-natured conversations and discussions carried on with students. Humor helps break down conversational barriers, establishes good rapport, and builds strong classroom communities.

You should be passionate. Good teachers are good because they not only have a love for children, but they also have a passion for the subjects they teach. If you're passionate about teaching, your students will know immediately. If you're less than excited about what you're doing, students will be able to determine that very rapidly, too. Your passion for teaching must be evident in everything you do.

Secondary Thoughts

Observations of successful secondary classrooms reveal that the teacher's knowledge of the subject is of considerably less importance (to students' learning) than her or his energy for teaching the subject.

I Wonder Why ...

Effective teachers are inquisitive. They continuously ask questions, looking for new explanations and myriad new answers. They serve as positive role models for students, helping them ask their own questions for exploration. They are content with not finding all the answers but rather with developing a classroom environment in which self-initiated questioning (by both teacher and students) predominates.

Good teachers are also creative. They're willing to explore new dimensions and seek new possibilities—never sure of what lies around the corner or down the next path. They're willing to experiment and try new approaches to learning—not because they've been done before but simply because they've never been tried at all.

Outstanding teachers seek help from others. They talk about new strategies with colleagues, seek input from administrators and education experts, read lots of educational magazines and periodicals, and access websites frequently. They don't try to go it alone.

Effective teachers are change-makers. They're not afraid of change and realize that change can be a positive element in every classroom. If something isn't working, these teachers are eager to strike out into new territories for exploration. They're never content with status quo; their classrooms are always evolving, always in a state of transition.

Flexibility

In preparation for this book, I interviewed scores of teachers all over the United States, from Maine to California and from Oregon to Florida—and a lot of places in between. I wanted to get their thoughts and impressions of good teaching and the characteristics they felt are essential in a quality-based classroom program.

To a person, they all told me the same thing: the number-one characteristic of a good teacher is flexibility or the ability to roll with the punches and not let the little things get you down.

It might come as no surprise to you, but there's no such thing as an average or typical day in teaching. Students come and go, clocks and other machines break, parents drop in unexpectedly, administrators have reports to file, meetings are scheduled at the last minute, you forget your lunch or your car gets a flat tire, the film you ordered didn't arrive, and a hundred other things can—and often do—go wrong.

However, it's the flexible teacher—the one who doesn't let these inevitable "roadblocks" get in her or his way—who survives and teaches best in the classroom. Yes, there will be "surprises," unanticipated and unplanned events, and glitches along the way. But if you are willing to compromise, bend, and adjust, you will give yourself an incredible opportunity to succeed.

Student Orientation

If you were to walk into the classroom of any outstanding teacher, regardless of her or his grade level, one thing will become immediately clear: students are respected, attended to, and clearly more important than the subject matter or the instructional materials used.

Showing You Care

The best teachers are those who truly care for their students. They exhibit empathy and try to see the world through their students' eyes. They know students have good days and bad days just like they do, and they adjust their instruction accordingly.

Expert Opinion

Well-known educator William Purkey once said, "Effective teachers let students know that they are somebody, not *some body*."

So, too, are good teachers sensitive to their students' cultural backgrounds. They respect students' languages, customs, traditions, and beliefs. They never make fun of students who are different but rather celebrate these new opportunities for enriching the learning experiences of all students.

Students need to know that they will never be embarrassed or ridiculed nor will they be intimidated or shown excessive favoritism. The best teachers have positive attitudes about everyone in the school—students, custodians, secretaries, aides, librarians, cafeteria workers, and fellow teachers. High-achieving classrooms are supportive, warm, and accepting.

Good teachers listen. They're aware of the "rule of two-thirds," which states that in traditional classrooms (regardless of grade or subject) two thirds of class time is taken up by talking, two thirds of that time is taken up by teacher talk, and two thirds of the teacher's talk is telling or demonstrating rather than interacting with students. These teachers know that students have much to contribute to the curriculum and to each other and provide numerous opportunities for them to do so.

Outstanding teachers know criticism has a negative impact on students' learning potential and use more encouragement than criticism. They maintain a high ratio of positive to negative comments (3:1—good; 5:1—better; 8:1—best).

Fire Alarm

It's been proven that 90 percent of the positive things students do go unrecognized in the classroom.

Effective teachers provide opportunities for students to get extra help. They are observant of students' needs and work to provide the instruction or materials that will help them succeed and flourish. Student progress is constantly monitored and adjusted as necessary.

Higher and Higher

The finest teachers are those who have high expectations for their students. They continually challenge their students, engaging them in higher-order thinking activities, problem-solving, creative-thinking extensions, and other instructional activities that s-t-r-e-t-c-h their minds.

I once worked for a principal who said, "Students don't fail, teachers do!" It was his belief that good teachers must take personal responsibility for their students' learning. Good teachers are sensitive to the instructional needs of every student and work for the success of each individual in the classroom.

Effective teachers match the difficulty of a lesson with the ability levels(s) of students. In addition, they vary the difficulty when necessary to attain moderate-to-high success rates (60 to 70 percent).

Using Student Ideas

Good teachers know they can significantly increase student engagement in the learning process by incorporating students' ideas in classroom discussions by:

- Using student ideas by repeating nouns and logical connections.
- Rephrasing student ideas in teacher words.
- Using student ideas to take the next step in problem-solving.
- Drawing relationships between student ideas and information shared earlier.
- Using what students say as a summary of important concepts.

Task Orientation

Task orientation is an emphasis on learning. The teacher concentrates on the instructional activities that cause learning to happen rather than on the procedural matters of running the classroom.

Focus, Focus, Focus

Effective teachers are able to handle administrative and clerical tasks efficiently, quickly, and without disrupting the classroom atmosphere. They spend more time teaching and less time on distractions and interruptions.

Good teachers present logical, clear, step-by-step lessons and include cycles of review, practice, and feedback. Lessons and units reflect the curriculum and are designed to help students master specific objectives. Time is not wasted.

Jabberwocky

Task orientation is the degree to which a teacher provides learning opportunities for students. Those learning opportunities take precedence over classroom management concerns.

The best teachers conduct their lessons in a businesslike, task-oriented manner. They maintain a strong academic focus in their classroom and are effective in designing lessons that enhance student mastery.

On Your Best Behavior

Effective teachers stop or prevent misbehavior with a minimum of disruptions. Small problems are not blown out of proportion and are dealt with quickly and efficiently.

Good teachers are in control of their classrooms. They invest time and effort in the prevention of discipline problems by developing positive student relationships and planning well-organized lessons.

Probing

Good teachers invite students as active participants in the dynamics of a lesson by *probing*. Simply stated, probing is a series of teacher statements or questions that encourage students to elaborate on their answers to previous questions. Probing is a way of shifting an individual conversation or class discussion to a higher level.

Good teachers use some of these probing questions frequently throughout a lesson:

- **Clarification.** "What do you mean by that?"

- **Obtaining more information.** "What's another word for that?"

- **Making connections.** "Is this like anything else you're familiar with?"

♦ **Comparison.** "How is your idea similar to or different from _____'s?"

♦ **Expansion.** "Is there any other information you can add to that?"

♦ **Validation.** "Why do you believe your response is correct?"

Classroom Management

Managing a classroom requires many tasks; however, it's important to remember that classroom management is not about achieving order for order's sake. It's about achieving order so productive learning can occur. The ultimate goal of classroom management is to promote learning.

Who's Responsible?

Effective teachers provide opportunities for students to make decisions and follow through on those decisions. Good classrooms are not teacher-dependent environments but rather independent student learning arenas. Teachers who provide students with multiple opportunities to make choices and accept the consequences of those choices are excellent instructional leaders.

Students who come up to your desk and ask, "Is this what you wanted?" or "What do I do next?" are saying they aren't allowed to make their own decisions. Teachers who empower students in making decisions are facilitating independent and responsible learners.

Expert Opinion

On average, a typical classroom teacher will make more than 1,500 educational decisions every day. These decisions can be minor (when to collect lunch money) or major (what to do when a student has an epileptic seizure).

Establishing Routines

Good classroom teachers teach their students classroom routines such as what to do when they finish an assignment early, how to get extra help, how to move in to and out of the classroom, and how to take care of their personal needs. This provides students with a sense of responsibility and allows them to make decisions that should be theirs rather than the teacher's.

Decibel by Decibel

Effective teachers know that a quiet classroom is not necessary a productive classroom. Learning is sometimes noisy and sometimes messy (just look at any science activity involving a bunch of kids and a tub full of earthworms). They recognize that learning can take place in many different types of environments. The activity level or noise level of a lesson may ebb and flow along with the level of involvement or participation on the part of students. Students need opportunities to share, communicate, and vocalize their educational experiences—all within previously established rules or expectations. Successful classrooms tend to involve significant amounts of class discussion and group exploration. A quiet classroom may be a dead classroom.

Majority Rules

Good teachers establish a set of expectations early in the school year. These expectations are clearly detailed and explained to students and are upheld consistently throughout the entire school year.

Effective teachers provide opportunities for students to take responsibility for establishing rules and the resultant consequences. They know that this ownership factor can be a positive motivator for all students.

Lifelong Learners

Good teachers are those who keep learning, who continually add to their knowledge base throughout their teaching career. My lifelong motto has always been, "Good teachers have as much to learn as they do to teach." Your education is a continual learning process. It doesn't stop just because you've graduated and have a teaching certificate. It means that if you are to provide the best possible education for your students, you need to provide yourself with a variety of learning opportunities, too.

It would be erroneous to think that your four or five years of college were all you needed to be successful in the classroom. There are too many developments within the field of education to think your college degree is the summation of all the skills, talents, and knowledge you'll need for the rest of your career. What you learn throughout the remainder of your teaching career might be significantly more important than the courses you've taken in college.

Good teachers keep current, stay active, and continually seek out new answers or new questions for exploration. Your desire to find out more about effective teaching methods and dynamic new discoveries within your field can add immeasurably to your talents as a teacher and can also add to your students' appreciation of education in their own lives.

Why Teachers Fail

Teachers sometimes fail. Teacher failure, whether dismissal, reprimand, or reassignment, is most frequently the result of poor human relations skills than lack of knowledge about their subject matter. The following reasons are most frequently mentioned:

- Inability to organize and control a classroom of students
- Lack of knowledge concerning how children grow and develop as pertaining to pupil-teacher interactions
- Inability to work effectively with other educators
- Inability to work effectively with parents
- Subject-matter inadequacies
- Other (immorality, insubordination, absenteeism, child abuse, senility, drugs, or alcohol)

The bottom line is this: your knowledge about a subject is considerably less important than your knowledge about students (or other people in the school). Regardless whether you're an elementary teacher or a secondary teacher, if you're more concerned about human relations than you are about your subject matter, you'll more than likely be a successful teacher.

The Least You Need to Know

- Students at all levels have some pretty definite ideas about the characteristics of effective teachers.
- All good teachers exhibit certain basic principles.
- Being an effective teacher involves a combination of five interrelated factors: you as a person, student orientation, task orientation, classroom management, and lifelong learning.
- Teachers more often fail because of a lack of personal attributes than because of a lack of knowledge about their subject matter.

Part 2

Making It Happen

Once upon a time there was a teacher. And once upon a time that teacher faced lots of decisions, lots of resources, and not very much time. That teacher was looking for answers—lots of answers. Guess what. That teacher is you!

Like thousands of teachers every year, you're wondering how to get started, how to begin each day, and how to begin this exciting career called teaching. In Part 2, I provide you with answers to all (well, almost all) your questions. We look at the first day of the new school year, ways to design exciting lesson plans, the incredible array of teaching resources at your disposal, and ways to assess your students. Most important, I show you how to get the most out of your time (including a few secrets you won't want to miss).

Peter's Law: If you don't know where you are going, you will wind up somewhere else.

Chapter 4

The First Day: Starting With Success

In This Chapter

- ◆ Will you be any good? Will your students like you: first-day jitters
- ◆ Use personality, community, routines and schedules, and determination to make your first day successful
- ◆ First day at the elementary level
- ◆ First day at the secondary level
- ◆ Ways to make a lasting impression

Do you remember your first kiss? Do you recall the anticipation, the fear, the anxiety, the trepidation? Do you remember all the various thoughts that were bouncing around in your head? *What if he doesn't like me? What if she doesn't do it right?* That was certainly a scary time, right?

Well, your first day of teaching can be a lot like your first kiss. You might have seen expert teachers create magic in a classroom and read all the latest books and resource materials. And still you're scared! Guess what—you're not alone. Of all the questions that teachers ask, "What do I do on the first day of school?" is probably the most common. Each year, more than 100,000 new teachers ask that same question.

First Questions First

As a beginning teacher, two questions will undoubtedly be circulating through your head: *Will they like me?* and *Will I be any good?* Interestingly, those are the same two questions that students have about new teachers at the beginning of each new school year. For students, the questions are *Will I like my teacher(s)?* and *Will my teacher(s) be any good?*

Expert Opinion

Parents will reinforce these two basic questions when their youngsters come home after the first day. They will typically ask, "How's your new teacher?" and "What did you learn in school today?"

Although you might have some fears and trepidations about your first day of teaching, please keep in mind that students, too, have similar fears about the first day of a new academic year. Whether they're entering school for the first time in the academic careers (kindergarten) or are just starting the last leg of a long educational experience (high school seniors), they'll have some concerns about their teacher(s) and what they can expect during the next nine months.

You can alleviate many of their fears as well as most of yours by focusing on four basic concepts. These are areas to focus on during the first day of classes, but they will also be important areas of concentration throughout the entire school year:

- Personality
- Building a community
- Routines and schedules
- Self-determination

Personality Plus!

Be sure your students see you as a human being first, rather than an authority figure in the classroom. Take time early during the first day to introduce yourself. Tell students something about yourself, particularly about your life outside the classroom. This can include the following:

- Your youth and educational experiences
- Your hobbies and interests
- Your family

- ◆ Places you've traveled
- ◆ Books you've read

It's important for students to know that you have experiences and interests not unlike those of other adults. In fact, I've often found it helpful to share a funny incident from my past, an embarrassing moment I had in school, or some self-deprecating humor. These humanizing touches cue students that their teacher does human things and is not always perfect.

It's Elementary

A very effective tool—even before school begins—is to send your students a brief newsletter to introduce yourself. As soon as you get your class list, compose a newsletter (*Mrs. Smith's Chronicle,* for example) that provides some inside information about who you are: hobbies, books you read during the summer, how excited you are to meet everyone, your family life, etc. This will help students and their parents get to know you even before they set foot in your classroom.

Building a Community

Besides knowing who you are as a person, students also need to know that the place in which they will spend much of their time (the classroom) will be safe, inviting, and comfortable. They need to know about the classroom environment very early during the first day. They also need to know that they are important and valued members of that environment.

Teachers from all types of schools have shared these ideas:

Meet and greet every student at the door. This sets the tone for the day and establishes a positive atmosphere. I prefer to shake the hand of every student, ask them their name, and personally welcome them to the class.

If you know ahead of time that you'll have second-language learners (those whose native language is something other than English) in your classroom, try to learn a greeting or welcome in his or her native language. A simple *Buenas dias, Carlos. ¿Como esta usted?* can mean a lot to a new student.

Provide opportunities for students to get to know each other early in the day. Here are some tried-and-true suggestions, but feel free to modify these according to the grade or age levels of the students with whom you work:

◆ Put some blank name tags in a box. Invite students to create a colorful name tag for someone sitting next to them.

◆ Invite each student to create a personal "coat of arms." Draw an outline of a crest and divide it into four sections. Duplicate it and distribute one to each student. Invite students to fill in each section with their name, a favorite activity or hobby, a favorite book, and a dream or wish. Invite students to talk about their crests with the entire class.

◆ Invite students to assemble into various small groups. Invite each group to discuss and agree on one favorite for each of the following: a musical group, a vacation spot, a favorite movie, a favorite movie/TV star, the best fast-food place in town, etc.

Routines and Schedules

One of the first things you'll need to address early on the first day are the rules and *routines* of the classroom. Some very interesting educational research suggests that when rules and procedures are established and discussed during the first days of school (and reinforced again during the first three weeks), the class runs more smoothly and behavior problems are minimized.

Ask yourself the following questions, then share the answers with your students on the first day:

◆ How will students respond in class? (raising hands, a signal or sign)

◆ What are the seating arrangements?

◆ How will students enter and exit the classroom?

◆ How will tardiness and absences be handled?

◆ How much can students interact with each other?

◆ How will homework be handled?

◆ How will missed work or makeup work be handled?

◆ What will happen when a rule is violated?

◆ How will classroom visitors be handled?

Jabberwocky

Routines are a way of managing the classroom. They are a set of expectations that save time and ensure a smooth-functioning classroom.

Equally important is the need to share with students a daily schedule of activities. Post this schedule in the front of the room, and use it to let students know a daily plan of action (for elementary students) or a sequence of procedures for an instructional period (for secondary students). This schedule offers students an expectation for each day. There's comfort in knowing how a lesson or day will be conducted. Students, just like adults, are creatures of habit, and enjoy having the security of a planned sequence of expectations.

CAUTION **Fire Alarm** _____

Remember the Rule of Five: there should be absolutely no more than five rules posted in the classroom. More than that will be confusing, overwhelming, difficult to remember, and perhaps even perceived as dictatorial by students.

Here are two sample daily routines.

Elementary	Secondary
Greet students	Greet students at door
Hang up coats	Go to seats
Go to seats	Quick motivational activity
Independent activity	Take attendance
Class welcome	Review lesson format
Salute flag, pledge	Go over lesson objectives
Take attendance	Begin the lesson
Sing a song	Incorporate group work
Discuss calendar, weather	Independent work
Lunch count	Collect assignments
Collect homework	Dismissal procedures
Discuss daily schedule	
Begin first lesson	
(Other activities will follow throughout the day.)	

The schedule you set on the first day will obviously be subject to change throughout the year as a result of unexpected events (guest speakers, assemblies, early dismissal, etc.). Nevertheless, students should have some expectations of how their day or a certain period will be framed. These predictable routines assure a well-managed and well-disciplined classroom.

Self-Determination

Teachers succeed when they share classroom management responsibility with their students. Giving students a sense of ownership in the affairs of the classroom is not only a powerful motivating force but is also a way to ensure harmony and promote group cohesiveness.

From day one, it is most valuable to let students know that they will be encouraged to make choices in your classroom. Some choices will be minor; others will be major. The important thing to convey to students is the fact that this is their classroom—a place that supports them in their learning just as you will support them in all their academic endeavors.

Expert Opinion

For early elementary students, limit the choices to two ("Which book should we read today—*In One Tidepool* by Anthony D. Fredericks or *Into the Sea* by Brenda Guiberson?"). Upper elementary students and middle school students can select from three or four choices. Secondary students can be provided with an unlimited menu of choices (within reason).

Share some of the choices with students:

◆ Choosing seats

◆ Choosing a read-aloud book

◆ Selecting a game to play

◆ Deciding on classroom rules

◆ Deciding on classroom procedures

◆ Selecting rainy-day activities

◆ Establishing ways to work in groups

◆ Setting routines for obtaining materials and supplies

◆ Determining procedures for trips to the restroom

First Day at the Elementary Level

If you're looking forward to your first day as an elementary teacher, you certainly have a lot to consider, everything from learning all your student's names to being sure you don't leave anybody behind on the playground after recess. Consider some of these suggestions for activities and procedures for your classroom:

◆ Meet parents and greet them with a smile and a welcome. Some will be reluctant to release their children into your care. Assure them that this will be a great year.

- Take time to introduce yourself and talk about who you are. If you have a difficult name, pronounce it several times for students and invite them to repeat it several times.

- Provide an opportunity for students to introduce themselves. Each student can stand and briefly (3 minutes maximum—use an egg timer) talk about his name, community, any summer adventures, books read, and/or family members.

It's Elementary

I like to have students do a name poem on the first day. Provide each student with a sheet of colored construction paper. Ask students (or assist them) to write their name vertically down the left side of the paper using large letters. Then invite them to write a self-descriptive adjective or phrase for each letter in their name. Here's an example:

J—Jumps rope
U—Understands Spanish
L—Loves cats
I—Intelligent
E—Energetic

These name poems can then be posted throughout the classroom. Take time during the first 2 to 3 weeks to refer to the name poems regularly.

- Let students know about early morning procedures—how attendance will be taken, collection of lunch or milk money, where to put their coats and book bags, etc.

- Take time to give students a tour of the classroom. Some teachers prefer to have students in their desks while they provide a visual tour of materials, computers, cabinets, supplies, bulletin boards, etc. Other teachers, like me, prefer a walking tour of the classroom to point out the specific locations of objects and items.

- Set up a classroom employment agency for various classroom jobs. Inform students about the assignments necessary to a well-functioning classroom. These can include botanist (waters plants), sanitation engineer (empties trash can), interior decorator (manages bulletin board), zoologist (cares for class pet[s]), etc. Invite students to apply for jobs (using a standard application form) on a set schedule, and rotate the assignments regularly.

- Read a book or a story to the students. Begin with a positive literary experience, and invite students to discuss their enjoyment or comprehension of the book.

- Engage students in a get-acquainted game such as a Human Scavenger Hunt. Make up a set of index cards, one for each student and then ask the students to find someone in the class who …

  - Has been in an airplane.

  - Has a baby sister.

  - Has a summer birthday.

  - Is wearing something blue.

  - Is from another country.

  - Is in an after-school sport.

- Take time to talk about rules and procedures. Show students a basic set of rules (remember the Rule of Five), and let them know that they will help decide on additional rules as the year progresses.

- Introduce the curriculum. Show students the books they'll be using and the subjects they'll be studying. Demonstrate various materials, point out the computer(s), and highlight the textbooks.

- Wrap up the day. Provide a final whole-class activity that encourages students to work together and get to know one another. Tie it to part of the curriculum. Better yet, provide students with part of an activity, but leave them hanging. That is, don't complete the activity on the first day, but let students know that when they return the next day, they will have an opportunity to finish the activity, project, or assignment.

- Send the students home with warm wishes and all the necessary forms to complete. Don't forget to send a letter home to parents telling them about your plans for the year and your wish to have them actively involved in their children's education.

First Day at the Secondary Level

First day at the secondary level is just as exciting and just as anxious as first day at the elementary level. There are so many names to learn, so many procedures to remember, and so many tasks to accomplish. Consider this suggested sequence of activities:

◆ Meet and greet your students at the door to your classroom. Shake their hand, call them by name, and welcome them into the room. This is a critical moment for preadolescents and teens as it sets the tone for the rest of the day and the rest of the year. It lets them know that their attendance is valued and that they are part of a community of learners. I suggest that you make this single act a regular part of your daily routine. You'll reap untold benefits.

◆ Establish a seating pattern or seating chart early on. Initially assign students to desks. You might want to do this alphabetically so you can learn their names quicker. Later, you can inform them that a class meeting will determine final or rotating seating assignments.

◆ Talk briefly about yourself. Let students see your human side by discussing your education, your family, and especially your philosophy.

Secondary Thoughts

Post a philosophical statement on the wall and use it to initiate some discussion with students on the first day. Select one that has personal meaning for you (you might want to use different statements with different classes or different periods). Here are a few I've used:

"You can't earn if you don't learn."

"Imagination is more important than knowledge." —Albert Einstein

"There is nothing more dangerous than a closed mind."

"Education is a process, never a product."

"Education is never about achieving perfection, but rather about meeting challenges."

◆ Take attendance. Spend some time learning the correct pronunciation of students' names. Make a positive comment about each students as you go through your class list ("Thanks for coming," "Good to see you," "How's the team look this year?").

◆ Share an initial set of rules and classroom expectations. Secondary students will quickly determine what kind of teacher you will be by how many rules you have, how precise those rules are, and the severity of the punishments you establish for infractions. Remember K.I.S.S.—Keep It Short and Sweet. Don't overload them with rules the first day. Let them know that they will be involved in establishing classroom procedures throughout the year.

◆ Inform students about your expectations for each class and each period. They need to know about bringing textbooks, note taking, expected quizzes and exams, homework assignments and procedures, getting your attention (raising hands), and bathroom procedures.

◆ Provide students with a syllabus or course outline for the semester or year. Inform them about the topics you'll cover; the projects they will complete; and any special activities such as field trips, guest speakers, or multimedia.

◆ Schedule a motivating or energizing activity related to your subject area. This can be in the form of a *Jeopardy!* game, a panel discussion, a scavenger hunt (see the earlier "First Day at the Elementary Level" section; adapt the hunt as necessary for secondary students), or a cliffhanger like one of these:

　　◆ Begin reading a book, but stop at a climatic point. Tell students that you'll read the conclusion tomorrow.

　　◆ Give students some brainteasers or puzzles related to a forthcoming topic. Tell students you will provide the answers in tomorrow's class.

　　◆ Engage students in a hands-on project (a mobile, diorama, poster, etc.). Tell them you'll provide time in tomorrow's class to complete the project.

◆ Provide a very short, but motivational, homework assignment. Here are some possibilities:

　　◆ *History:* Interview your parents or grandparents about a recent historical event.

　　◆ *Science:* Locate a discovery or invention that was not around 20 years ago.

　　◆ *English:* Write your own epitaph.

　　◆ *Math:* Find three mathematical equations used in popular media (billboards, magazine advertisements, TV commercials, etc.).

- ◆ *P.E.:* Discover what the world record for the hammer throw is or what is the hammer throw? For men? For women?

- ◆ *Art:* Find a Salvador Dali painting and tell what it means to you.

◆ Wrap up the period by giving students a preview of things to come. Whet their appetite for the coming week, the coming month, and the coming year. Leave them with a feeling of anticipation.

And in Conclusion ...

If it's true that first impressions are lasting impressions, then what you do during that all-important first day of school helps set the tone (and the expectations) for the year to follow. These final tips will help you make this day a successful one.

Plan out a sequence of administrative tasks that you must do the first day. Frame these as a checklist, and check them off as you complete them. Among others, these may include the following:

- ❏ Attendance
- ❏ Seating chart
- ❏ Health forms
- ❏ Free and reduced lunch lists
- ❏ "Specials" forms (forms for the music, P.E., art, library programs)
- ❏ Homeroom lists
- ❏ Special education forms
- ❏ Permission slips
- ❏ P.E. exemption forms

Be sure to provide students with first-day activities and assignments that you're confident they'll complete successfully. It's vital that students achieve a measure of success on the first day—whether that success is being able to hang their coat on the proper hook in the kindergarten classroom or discover the solution to a brain puzzler in the advanced algebra class.

The Least You Need to Know

- ◆ Everyone will be asking two critical questions on the first day, will you be any good and will they like you. With a little planning, you can answer "yes" to both.

- ◆ Your personality, the community, routines, and your determination will all help set the tone for a successful first day of school.

- ◆ The first day in an elementary classroom is fast-paced, hectic, and seemingly without end—but you'll love it!

- ◆ The first day at the secondary level will leave you gasping, somewhat lost, and slightly dazed—but you'll love it!

- ◆ First impressions are often lasting impressions. A great first day can lead to many other great days.

Chapter 5

Lesson Plans: The Nitty-Gritty of Teaching

In This Chapter

- Lesson plans, defined
- All the lesson plan parts, from start to finish

Imagine you want to take a driving trip from the East or West Coast to Colorado. What would be one of the first things you would do? Like most people, you would probably obtain a road map. The map is your guide; it helps you locate the highways you'll travel, points of interest along the way, and the fastest (or most scenic) way to get to your destination.

A lesson plan is a roadmap for teachers. It is your instructional guide in the classroom, a way to map out what you want your students to learn, how you'll help them learn the material, and how you'll know if they actually learned that material. Let's take a look at good lesson planning and how you can make it happen in your classroom.

Understanding Lesson Plans

"Why should we write lesson plans when the textbook has all the information we need to teach our students?" Many teachers typically ask this question which reflects their concern not only for the content of their course(s) but also for the time necessary to create lesson plans.

But a lesson plan is just that: a plan or a blueprint, subject to modification and revision from year to year and from one group of students to another. In essence, a lesson plan is a sketch that provides a sense of direction and the means to help students achieve appropriate levels of understanding.

No textbook or set of printed materials can be written to serve the needs of all students. The students you will have in your classroom are unique and have their own particular learning styles, attitudes, and aptitudes. No textbook publisher can plan for that. Your experience in teaching at your grade level or subject area, in knowing your own strengths and weaknesses, and in tailoring lessons to the special characteristics of students are important in ensuring the success of your curriculum.

A lesson plan is a *guide* and a guide only. A well-designed lesson plan is flexible, subject to change, and reflective of the individual needs of each and every student in the classroom.

A good lesson plan provides an outline for the accomplishment of specific tasks, while at the same time allowing for a measure of flexibility in terms of student interests and needs. Lesson plans exist for several reasons:

- ◆ To ensure that students are taught what they need to know (as established by the school, the district, or the state)

- ◆ To prepare for and attend to individual differences between and among students

- ◆ To ensure effective and efficient teaching so classroom time is used appropriately

- ◆ To provide others (e.g., substitute teachers) with an appropriate instructional plan

- ◆ To serve as a way for teachers to evaluate their teaching effectiveness

Lesson plans can take many different designs and allow for a variety of options. Your school or district might dictate the design; however, most lesson plans will follow this basic outline. Let's look at the outline first; then I'll address each of its components.

Lesson Plan

Class/subject: _____

Date of lesson: _____

Period/time: _____

Topic: _____

Objectives: _____

Assessment: _____

Standard(s): _____

Resources: _____

Procedures:

  1. Motivational opening: _____

  2. Development of lesson: _____

  3. Closure/outside work: _____

Evaluation (personal reflection): _____

Adaptations: _____

First Things

When preparing a lesson plan, you need to clearly state some initial information:

- **Class/subject.** What is the class you are teaching (elementary) or the subject (secondary)?

- **Date of lesson.** What day of the week and actual date on the calendar will you be teaching this lesson?

- **Period/time.** What period of the day (secondary) or time of the day (elementary) will you be teaching this lesson?

- **Topic.** What is the focus or main idea of the lesson?

Expert Opinion

Many schools or districts ask you to prepare your lessons one week in advance and turn them in to the building principal to be checked and recorded. The preliminary information is important if the principal is planning to visit your classroom (for an observation) or there's a need for a substitute teacher in your room.

What to Teach

One item you won't see on the lesson plan here might be the one you control the least: the content of the material you'll teach. The subject content (the information you'll teach) might come from a variety of sources. These sources may include but are not limited to textbooks, state curriculum guides, and/or district curriculum guides. Although the content might be fairly standardized within a grade or subject area, the ways in which that content can be taught are as varied as the number of teachers teaching it.

Expert Opinion

To find out the recommended or required content for any grade or subject area, log on to your state's Department of Education website and obtain that information directly.

Jabberwocky

Your lesson plan's **objectives** describes what the students will be able to do upon completion of the instructional experience.

Objectively Speaking

The crux of a good lesson plan is its *objectives*. Continuing with the roadmap analogy, getting to your final destination (Carbondale, Colorado, for example) is your objective. In a lesson plan, the final destination (identifying iambic pentameter *or* listing important events in the life of Benjamin Franklin, for example) for your students is the objective(s) of the lesson.

To take the analogy one step further, objectives are what drive a lesson. They power it forward. Most important, everything you do in a lesson must be tied to one or more objectives. Every activity, every instructional devise, every teaching resource, and every means of evaluation and assessment must be linked to the lesson's objective(s).

Writing good objectives will be challenging at first. However, everything in the lesson must revolve around the objectives; thus, you must construct them with care and attention to detail. A well-crafted objective has two components:

- **The audience:** The students for whom the objective is intended
- **The terminal behavior:** The anticipated performance

Here's an example of an objective for a third-grade science lesson: students will list the nine planets of our known solar system.

CAUTION **Fire Alarm** _____

For purposes of clarity, I am not describing the traditional behavioral objective used by many schools. A behavioral objective has four elements:

- ◆ The audience
- ◆ The terminal behavior
- ◆ The observable conditions or the setting in which the behavior is to be demonstrated
- ◆ The degree of proficiency or performance level

Here's an example of a behavioral objective: All students will write an essay summarizing three major factors that lead to the start of World War II.

Objectives are built around good verbs. I like to think of verbs as the gasoline that keeps a lesson moving forward. Thus, the verbs you use in your lesson objectives should be action verbs or verbs you can use to measure performance. Passive verbs are often immeasurable and make an objective weak. These are just a few sample verbs (among hundreds possible).

Passive Verbs to Avoid			
appreciate	enjoy	learn	realize
believe	know	like	understand

Active Verbs to Use			
add	compute	inspect	rate
alphabetize	construct	list	review
assemble	debate	locate	say
assess	define	match	select
build	design	measure	show
calculate	discuss	operate	solve
collect	draw	place	speak
color	explain	plan	write
compare	grow	point	

As you'll note in these examples, it would be relatively easy to assess students' ability to add (e.g., Students will be able to add a column of two-digit numbers), but quite difficult to assess a students' ability to realize (e.g., Students will be able to realize Lee's defeat at Gettysburg). Action verbs in your objectives help you assess students and be sure they know or can do what you taught them.

Assessment

You want students to learn, but how will you know if they have learned what you taught them? You need to assess or evaluate how well they have learned the material you presented. Unfortunately, many teachers think assessment is simply the administration of a test or quiz at the end of a lesson. Nothing could be further from the truth. Effective assessment is composed of several decisions that you must make while writing a lesson:

- ◆ How often during the course of the lesson will I assess my students?

- ◆ What will be the format (informal vs. formal) of my assessments?

- ◆ At what points in the lesson should I assess students?

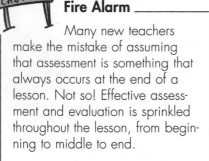

Fire Alarm

Many new teachers make the mistake of assuming that assessment is something that always occurs at the end of a lesson. Not so! Effective assessment and evaluation is sprinkled throughout the lesson, from beginning to middle to end.

The bottom line of assessments is this: what do you need to know about your students, and when do you need to know it? The well-designed lesson will provide opportunities for both you and your students to evaluate progress within the lesson. Any and all assessment tools must be designed and placed within a lesson to determine if your students are mastering the objectives or are in the process of learning those objectives. (Chapter 9 addresses assessment and evaluation in greater detail.)

Standards

Depending on the requirements of your school or district, you might be asked to include local, state, or national *standards* in each of the lessons you plan. Understand that standards and objectives are not the same thing.

Jabberwocky

Generally speaking, **standards** describe what students should know and be able to do. *Academic or content standards* provide a clear description of the knowledge and skills students should be developing through instruction in specific content (or academic) areas. *Performance standards* describe what it will take for a student to demonstrate mastery of a standard (sometimes called benchmarks).

I spend more time and detail in describing standards in Chapter 6. It's important, however, for you to find out if your school or district requires the addition of standards to your lesson plans.

Resources

In this section of your lesson plan, you need to list all the materials and resources you want to use in teaching the lesson. Fortunately, many resources are available to help you create your lessons (I'll address these in more detail in Chapter 6).

You will undoubtedly discover that your biggest decision when planning your lesson is deciding which resources to use from the hundreds available. Effective lessons combine several different resources to provide for a variety of learning (and teaching) opportunities.

Fire Alarm

Boring lessons often over-rely on a single resource (the textbook, for example) for the entire lesson.

Consider these resources for your lessons:

- ◆ Textbook(s)
- ◆ Supplemental textbooks
- ◆ Children's or adolescent literature; trade books
- ◆ Commercial teacher resource books (see Appendix C)
- ◆ Materials from a teacher supply store or online store
- ◆ Online resources
- ◆ Other teachers
- ◆ Community resources (guest speakers, printed materials)
- ◆ Students

Procedures

This is the body of your lesson plan, the ways in which you'll share information with students and the methods you'll use to help them assume a measure of mastery of that material. The three stages (a motivational opening, the development of the lesson, and the closing), although instructional in nature, can also involve some formal or informal assessment periodically. Periodic assessment throughout a lesson will alert you to any misconceptions or misunderstandings students may have long before they reach the conclusion of the lesson (when it may be too late).

Let's take a look at the three major stages of this section of effective lesson planning.

Motivational Opening

This stage of a lesson is critical! It's how you stimulate students' interest in a topic or subject. It may involve asking students a thought-provoking question such as, "How would you like to sleep for four months every year?" or "Did you know we can measure any tree on the playground without climbing it?" Other attention-gaining devises can include models, maps, globes, a piece of apparatus, or a demonstration. It is important that each and every lesson include some method to stimulate the students' interests.

Here are some other methods to consider for this all-important first stage:

♦ **Tapping background knowledge.** Students bring a certain amount of background knowledge or prior experiences to any lesson. Use this opportunity to find out what students know before beginning any lesson.

♦ **Self-questioning.** I've found that when students of any age are provided opportunities to generate their own questions about a topic, they will be motivated to seek the answers to those questions.

Secondary Thoughts _____

Don't make the mistake of assuming what students know. Take the time to assess their background knowledge, and you'll be rewarded with more successful lessons. For example, just because students studied American history in elementary school, had a basic history course in middle school, and are now in your high school history class, don't assume they know all there is to know about American history. Take the time to find out. Bottom line: Always know what your students know!

- **Predicting.** Predictions are educated guesses about what might or might not happen. Predictions are valuable for providing students with some self-initiated directions for a lesson.

- **Brainstorming.** Brainstorming allows students to share much of their prior knowledge in a supportive arena. Encourage students to brainstorm for everything they may know about a topic. Remember that the emphasis in brainstorming is on gathering a quantity of ideas, regardless of their quality.

- **Reading aloud.** Read a book, a piece of children's or adolescent literature, or other written resource to students to pique their interest and stimulate their curiosity.

- **Establishing relationships.** It's valuable for you to demonstrate how a lesson is related to other lessons. Students must understand that no single lesson exists apart from other lessons, but has a relationship with other previously presented material.

- **Organizing graphically.** Use graphic organizers (charts, graphs, or outlines of the essential information in a lesson) to provide students with a pictorial representation of the major points in a lesson and how those points are related to each other.

- **Stating the lesson objectives.** Often students perceive a lesson as something a teacher concocts on the spot. Unfortunately, that perception sends a signal that lessons are not designed with students' needs and interests in mind. It's vital, therefore, to let your students know exactly what they will be taught and what you plan to have them learn. When students are aware of the objectives, they will be able to understand the direction and scope of a lesson and work with you in achieving those learning experiences.

Development of the Lesson

This is the heart of any lesson—that portion where you teach and where students learn. This is where students obtain valuable information, manipulate data, and engage in active discovery through total involvement. Include some of the following elements in this stage:

- **Lesson methodologies.** Not only is it important to give some thought as to what you're going to teach, it is equally significant that you consider the methods of presentation as well. I'm sure you've been in a class where the only method of instruction was dry, stale lectures. You undoubtedly found the class boring and wearying. The same fate awaits your students if you provide them with an over-abundance of one type of teaching methodology to the exclusion of others. (These are addressed in considerable detail in Chapter 10.)

◆ **Problem-solving.** As I discuss in Chapter 13, problem-solving is an inherent part of any lesson. Providing students with the opportunities to solve their own problems in their own way is a valuable motivational technique.

◆ **Creative thinking.** Learning is much more than the memorization of facts. Any lesson must allow students opportunities to manipulate data in new and unusual ways.

◆ **Hands-on activities.** It's critical that students have sufficient opportunities to create products based on what they learn. These might include but are not limited to posters, dioramas, charts, graphs, mobiles, notebooks, portfolios, and models.

◆ **Student engagement.** Successful lessons include several ways in which students can practice the desired behavior(s). Here are just a few suggestions:

◆ Students critique the directions or set up for a presentation or demonstration.

◆ Students verbalize the steps they're taking during the completion of an activity.

◆ Students manipulate objects or devices and verbalize their feelings about their actions.

◆ Students work in small groups to share information learned and how it relates to prior knowledge.

◆ Students graph or illustrate significant points on the chalkboard for class critique.

It's Elementary

Consider both short-term as well as long-term projects in which students can participate according to their interest and ability levels. You might want to include a variety of activities within a lesson as well as some activities that can extend over longer periods of time.

Closure

Effective public speakers always follow three essential rules of a good presentation:

1. Tell the audience what you're going to tell them.

2. Tell them.

3. Tell them what you've told them.

Those same rules are important in the well-designed lesson, too. It's essential that you incorporate some sort of closure into the lesson. This might mean a few minutes at the end of the lesson during which you or your students summarize some of the significant points, an activity in which students share perceptions with each other, or a time during which students recall their positive or negative perceptions of a lesson.

Here are some closure suggestions:

♦ **Teacher summary.** Be sure to summarize the important points or critical elements of a lesson for students. Discuss what you taught and what they learned. This might be the most valuable 3 to 5 minutes of any lesson.

♦ **Student summary.** Provide opportunities for students to summarize a lesson as well. Inviting them to put a lesson into their own words can be helpful to you in determining how well they learned the material.

♦ **Lesson product.** Invite students to incorporate the major elements of a lesson into a final product. As described earlier, this product may take the form of a poster, brochure, model, or portfolio.

Expert Opinion

Whenever possible, use a cliffhanger at the end of a lesson. This can be an unanswered question you write on the board, an unfinished project, or an enticing bit of information ("Tomorrow I'll bring in a creature with eight eyes. You won't want to miss it!")

Self-Evaluation

As you write lessons, include a brief section at the end that allows you to self-evaluate. This will be important when and if you decide to teach the lesson again. It will also provide you with some important insights relative to your perceived level of success.

You might consider some of these self-evaluative questions:

"How was my pacing?"

"Did students understand the content?"

"Did students understand the important concepts?"

"Did I use my time appropriately?"

"What changes should I make the next time I teach this lesson?"

"Were students engaged and involved?"

"What new activities or procedures could I include?"

"Did I present the lesson well?"

Adaptations

As you'll discover in Chapter 18, you will undoubtedly have a wide variety of students who will exhibit various talents, skills, emotions, physical and mental attributes, languages, and perceptions. You'll need to make accommodations or create specialized learning opportunities for some of those students. You should include any special materials, procedures, or techniques in this section of a lesson plan.

The Least You Need to Know

- A lesson plan is a basic outline of what you will teach and how you will teach it.

- A well-designed lesson plan has several elements—all of which work together.

- A lesson plan is built around active verbs—verbs that can be assessed and evaluated.

- The heart and soul of lesson plans are the motivational opening, the development of the lesson, and a lesson's closure.

Chapter 6

Resources: So Much to Choose From

In This Chapter

- ◆ Textbook use

- ◆ Community and local resources

- ◆ Standards-based education

- ◆ Copyright law—what you need to know

- ◆ Free stuff for you

Teaching is very much a "people activity," but you know you'll need some assistance helping students learn. That assistance usually takes the form of the resources, materials, and textbooks available in the classroom. What you use and how you use it will be a major factor in the construction of your classroom program; just as it will be a major element in the overall success of your program.

This chapter provides you with an overview of some of the resources, materials, and textual items available to you and your students. Consider them as possibilities, not absolutes, for the design of your individual instructional program.

Textbooks: Open 'Em Up and Check 'Em Out

As you visit classrooms, you probably notice that most, if not all, of those classrooms use a standard *textbook* series. The reasons for this are many, depending on the design and focus of the curriculum, the mandates of the administration, and/or the level of expertise on the part of classroom teachers.

Jabberwocky _____

A **textbook** is a collection of the knowledge, concepts, and principles of a selected topic or course. It's usually written by one or more teachers, college professors, or education experts who are authorities in a specific field. Most textbooks are accompanied by teacher guides, which provide you with supplemental teaching materials, ideas, and activities to use throughout the academic year.

Textbooks provide you with several advantages in the classroom:

- ◆ Textbooks are especially helpful for beginning teachers. The material to be covered and the design of each lesson are carefully spelled out in detail.

- ◆ Textbooks provide organized units of work. A textbook gives you all the plans and lessons you need to cover a topic in some detail.

- ◆ A textbook series provides you with a balanced, chronological presentation of information.

- ◆ Textbooks are a detailed sequence of teaching procedures that tell you what to do and when to do it. There are no surprises—everything is carefully spelled out.

- ◆ Textbooks provide administrators and teachers with a complete program. The series is typically based on the latest research and teaching strategies.

- ◆ Good textbooks are excellent teaching aids. They're a resource for both teachers and students.

Use Textbooks Wisely

A textbook is only as good as the teacher who uses it. And it's important to remember that a textbook is just one tool, perhaps a very important tool, in your teaching arsenal.

Sometimes, teachers over-rely on textbooks and don't consider other aids or other materials for the classroom. Some teachers reject a textbook approach to learning because the textbook is outdated or insufficiently covers a topic or subject area.

As a teacher, you'll need to make many decisions, and one of those is how you want to use the textbook. As good as they may appear on the surface, textbooks do have some limitations. The following table lists some of the most common weaknesses of textbooks, along with ways of overcoming those difficulties.

CAUTION

Fire Alarm

Some textbooks may fail to arouse student interest. It is not unusual for students to reject textbooks simply because of what they are—compendiums of large masses of data for large masses of students. Students may find it difficult to understand the relevance of so much data to their personal lives.

Weakness	Student Difficulty	Ways of Overcoming Problem
The textbook is designed as the sole source of information.	Students only see one perspective on a concept or issue.	Provide students with lots of information sources such as trade books, CD-ROMs, websites, encyclopedias, etc.
Textbook is old or outdated.	Information shared with students is not current or relevant.	Use textbook sparingly or supplement with other materials.
Textbook questions tend to be low level or fact-based.	Students assume that learning is simply a collection of facts and figures.	Ask higher-level questions and provide creative thinking and problem-solving activities.
Textbook doesn't take students' background knowledge into account.	Teacher does not tailor lessons to the specific attributes and interests of students.	Discover what students know about a topic prior to teaching. Design the lesson based on that knowledge.
Reading level of the textbook is too difficult.	Students cannot read or understand important concepts.	Use lots of supplemental materials such as library books, Internet, CD-ROMs, etc.
The textbook has all the answers to all the questions.	Students tend to see learning as an accumulation of correct answers.	Involve students in problem-solving activities, higher-level thinking questions, and extending activities.

continues

continued

Weakness	Student Difficulty	Ways of Overcoming Problem
The text is superficial, inadequate, or shallow.	Students do not have opportunities to pursue a topic in depth.	Spend more time on fewer topics to develop deep-rooted concepts and comprehension.

Think of a Textbook as a Tool

I like to think of textbooks as tools—they are only as good as the person using them. A hammer in the hands of a competent carpenter can be used to create a great cathedral or an exquisite piece of furniture. In the hands of someone else, the result may be a rundown shack or a rickety bench. How you decide to use textbooks will depend on many factors.

I would like to add a personal note of caution here: do not make the mistake of basing your entire classroom curriculum on a single textbook. The textbook needs to be used judiciously. A carpenter, for example, doesn't use only a hammer to build a magnificent oak chest. She may use a plane, chisel, saw, sander, or any number of tools to create the masterpiece she wishes to build. A great classroom program, just like a great piece of furniture, needs many tools in its construction.

When thinking about how you want to use textbooks, consider the following:

♦ Use the textbook as a resource for students, but not the *only* resource.

♦ Use a textbook as a guide, not a mandate, for instruction.

♦ Be free to modify, change, eliminate, or add to the material in the textbook.

♦ Supplement the textbook with lots of outside readings.

♦ Supplement teacher information in the textbook with teacher resource books (see Appendix C); attendance at local, regional, or national conferences; articles in professional periodicals; and conversations with experienced teachers.

Expert Opinion

Remember, no textbook is perfect, and no textbook is complete. It is but one resource at your disposal. Use it as a blueprint, a guidebook, or an outline.

Standards, Schmandards

One of the major movements in schools everywhere is standards-based education. Generally speaking, a standard is a description of what students should know and be able to do.

Expert Opinion _____

A mathematics standard for students in grades 6 though 8 is to "compare and order fractions, decimals, and percents efficiently and find their approximate locations on a number line." An example of a writing standard for students in grade 11 is to "write a persuasive piece that includes a clearly stated position or opinion along with convincing, elaborated and properly cited evidence."

By definition, educational standards let everyone—students, teachers, parents, administrators—know what students are expected to learn.

Educational standards have been developed by a number of professional organizations (see Appendix B) in addition to those created by state departments of education and local school districts. Standards are designed to answer four questions:

- What do we want students to know and be able to do?
- How well do we want them to know/do those things?
- How will we know if students know and can do those things?
- How can we redesign schooling to ensure that we get the results we want?

Let's take a look at each of these questions in a little more detail.

Learn to Earn

Standards make clear to everyone, including students, the expectations for learning. They are designed to help students be responsible for their own learning, become a good thinker and problem-solver, and know what quality work looks like. They are based on three primary concepts:

- **Content standards.** These describe what students should know or be able to do in 10 content areas: language arts, mathematics, science, social studies, fine arts, health, physical education, world languages, career and life skills, and educational technology.

- ◆ **Benchmarks.** These make clear what students should know and be able to do at grade levels K to 3, 4 to 5, 6 to 8, and 9 to 12.

- ◆ **Performance standards.** These answer the questions, "What does good performance look like?" and "How good is good enough?"

Higher and Higher

Standards-based education engages students, not only in the learning process, but also in knowing what is expected of them. Students know, before a lesson begins, what they should do to achieve competence. They also know that you, as their teacher, will do whatever it takes to help them achieve the standards of a lesson or unit.

Accountability Counts

In a standards-based school, everyone is accountable. Students are responsible for their own learning, parents know what is expected of their children, teachers provide a positive learning environment, administrators provide the necessary leadership, and community members work to support the learning. Everybody has a role, and everybody is responsible for learning to happen.

Teach Them, and They Will Come

Standards-based teaching is different from some of the more traditional forms of teaching with which you may be familiar. It is a sequential and developmental process in which academic standards become the focus, or pillars, around which all instruction revolves. Here's how you would develop a standards-based lesson:

Jabberwocky

Standards-based teach- **ing** is when teachers use activities and lessons to ensure that students master a predetermined set of requirements or standards.

1. Define the content standards and the accompanying benchmarks.

2. Write the learning objectives.

3. Develop the appropriate assessments.

4. Establish the performance standards or levels.

5. Design the lesson.

6. Plan the instructional strategies and/or activities.

7. Implement the instruction (teach).

8. Assess students.

9. Evaluate and refine the teaching/learning process.

And the Difference Is ...?

There are two major differences between standards-based teaching and traditional forms of teaching. In standards-based education ...

♦ Teachers identify key knowledge and skills *first* and use them to focus all instructional and assessment activities.

♦ Teachers determine performance standards and share these with students *before* instruction begins.

It is important to note that standards-based reforms have met with both success and controversy. Many school districts across the United States report that standards-based efforts have resulted in higher overall achievement test results. Another benefit is that community members are more engaged in the affairs of the school.

There are also some negative views on standards-based education. Teachers have concerns because of the sheer number of standards in place within a single content area or at a single grade level. Some teachers feel as though they have to "teach for the test" so their students will have higher test scores. There are also concerns about the lack of emphasis on problem-solving skills and critical-thinking abilities. Some communities are concerned that their urban schools are not being treated fairly and that the higher standards are causing higher failure rates.

Standards, whether those from professional organizations, your state, or your school district, are another form of instructional resource for your classroom. They can guide you in developing appropriate lessons and assist you in helping your students achieve academically. However, just as with any other resource, they are teaching tools. Just as you would select one set of tools to build a log cabin, so, too, would you select another set of tools to build a condominium. The same is true of the teaching tools at your disposal.

Copyright and Copy Wrong

You can use lots of printed and nonprint resources in your classroom. Because many of these materials are protected by copyright laws, your school or district may have policies in place to ensure that everyone is in compliance with current copyright laws.

Fire Alarm _____

To be sure you're in compliance with the most current copyright laws, please log on to the U.S. Copyright Office at website at www.copyright.gov.

When copying any material, it's important that the reproduction is allowed under the category of "permitted use."

Because of space, I'm not able to provide all the legal guidelines, so please check current laws as well as the guidelines used by your school. Following are some copyright do's and don'ts (from section 107 of the 1976 Omnibus Copyright Revision Act).

You may …

◆ Make single copies of a chapter of a book; an article from a periodical, magazine, or newspaper; a short story; a short essay; a short poem, whether or not from a collected work; or a chart, graph, diagram, drawing, cartoon, or an illustration from a book, magazine, or newspaper.

◆ Make multiple copies for classroom use (not to exceed one copy per student in a course) of a complete poem if less than 250 words; an excerpt from a longer poem, but not to exceed 250 words; a complete article, story, or essay of less than 2,500 words; an excerpt from a larger printed work not to exceed 10 percent of the whole or 1,000 words; or one chart, graph, diagram, cartoon, or picture per book or magazine issue.

You may not …

◆ Copy more than one work or two excerpts from a single author during one class term.

◆ Copy more than three works from a collective work or periodical volume during one class term.

◆ Reproduce more than nine sets of multiple copies for distribution to students in one class term.

◆ Copy to create or replace or substitute for anthologies of collective works.

◆ Copy "consumable" works, e.g. workbooks, standardized tests, or answer sheets.

◆ Copy the same work from term to term.

On the Hunt for Supplies

In addition to textbooks and other instructional materials, you'll also need nontext supplies to help teach your students.

One of the first things you want to do when you get your first teaching job is to check out the school's supply room or materials center. Survey the various types of supplies available for teachers—everything from pencils to computers. Find out early the procedures and rules for obtaining regular classroom supplies (paper, pencils, cellophane tape, paper clips, etc.) as well as those materials used infrequently (science equipment, maps and globes, charts, etc.).

Chapter 7 deals with educational technology, but it's important for you to discover early on where you can obtain various types of technological aides, including such items as videos, films, and filmstrips; computer software; DVDs and CD-ROMs; videodiscs and laser discs; and audiotapes, records, and recorded music.

By locating and determining the availability of these items early, you can make some important decisions regarding the development of your lessons. The success of teaching a specific topic may be determined by the availability of technological materials. Survey early and survey often so you are always prepared.

Your Community: Where the Action Is

Your local community has a wealth of resources available for your classroom. It doesn't matter whether you teach elementary school, middle school, or high school; you can and should take advantage of some of the resources right in your own backyard.

Power to the People!

One very valuable resource, often overlooked by classroom teachers, is people in their local communities. No matter whether you live in a large or small community, you can always find people who can add to your classroom program. These individuals can serve as guest speakers, panel members, seminar leaders, etc. Some potential people resources you may want to consider for various aspects of your classroom program include the following:

airplane pilots	environmentalists	musicians
astronomers	factory workers	nurses
biologists	farmers	nursing home staff
cartographers	flight controllers	park rangers
college instructors	gardeners	plumbers
college students	geologists	professors
conservationists	lawyers	sanitation workers
cooks	librarians	scientists
doctors	mechanics	store owners
druggists	medical personnel	telephone engineers
ecologists	meteorologists	veterinarians
electricians	museum personnel	vocational teachers

On the Home Front

Parents are also a valuable resource for any classroom teacher. You might want to solicit the involvement and contributions of parents with a letter similar to the following:

Can You Help Us?

Parents or guardians: Please complete the following survey and return it to school at your earliest convenience. Thank you.

Name: _____

Address: _____

Phone number: _____ E-mail: _____

Do you have any special skills you can share as part of our classroom program? These may include model building, electrical knowledge, weaving, fishing or hunting, cooking, writing, and the like. *I'd be willing to share the following:*

_____

_____

Do you collect any special objects you can share with students? These may include shells, coins, stamps, bottles, photographs, or postcards. *I'd be happy to demonstrate my collection of:*

_____

_____

Does any part of your work or job involve something related to our class or subject? This may include electricians, lawyers, doctors, store owners, beauticians, plumbers, carpenters, machinists, architects, etc. *I can share the following parts about my job:*

_____

_____

Do you have an association with any special places we may visit as part of our classroom program? These may include construction sites, museums, galleries, hospitals, industrial sites, and so on. *Yes, I can arrange a visit to:*

_____

_____

Do you know of other individuals in the community (friends, relatives, co-workers) who have a special hobby or talent they could share with our class?

Their name: _____

Phone number: _____ E-mail: _____

Do you have any special materials at home we could borrow as part of our instructional program? These may include antiques, memorabilia, special tools, gadgets, etc. *Yes, I could loan you:*

_____

_____

Is there any other information, materials, places, or data you can share with us that will help our classroom program?

_____

_____

Sincerely,

[your name]

I discuss the role of parents in education in greater detail in Chapter 23.

All Around You

One of the easiest ways to obtain resources and materials for your classroom is to tap into the local merchants in your area. I have used this strategy for many years with incredible success. I've gotten wallpaper samples from the local paint supply store, which we used to create our own homemade books. I've begged for travel brochures from the local travel agency as part of our study of European countries. By asking (pleading, begging) for materials and supplies from your hometown merchants, you can quickly make up for any deficiencies in the school budget.

Here are a few suggestions of places I've found helpful to seek supplies from:

- **Appliance store:** large boxes, cartons, cardboard
- **Carpet store:** carpet squares, rug samples
- **Florist:** ribbon, plastic ties, foil paper
- **Newspaper:** newsprint, old newspapers
- **Paint store:** paint samples, empty cans, stirrers, wallpaper samples
- **Art supply store:** rags, paint, crayons, ink
- **Pizza parlor:** pizza boxes, cardboard circles
- **Bank:** coin wrappers, deposit forms
- **Hospital:** x-rays, colored file folders
- **Camera shop:** 35mm film canisters
- **Liquor store:** cartons, boxes
- **Contractor:** wood pieces, plastic tubing, bricks

- ◆ **Hardware store:** buckets, tools, cleaners, brushes

- ◆ **Cleaners:** hangers

- ◆ **Travel agency:** travel brochures, pamphlets, maps

- ◆ **Supermarket:** egg cartons, boxes, paper bags

- ◆ **Doctor/dentist:** old magazines

- ◆ **Drug store:** empty pill bottles, posters, signs

Ask around your local community, and you might be surprised by what you can obtain. When local businesses and merchants know that some of the materials they would normally discard are being used for educational purposes, they are often more than willing to make contributions to your classroom. Make your requests in person, and build a personal relationship with several small businesses in your area. The results can be quite rewarding.

It's Free!

To freely or inexpensively supplement the teaching and supply materials you get from your school or district when budgets are tight, check out some of the professional resources you subscribe to. Many of the newsletters and newspapers published by these groups have sections offering free and low-cost materials. Usually, all it takes is a letter (or e-mail), and you can obtain all sorts of printed materials for your classroom. In each edition of *NSTA Reports*, the newspaper for members of the National Science Teachers Association (NSTA), a section lists a wide variety of materials, audiovisual aids, brochures, pamphlets, and other items that are either free or modestly priced. Check out professional newspapers—there's lots of stuff free for the asking.

Educators Progress Service is a company that publishes guides for teachers interested in obtaining free or inexpensive teaching materials. Contact them at 214 Center Street, Randolph, WI 53956; 1-888-951-4469; or www.freeteachingaids.com, and order a few of their guides for your classroom.

Expert Opinion

Check out www.freebies.com for some of the latest offers and latest materials you can obtain free of charge.

The Least You Need to Know

- ◆ Textbooks are just one of many resources you can use in your classroom.

- ◆ Standards-based education is a hot-button topic in schools today.

- ◆ Trade books and librarians are valuable resources.

- ◆ Be aware of current copyright laws.

- ◆ Your local community has people and material available to enhance your teaching effectiveness.

- ◆ Knowing where to look and how to ask can net you some free stuff for your classroom.

Teaching With Technology

In This Chapter

In the "good old days," a typical classroom held a chalkboard, some books, and rows of desks, sometimes bolted to the floor. Teachers were expected to do a good job regardless of the lack of materials or resources.

Technology in the classroom has come a long way since the days of horn-books, quill pens, and creaky wooden desks (can you even call those things "technology"?). Some teachers argue that we have too many resources at our disposal. Others say the cost of technology puts far too many resources out of reach of many school budgets. And some say that teachers under-utilize and underappreciate much of the available technology. Let's take a look and see what all the fuss is about.

Technology Defined

Many people tend to have a narrow focus of technology. That is, they believe that technology consists of computers and any materials associated with computers (CD-ROMs, computer disks, etc.). In reality, technology is considerably more.

Educational technology is very broad and expansive. If you use a television in your classroom to show a video about an environmental issue, you're using technology. If you use an overhead projector to illustrate a mathematical concept, you're using technology. If you ask a small group of students to access a website on the ancient Incas with the classroom computer, you're using technology.

Jabberwocky

Educational technology is any instructional aid(s) or media used by teachers that supports the teaching and learning process.

Expert Opinion

According to Dave Kochik, technology is simply another tool for teachers. He says that the best question teachers should ask is, "What tools will help me help my students?"

Anytime you or your students use a device, apparatus, or piece of equipment to enhance what you teach or what students learn, you are taking advantage of educational technology. The narrow view of technology (classroom computers) limits the options you have available to make learning happen in your classroom.

The current emphasis on educational technology and especially on the use of computers in the classroom makes it seem as though some of these tools are absolutely essential for good teaching and good learning to take place. However, it is vitally important to keep in mind that good educational programs are not built around technology; rather, technology is one of the elements (or tools) of a well-designed instructional program.

Computer Technology

Like many teachers, you might be somewhat fearful of your classroom computer. You might also be wondering how this instructional tool can best be used in your classroom to enhance your teaching and motivate your students. You might be concerned about the amount of time your students will spend on a computer and whether that time will be educationally productive. Or you might be worried simply about whether you will break the darn thing if you use it in the wrong way.

Your concerns are normal. Thousands of teachers every year have the same worries simply because computers are a relatively new tool for classroom teachers (chalk, on the other hand, has been around since the time of the dinosaurs). And as with any new tool, the operator (you) might be somewhat hesitant to use it.

Consider the uses for a computer in your classroom.

Student uses	Teacher uses
Desktop publishing	Preparing instructional materials
Word processing	Locating lesson plans
esting and assessment	Communicating with parents
Reinforcing skills (multiplication tables, spelling words)	Tracking student progress
E-mailing students in other schools	Creating tests and exams
Using multimedia encyclopedias	Creating multimedia presentations
Playing games and simulations	Generating student assignments
Researching homework	Contacting teachers around the world
Taking virtual field trips	Keeping records
Creating maps and other visual aids	Displaying slide shows
Completing graphic organizers	Creating curriculum guides
Accessing the Internet	Generating schedules, duties, and assignments
Using information databases	Accessing worldwide web cams
Participating in educational chat rooms	Grading
Creating banners and posters	Producing newsletters and other communication tools

The One-Computer Classroom

Many classrooms, both at the elementary and secondary levels, are equipped with a single computer. The question many teachers ask is, "How can I effectively use my single computer in a room full of 20, 25, or even 30 students?" Here are some ideas you can use in your classroom:

◆ Divide the class into pairs of computer buddies. Designate one period of time each day as computer time. Assign each pair use of the computer on a rotating basis.

- Set up the computer as a learning center (see Chapter 19). Students can use the computer during center time, rotating to the center at scheduled times.

- Small cooperative groups of students can work on the computer to access information, check out websites, and do necessary research on a rotating basis.

- Open the computer during morning arrival or afternoon dismissal for independent use. Again, rotate use among individuals or groups.

- Use the computer for whole-class activities. If you have access to a projection system or multimedia program, use it to project a word processing program, simulation, interactive map, or other visual aids for the entire class.

- Write each student's name on an index card or craft stick. Randomly draw three, four, or five names each day. Provide those students with computer access during the day. Go all the way through your class list and then start over. Rather than have each student use the computer once a week, you're providing access in concert with your daily schedule.

The Internet and Your Classroom

The Internet is a powerful, worldwide communications system. Often referred to as a "network of networks," it connects thousands of computer networks all over the world. It does this through data lines that can transmit information at high rates of speed.

I like to think of the Internet as a very large library. In a large library, the researcher has a plethora of resources, books, periodicals, microfiche, and the like at his or her fingertips.

The Internet houses literally billions of pages of text, and that number is growing every day. To say that there's a lot of information on the Internet would be a gross understatement. But just because it's online doesn't mean the information is useful or appropriate.

Check It Out!

Check out each and every website and even every *search engine* before presenting it to your students. The Internet is always changing, always evolving. It's quite possible that an address has changed or is no longer current. Pages might have been eliminated, and new pages might have been added. Knowing what your students are looking at will save problems later on.

Check any sites for their grade appropriate-ness. Be sure the content and the vocabu-lary is appropriate for your students' reading levels.

You might want to set up specific websites as bookmarks or favorites and limit students to those sites only. This will also enable your students to organize their searches more effi-ciently within a specific area of study.

Expert Opinion

Perhaps the best search engine for any classroom teacher is www.yahooligans.com. This site lists only prescreened, educator-approved, and kid-friendly web-sites. It's one of the few websites I can recommend without any reservations. Check it out!

Jabberwocky

A **search engine** is a program designed to find websites based on keywords you enter. For example, enter the keyword *volcanoes* into the search engine www.yahooligans.com, and you get a listing of more than five dozen websites.

For complex topics, students can save a lot of time by utilizing a *metasearch engine*. A metasearch engine submits a request for information to several different search engines at the same time. The results are arranged on a list from high-frequency to low-frequency citations. Some excellent metasearch engines include www.allonesearch.com, www.metacrawler.com, www.ask.com, and www.google.com.

Evaluating Websites

You'll find a lot of excellent material available on the web. By the same token, you'll also find a lot of inaccurate and inappropriate material, as well as a lot of dangerous material.

When evaluating the appropriateness of any website for your students, ask yourself the following questions:

- ◆ Does the website load quickly and easily?

- ◆ Is the website associated with a product, or does it contain advertising?

- ◆ Is the website easy to navigate for students of varying abilities?

Fire Alarm

Never allow your students to access a website until you have accessed and previewed it first. For example, using www.whitehouse.com will open up a pornographic site. Using www.whitehouse.gov will open up the official website of the White House in Washington, D.C. Please be advised.

◆ Is the author an authority in the field? What are her or his credentials?

◆ Is the website current and up-to-date?

◆ Does the content provide thorough and complete coverage of the topic?

◆ Does the website provide links to other sites?

◆ Does the website meet the instructional objectives of a specific lesson?

Bulletin Boards

Walk into most classrooms and you'll see one or more bulletin boards. Some will be creatively designed with eye-popping colors, dynamic illustrations, and three-dimensional letters. Others will simply be a hodge-podge of old, faded, and worn-out bulletins.

The difference is clear. Classrooms that are visually appealing and intellectually stimulating are those in which teachers have devoted considerable attention to their classroom bulletin boards. Your students will spend a significant portion of their waking hours in your classroom. It's important, therefore, that your classroom be one that excites, stimulates, and motivates students in a host of learning opportunities.

Elementary Bulletin Boards

Bulletin boards in elementary classrooms come in all shapes, sizes, and dimensions. Many teachers typically use these bulletin boards and bulletin board items:

alphabet charts	handwriting chart	Pledge of Allegiance
attendance chart	letter charts	rules
birthdays	number chart	school calendar
classroom calendar	outstanding work	weather chart
classroom helpers	phonics chart	word wall
current events	photo gallery	writing guidelines

Secondary Bulletin Boards

Middle school and high school bulletin boards are often reflective of specific subjects or topics and, thus, can vary widely. Here are some standard examples:

assignments	motivational posters
bell or period schedule	newspaper clippings
calendar	periodic table (science class)
classroom rules	Pledge of Allegiance
current events	school news
famous people/sayings	student writing(s)
homework policy	team schedules

Other Bulletin Board Ideas

Need more tips and possibilities for the bulletin boards in your classroom?

◆ Plan to change your bulletin boards, at the very least, once a month. Bulletin board displays lose their effectiveness if left standing for the entire school year!

◆ Whenever possible, create interactive bulletin boards. Provide flaps to lift, pockets to fill, Velcro pull-offs, puzzles to complete, or dials to spin. These bulletin boards directly involve students in a host of learning opportunities.

◆ Use a variety of bright colors, large letters, and lots of illustrations. Don't overload the visuals, however. Be sure there's sufficient "white space" on the bulletin board, too.

◆ Provide lots of opportunities for students to design and assemble bulletin boards. Encourage them to post their work and celebrate their accomplishments.

◆ Create extra bulletin boards by covering a wall of the classroom with butcher paper or newsprint. Students can write announcements, vocabulary words, or sayings on the paper. You can easily remove and replace the paper throughout the year.

Expert Opinion

You can obtain newsprint by visiting your local newspaper office on a regular basis. They often have excess rolls of newsprint after a print run of the newspaper. You can obtain this newsprint for free, just for asking.

- Create hanging bulletin boards by stringing a wire or heavy twine from corner to corner of your classroom. Put clothespins on the wire and hang student work, inspirational posters, decorations, or other items.

- Create a simple bulletin board that you can change each week. Post a series of different puzzles, mini-mysteries, word searches, or brainteasers each week for students to tackle during their free moments.

- Consider creating at least one "special events" bulletin board. This can be used to celebrate birthdays, the loss of a first tooth, new sisters or brothers (elementary); an historical event, a sports team victory, or a Student of the Week (secondary).

Overhead Projectors

One piece of technology that's been around for a long time is the overhead projector. This instrument is used to project information or data onto a screen in the front of the classroom. The information is printed on a transparency master (a thin sheet of acetate or plastic), and the transparency is laid on top of the projection surface. A bright light shines through it, and an enlarged image is projected on the screen.

Fire Alarm

The minimum font size for any overhead transparency is 24 points—no less! If you don't know whether a transparency is 24-point font or not, lay the transparency on the floor and stand over it. If you can't read it (without bending over), the font is too small. If you can read it, the font size is an appropriate size for projection.

Overhead projectors have a number of advantages. You can face your students as you project an image and write on the transparency. The projection also allows all students in the room to see important material. It also enables you to present visual information and lecture at the same time.

The effectiveness of an overhead projector as a classroom aid is determined by one factor—students in every part of the classroom must be able to see what you're projecting onto the screen. If the print is too small, the overhead isn't very effective.

Other Audio and Visual Technologies

You can use a wide variety of technologies to enhance your teaching effectiveness. Be aware of the increasing availability of these tools, and you'll be able to offer your students multidimensional learning opportunities.

But there's no magic formula or magic combination that will work in every situation in every classroom. Your increasing level of expertise in concert with your level of comfortableness will ultimately determine how much or how often you will want to use these instruments.

Some of the following technologies are traditional—they've been around for a long time. Others are relatively new. Still others, yet to be developed, will provide you with a wealth of instructional possibilities yet to be realized.

- **Audiocassettes.** These allow you to provide recorded music, voices, and sounds to your students. Tape players are inexpensive and easily used as adjuncts to any part of the classroom curriculum.

- **Broadcast radio.** Commercial and public service radio allow you to introduce current and past events into the curriculum. Weather broadcasts, National Public Radio, and breaking news events can be positive additions to social studies and science programs.

- **Speakerphones.** Several schools have effectively used speakerphones to bring guests into the classroom via conversations, interviews, and question-and-answer sessions.

- **CD-ROMs.** These discs of digitized sounds and pictures offer students relevant and current information in an easy-to-use format. They can be used independently by students and are frequently specific to selected areas of the curriculum.

- **MP3.** *MP3* stands for "Moving Picture Experts Group Audio Layer 3." These compressed audio files are easy to customize. The utility of MP3s as a classroom aid is still in its infancy, but it holds promise as an aid in music appreciation and speech instruction.

- **Instructional TV.** *Sesame Street*, the Discovery Channel, Channel One, and other educational programs on public televisions stations provide classroom teachers with a wide array of instructional possibilities.

- **Slide projectors and digital projectors.** These devices allow you to project photographed images onto a large screen. You can alter and vary the sequence of projections and easily insert new images into the slide show.

- **Video cameras.** Video cameras are being used in more and more classrooms. Not only can teachers record and show specific information relative to a particular concept, but students can also record interviews, nature scenes, and items of local interest in creating their own interpretations of a lesson or concept.

The Least You Need to Know

- Educational technology is broadly defined and broadly used in many classrooms.

- Computers offer you and your students incredible teaching and learning opportunities.

- The Internet opens doors, opens minds, and opens possibilities.

- Dynamic bulletin boards can send powerful messages to your students.

- Lots of technology is available to you. Go slow and get to know it.

Time: Just Another Four-Letter Word

In This Chapter

- ◆ Time robbers
- ◆ Taking control
- ◆ Saying "No"
- ◆ Giving students responsibility
- ◆ Time management tips

Have you ever said, "There just isn't enough time," or "I wish I had more time!" Often, it seems as though there aren't enough hours in the day to do all the tasks on our to-do lists. We often run out of time whenever we tackle a new chore or duty. Time, or the lack of time, seems to be the master of our lives.

However, I've learned that I can take control of my time, instead of time taking control of me, and so I'll show you some ways you can take charge of your time.

Too Many Tasks, Not Enough Day

I always chuckle to myself when people tell me that teachers have it easy. They say teachers just work a couple hours a day and then they have all those vacations off. Oh, if they only knew! I don't think it would surprise you to learn that teachers work many more hours, many more days, and many more weeks than the general public thinks.

Fire Alarm

The average classroom teacher will make more than 1,500 educational decisions every school day. In an average 6-hour school day, that's more than 4 decisions every minute.

Grading papers after school and on weekends, volunteering to coach various athletic or academic teams, coming in early to set up a special lesson, and spending holidays and vacations doing research or looking for new teaching ideas are all part and parcel of the life of a teacher. On top of that, you can add all the daily interruptions, distractions, unanticipated problems, or visitors and the myriad decisions that must be made. It's no wonder many teachers feel stretched to their limit by the end of the day.

What steals your time? Or what consumes your time so you're out of time for other tasks and duties? In conversations with teachers at all levels and in all types of schools, I have found that they most often cited the following chores, duties, and assignments:

- Classroom discipline
- Taking attendance
- Noninstructional activities

Secondary Thoughts

Educational studies and conversations with teachers have shown that the number-one time robber is classroom discipline. Studies revealed that more than 15 percent of an average high school day is devoted to discipline or student behavior matters.

- Visitors
- Noises, distractions, and unplanned interruptions
- Distributing and collecting papers
- Talking and telephone calls
- PA announcements
- Paperwork and clerical tasks
- Bus duty, hall duty, or cafeteria duty
- Grading and record keeping

A number of educational research studies have shown that more than half of a typical school day is consumed by noninstructional matters.

Taking Control of Your Time

Think about this: time is about control. When you allow time to control you, you never have enough of it. On the other hand, when you control your own time, you can allocate your time available to complete tasks and duties.

Time Chunks

When your friendly author (that's me) was asked to write this book, I was quite excited. Then, my friendly editor told me I had to write the 25 chapters of this book in just 12 weeks (in addition to holding down a full-time teaching position). Was I disheartened? No, because after writing around 90 books, I've learned that the best way to write a multi-chapter book is to break it into chunks.

By dividing an assignment (such as a book project) into smaller pieces, it becomes more manageable. I didn't look at this book as a 25-chapter project; rather I looked at it as a series of magazine articles. Each "article" would be between 12 to 14 single-spaced manuscript pages long; would have about 4,600 words, and would go through approximately 12 to 15 drafts. I pictured this project as a collection of short articles, rather than an overwhelming 115,000-word book.

"Chunking" a task or assignment into smaller pieces helps make the overall assignment more manageable. You can do as I do: after I finished each "article" for this book, I checked it off a master list. As I went along, I saw more and more check marks on my list. That was a positive stimulus and a positive incentive. Imagine how I would have felt if I just listed the entire book on my "To Do" list. It never would have been checked off until the end, and I might have become weighted down by the enormity of the project.

Here are some tips you can use for managing any major project:

+ Divide the project into smaller, more manageable chunks (lessons instead of a whole unit; paragraphs instead of a whole report; columns instead of a whole spreadsheet).

+ Record each individual chunk separately on a list.

+ Focus on completing one chunk at a time.

+ Check off each individual chunk as you complete it; then move on to the next chunk.

+ Look at how rapidly your check marks accumulate on your list, and use that as motivation to keep going.

♦ Give yourself a reward for the completion of two, three, or five chunks (I reward myself with macadamia nut cookies for every three chapters [or "articles"] I write).

Just Say "No"!

Teachers are special people. We love working with others—students, parents, colleagues, and maybe even our administrators. By our very nature, we are "people persons." We like to go out of our way to help others and especially to help our students succeed.

But as teachers, we have a tendency to say "Yes" too many times. We volunteer for too many projects; we get on too many committees; we get involved in the lessons or units of our colleagues; or we willingly take on duties simply because somebody asked us to. In the words of a former first lady, teachers need to "Just say *no!*"

Teachers tend to be workaholics—it's the nature of the job. As a result, you're likely to be confronted with lots of requests and lots of "invitations." Use these ideas for saying "No" with style and grace:

"I'd really like to, but I'm overcommitted right now and don't think I'd be able to do it justice."

"Thanks for asking, but I really need to spend some more quality time with my children … my spouse … my friends … myself."

"I appreciate your confidence in me, but I have other tasks that demand a lot of my time."

"I have a lot of assignments already on my calendar. Can I get back to you at a later time?"

"No thank you. I'm not ready to take on that additional responsibility just yet."

Share Responsibility to Save Time

One of the best ways you can increase the amount of time available to you in your classroom is to share the responsibility of certain (often daily or repetitive) tasks with your students. I mentioned that teachers traditionally make more than 1,500 educational decisions every day, but you don't need to! Give your students classroom responsibilities and decision-making power, and you'll increase your available time.

So Much to Do, So Little Time

Numerous tasks, chores, and assignments must be accomplished every day, from taking attendance to taking lunch count to handling late-arriving students or getting instructional materials. Most teachers do these out of habit or because they see them as "teacher jobs" or responsibilities.

Tip-Top Time Tips

You have a lot of things to do every day in your classroom. How can you get a grip on it all? The answer: turn some of those responsibilities over to your students. "But my students are too young … too old … too dependent … too …," you wail. Not to worry; *any* child can benefit from taking on classroom responsibilities. The ultimate benefit will be more time for teaching and more time for learning. These suggestions are for saving time (and your sanity); feel free to modify and adapt them to other daily duties and chores in your classroom:

- Post library pockets on a special bulletin board. In each pocket, place a colored index card with a student's name printed on it. When each student arrives in the morning, she or he is responsible for removing her or his card, turning it over, and putting it back in the pocket. A quick glance at the bulletin board will show you who is absent. You've just taken attendance.

It's Elementary _____

When students arrive in the morning, have each student remove a clothespin with his name printed on it from a special coffee can. Then he clips his clothespin to one of two strings strung across a bulletin board. One string is labeled "Packers," the other string is labeled "Buyers." You quickly have a count of who brought their lunch and who is buying it in the cafeteria.

- Purchase small Styrofoam cubes from a local hobby store. Glue a 1×1-inch square of red paper to a toothpick, then stick the toothpick into a cube. Make enough for all your students, and distribute them to the students. When a student needs assistance with an assignment or doesn't understand a task, she or he can pull the flag out of his or her desk and place it on the desktop. By glancing around the room frequently, you can determine who needs individual help. Students don't need to call out and disrupt the flow of instruction.

◆ Assign and rotate the job of "classroom greeter" to students on a weekly basis. This person's responsibility is to greet any and all persons who come into your classroom. This frees you to continue with a lesson rather than taking time out to attend to the visitor. Most visitors are there to deliver information (the buses are late) or obtain information (the lunch count). Students can easily handle these tasks.

◆ Place all your materials and supplies in properly labeled drawers, cubbies, cabinets, compartments, and storage bins. Assign the task of "materials engineer" to two students each week on a rotating basis. Those students are responsible for obtaining the necessary materials for selected assignments, experiments, or other instructional tasks to be completed by a small group or the entire class.

◆ In some classrooms, there are many tasks to accomplish in the morning (hang up jackets, put notebook inside desk, use the attendance chart, put homework in a basket, get a book, etc.). I found it advantageous, particularly at the beginning of the school year, to make a list of all those duties. I duplicated the list onto sheets of card stock (65-pound paper) and laminated them. I taped one of these cards in the upper right corner of each student's desk. When a student came in, he or she would use a crayon or wax pencil to check off each item as it was completed. Later in the day, we wiped off the cards so they were ready for the next day.

◆ Glue a picture of a boy on one sheet of card stock and a picture of a girl on another sheet. Laminate both sheets, and hang them by a string on hooks in the back of the classroom. When a student needs to use the restroom, she or he goes to the back of the room, turns over the appropriate card, and leaves. Upon returning to the classroom, the student flips the card back to the picture side. You can continue teaching without any unnecessary interruptions.

Secondary Thoughts

Instead of using paper passes for students to leave and use the restroom, make a large block of wood for the restroom pass. Make the block large enough so it won't fit inside a student's pocket. Paint it a special color, and print your name in large letters along the side. Hang it by a chain in the back of the classroom. Provide a single block rather than two separate blocks (only one student out of the room at a time).

◆ Pencil sharpeners can be a frequent interruption in any classroom. Rather than have students use the pencil sharpener during the day or during a lesson, assign one student each week as the "tool master." That student is responsible for sharpening a collection of pencils at the beginning of the day and placing them in a special container (an empty coffee can, a shoebox, etc.). Students who need a pencil can obtain them from the container on their own.

◆ Obtain colored baskets or trays from your local office supply store. Designate these as homework bins for your students by color:

  ◆ *Red:* Place completed homework here.

  ◆ *Green:* Get your homework assignment from here.

  ◆ *Blue:* Obtain homework assignments that were given out when you were absent from this bin.

  ◆ *Yellow:* Place uncompleted homework here. (This can alert you to students who did not understand the assignment, had difficulty completing it, or simply chose not to do it.)

Creating these routines and procedures will mean little unless you take the time to teach or train your students in how to use them. Clearly explain a routine to students and provide sufficient opportunities for students to practice it under your supervision (you might need to model some routines before encouraging students to practice them). This training time early in the school year will save you countless hours during the remainder of the year.

The Paperwork Conspiracy

What's the number-one time management problem for most teachers? You guessed it—dealing with paperwork. That includes all the reports, tests, attendance forms, graphs, letters, memos, mail, announcements, materials, and requests that consume not only our time but our desk space as well.

It's obvious that we're "paper packrats." We hate to throw away anything, and we hoard paper, save paper, move paper from one place (on our desks) to another and file, catalog, and store paper until the proverbial molehill becomes an actual mountain.

Fire Alarm

One efficiency expert estimated that of all the pieces of paper that go into our filing cabinets every year, fully 95 percent of it will never come out again—or only come out to go into the trash can!

Are you buried under mountains of forms? Did you finally discover a 4-week-old missing sandwich under a pile of papers? Do you spend most of your day shuffling, arranging, or filing 8½×11 sheets of paper? Welcome to the club!

There are ways of gaining control over the Mt. Everest of paperwork you must deal with every day. Try these suggestions:

- Use colored file folders to file papers. Select a different color for each subject or for each period of the day.

- If you haven't looked at a piece of paper in more than a year, throw it away. It's not that important.

- Business management experts coach you to handle a piece of paper only once. It's tough to follow, particularly for teachers, but try to keep it in mind the next time you stuff your briefcase with papers.

- Use a Rolodex file for phone numbers, addresses, PINs, e-mail addresses, and other frequently used information. A Rolodex file takes up less room than a pile of papers.

- Like most teachers, you probably have lots of books. These may be professional books, old textbooks, or resource books. If you haven't looked at a book in 2 years, donate it to your local library or community fund drive.

- Designate 1 day every month (for example, the third Tuesday of the month) as "filing day." Use it to file all the papers that have accumulated on your desk during the month.

- Designate 1 day every 6 months as "purging day." Use it to get rid of all the files and papers you haven't used in the last 12 months.

- Use your computer as a filing system. Use your word processing program to organize frequently used forms, exams, and records.

- Designate a special file drawer for each subject you teach. Organize it with colored files:

    Red: Lesson plans

    Green: Tests, quizzes, and exams

    Blue: Handouts and worksheets

    Yellow: Transparencies and PowerPoint disks

    Black: Unit plans

    Gray: Supplemental resources and websites

◆ Purchase two file baskets from a local office supply store. Label one "To and from the School Office"; the other "To and from Home." Place them on your desk, and keep the papers you typically handle moving in and out of them daily.

◆ Photocopy your class roster and laminate it. Use it for multiple purposes: to record incoming homework, parent permission slips, lunch money, etc. Use a wax crayon to mark each task, and then erase it when the task is complete.

◆ Many efficiency experts suggest that you establish time limits on how long you'll keep various types of paperwork. Here are a few suggestions:

> *Memos:* 1 week
>
> *Minutes of meetings:* 4 weeks
>
> *Letters to parents:* 3 months
>
> *Attendance records:* 1 year
>
> *Professional articles:* 2 years
>
> *Lesson plans:* 2 years
>
> *Grade books:* 3 years

Date each piece of paper you receive. When its "expiration date" arrives, get rid of it.

◆ Sort all incoming paperwork into three piles. The "A" pile gets your attention right away; the "B" pile gets your attention within the next 48 hours; and the "C" pile can wait until sometime in the future.

Maximize Your Instructional Time

As a classroom teacher, you want to engage your students in productive learning time. This is time when your students are engaged in meaningful and appropriate work. The more productive learning time you have, the more your students will learn. The challenge, of course, is in creating a classroom that maximizes that time.

Keep Things Flowing

Flow refers to the way in which learning activities move smoothly and briskly. There's no stop-and-start rhythm to the class, but rather one activity leads naturally into another activity. You can maintain that flow through an awareness of the following:

- Ignore minor behaviors that have nothing to do with the lesson. For example, a student is twisting a strand of her hair. It's not necessary to stop the lesson and point out that behavior to the student. Move over to the student, put a hand on her back, nod, and keep the lesson going.

- Some teachers jump back and forth between activities. They start one activity or lesson, go back and make a comment about a previous lesson or activity, and then return to the new activity. Keep your lessons flowing in a forward direction.

- Often teachers will continue to explain a point or concept until, as students would say, "it's been beaten into the ground." The trick is to know when students understand and then stop at that point.

Teach Transitions

Transitions are those times during the day when you move from one activity to the next. Because students work at different paces and different levels, some may be able to make the transitions faster than others. Thus, transition time often leaves openings for misbehavior and disruptions. To avoid this, consider the following:

- Let students know when (in 2 minutes, for example) an activity will end: "We'll have a whole-class review of triangles in two minutes."

- Let students know what they can expect in any subsequent or follow-up activity: "After lunch, we're going to continue looking at the structure of onion cells."

- Be sure your lessons have clear beginnings and endings. Review the lesson objectives before the lesson begins and again at the conclusion of the lesson. Verbal cues are also valuable: "It's time for science to begin. I hope you're ready for the adventure."

- Establish clearly outlined routines for transition times. Provide opportunities for students to practice those routines: "When you come in, be sure you complete your 'Fabulous Five' chores before you sit down."

Be Clear, Be Close

Students achieve when they know exactly what is expected of them. Incomplete assignments are often the result of incomplete directions. As a result, time is wasted. It's equally important that students know you are available at all times. The amount of learning that takes place in a classroom is often related to the distance you maintain with your students. Time is saved when you are readily available. Here are two considerations for you:

- Always provide clear, precise, and thorough directions to any assignment. If students are asking lots of questions about what they're supposed to do, the directions were not clear and precise.

- Closely monitor student progress by circulating throughout the room and maintaining a physical presence with the students. Your desk should just be a place to put papers, not a sanctuary from students.

Get a Handle on Pull-Outs

Pull-outs are those students who must leave the classroom and may include students who have appointments with the guidance counselor, lessons with the reading specialist or music teacher, or instruction for gifted students. With so many comings and goings, it's often difficult to keep track of everyone, much less teach a complete lesson to every student. Here are some suggestions:

- Laminate a personal schedule for each pull-out student and tape it to the corner of her or his desk. Teach the student how to exit the classroom with no disruption to the class. Make each student responsible for her or his own schedule. This is not something you have to monitor all the time.

- Work closely with the teachers your students are leaving class to see. Try to arrive at a schedule that will cause the least disruption to your classroom.

- Check with the administration or other teachers about any procedures for students needing to make up missed classroom work. Initiate a "study buddy" program in your classroom so that each time a student leaves, she or he has a buddy who is responsible for obtaining the necessary information and passing it along. If feasible, provide time in class for this exchange to take place.

Remember, time can be your ally or your enemy. It's all in how you look at it. Teach your students how to use it wisely, and master the ideas in this chapter. You'll be more in control of your classroom—and your life.

The Least You Need to Know

- You are in control of your time, not the other way around.

- People, paperwork, and interruptions will consume a major part of your instructional time.

- If you break a task into chunks, you can control the time available for its completion.

- Give students more responsibility, and you'll have more time to teach.

- You can handle paperwork (and avoid procrastination) with systematic organization and lots of purging.

- Maximizing your instructional time requires attention to flow, transitions, clarity in your directions and closeness with your students, and handling pullouts.

9

Testing, Testing: Assessment and Evaluation

In This Chapter

- Evaluation versus assessment
- Ways of gauging student learning
- Preparing good assessment tools
- Ways of evaluating students
- The pluses and minuses of high-stakes testing

Testing is very much a part of the learning cycle. By some estimates, the average student will take nearly 2,500 tests, quizzes, and exams during her or his school years. For the most part, those measurement devices are designed to determine how much students know about a particular topic.

However, that assessment does not have to be the dull, dry, pedantic monster it's often perceived to be by both students and teachers. Sure, assessment is a necessary part of any curriculum, but in the hands of a classroom teacher seeking to promote a dynamic and engaging curriculum, testing can also be a useful tool.

Assessment vs. Evaluation

Assessment is, most likely, not a new concept for you; however, in most previous assessment situations, you were probably the one being tested. As you move into your teaching position, you will assume the responsibilities of an evaluator and an assessor. You will be required to determine how well your students are learning, gauge their performance, and measure the appropriateness of the content and the effectiveness of the methods and techniques utilized in your classroom.

Jabberwocky

When you **assess** your individual students, you gather information about their level of performance or achievement. **Evaluation** is comparing a student's achievement with other students or with a set of standards.

Effective assessment is a continuous process. It's not simply something that's done at the conclusion of a unit of study or at the end of a lesson. Effective assessment and *evaluation* are integrated into all aspects of the curriculum, providing both teachers and students with relevant and useful data to gauge progress and determine the effectiveness of materials and procedures.

Here are some criteria to consider for your own classroom:

◆ Effective evaluation is a continuous, on-going process. Much more than determining the outcome of learning, it is rather a way of gauging learning over time. Learning and evaluation are never completed; they are always evolving and developing.

◆ A variety of evaluative tools is necessary to provide the most accurate assessment of students' learning and progress. Dependence on one type of tool to the exclusion of others deprives students of valuable learning opportunities and robs you of measures that help both students and the overall program grow.

◆ Evaluation must be a collaborative activity between teachers and students. Students must be able to assume an active role in evaluation so they can begin to develop individual responsibilities for development and self-monitoring.

◆ Evaluation needs to be authentic. It must be based on the natural activities and processes students do both in the classroom and in their everyday lives. For example, relying solely on formalized testing procedures might send a signal to children that learning is simply a search for "right answers."

Evaluation is intrinsically more complex than writing a test, giving it to a group of students, scoring it, and handing it back with some sort of letter grade. Indeed, it involves a combination of procedures and designs that not only gauge students' work but also help them grow in the process.

Categories of Evaluation

You have many ways of gauging student progress within your classroom. In this section, we'll concentrate on two very broad categories:

- **Product evaluation.** You are probably most familiar with product evaluation. Typically, it takes place at the conclusion of a lesson and involves some sort of paper-and-pencil test or quiz on the material learned. Well-designed product-oriented measures will be matched with the learning objectives of a lesson. What was taught is what will be tested; if it wasn't taught, it can't be tested.

- **Process evaluation.** Process evaluation concentrates not so much on what students have learned, but instead on how they learn or how they pursue learning. Process evaluation may include the development of teacher- or student-initiated projects (science fair projects) in which students pursue a particular area of interest. It may also include performance measures in which the teacher provides materials and procedures for using those materials and then observes how students perform on the specified tasks. The objective in process-oriented evaluation is not on whether students have learned a series of right answers but more so on how they go about learning.

We can further define these two forms of evaluation according to type:

- **Formative evaluation.** Formative evaluation is utilized concurrently with instruction. It is used to assess student progress with the material being presented, as a diagnostic instrument to determine student strengths and weaknesses, and to provide feedback for the student and teacher. It is the evaluation that occurs between the introduction of a unit of work and its conclusion.

Expert Opinion

The feedback provided by formative evaluation will help you determine the effectiveness of the content with a series of questions; for example, "Is the material too difficult or too easy?" "Are there gaps that need to be covered before we move on?" and "Do any concepts or vocabulary need to be clarified?"

♦ **Summative evaluation.** Summative evaluation is used frequently at the conclusion of a unit of study. Basically, it serves three primary functions:

1. It assesses the extent of pupils' achievement or competency at the end of instruction.

2. It provides a basis on which grades or course marks can be fairly assigned.

3. It provides the data from which reports to parents and transcripts can be prepared.

One way to distinguish between formative and summative evaluation is based on the utilization of the data collected through the evaluation instrument. If it is to be used to determine a final grade or assess the final achievement or performance of a student or a group of students, it is summative. If, however, the information is for planning purposes, it is formative.

Product-Oriented Evaluation

The majority of data gathered in summative evaluation comes from teacher-made tests. However, writing good tests is a skill that you must learn and practice if the instruments are to yield data of any use to you or your students.

Preparing Measuring Instruments

Construction of a good test takes careful planning. You must design the instrument to measure the objectives you have established for a specific unit of work. The objectives might be …

♦ The particular skills you want the students to perform (design a scientific experiment).

♦ The body of knowledge you've established for the class (knowing state capitals).

♦ The level of knowledge you desire your students to achieve (the application of specific forms of punctuation on a written assignment).

♦ The attitude or value you want your students to acquire (using relationships to defend answers on an essay examination).

In addition to evaluating the objectives you've established, you'll need to measure how well your students have acquired the body of facts, concepts, principles, and generalizations appropriate for the material you're presenting. The source of this body of information might be the curriculum guide you're following, the textbook you're using, or a unit you've designed.

Types of Product-Oriented Tests

You're probably familiar with two types of examinations: objective tests and essay tests. These two tests are widely used; however, you have many other assessment options:

♦ Multiple-choice

♦ True-false

♦ Short answer completion

♦ Matching

Fire Alarm

Essay exams have their disadvantages. They require more time to evaluate than is required for objective tests, and the "halo effect" (expecting better students to do well) may also influence your evaluation of essay responses.

Evaluating Product-Oriented Evaluation

It's important to keep in mind that evaluation, to be thorough, must occur before, during, and after instruction. One of the dangers of some of the more formal methods of evaluation is that they often take place at the conclusion of a lesson or activity. This tends to underscore learning as simply an accumulation of facts and figures to be memorized and regurgitated on various written instruments.

Secondary Thoughts

There's often a tendency for teachers to over-rely on written or summative type evaluation procedures. Remember that good evaluation includes a multiplicity of options and strategies.

Process-Oriented Evaluation

Much of what you will assess or evaluate in your classroom will be oriented to the products of learning. However, to have a well-rounded evaluation program, you must give equal attention to process-oriented evaluation as well.

A process approach to evaluation can provide both you and your students with valuable and useful information to gauge progress and assess the effectiveness of the entire curriculum. In so doing, you can help your students assume an active role in the evaluation process and can help make your classroom program more of a collaborative effort, instead of one in which you assume all the responsibilities for teaching and evaluating.

There are many forms of process evaluation, but here I will concentrate on just a few. I don't mean to imply that these are the only forms and formats, but rather that these have been proven over time to yield important data for teachers and students alike. Consider these (or modifications thereof) for your own classroom. You should also be willing to attempt other evaluative measures in keeping with your philosophy of teaching and your students' abilities and attitudes.

Performance Assessment

Performance assessment can easily be built into almost any lesson. It is, in effect, a "hands-on" form of evaluation allowing students the opportunity to demonstrate their understanding or mastery of important concepts through the manipulation of objects and concepts.

In a lesson on simple machines, for example, you can provide students with inclined planes (ramps), a weight, and a spring gauge. They can demonstrate their understanding of the inclined plane by pulling a weight up different ramps of different lengths and different heights. In other words, students have opportunities to apply their scientific knowledge in real-life events as opposed to a paper-and-pencil test, which may only indicate the factual data memorized.

Secondary Thoughts

Teachers often use a *grade contract* with secondary students. This agreement between the teacher and students stipulates that when a specified event(s) has occurred, a particular positive consequence will follow. For example, students can obtain a specific grade in a course (A, B, C) when they complete a certain number of assignments satisfactorily.

Project Assessment

You can do this form of assessment when students are relatively independent and can work by themselves or in small groups. In this evaluative procedure, students are provided access to all sorts of materials and supplies, and using their creativity, they must design or devise a project that illustrates a specific principle or concept. This form of assessment is long term and allows students to formulate plans of action and carry them out to their conclusion. Science fair projects, for example, are an excellent example of the project approach to evaluation.

Anecdotal Records

As I alluded to earlier, evaluation is not a "once-and-done" process. Rather, it occurs over time and tracks a student's development and competence over many days, weeks, or months. *Anecdotal records*, or narrative descriptions of students' behavior and academic performance, can be some of the most valuable evaluation tools available. Through anecdotal records, you can keep a running record of each individual student to determine likes and dislikes, advancement or regression, and growth and development.

By their nature, anecdotal records are subjective assessments of students. However, they have the advantage of "tracking" students over many occasions and many learning opportunities. In this way, they serve as an accurate record of performance that the teacher can share with administrators and parents. Here are some guidelines for using anecdotal records:

Jabberwocky

Anecdotal records are observational notes a teacher takes about a specific student's performance or behavior.

- ◆ Don't try to write a description of each student's behavior and performance every day. Identify four or five students a day, and concentrate on them.

- ◆ Keep your comments short and to the point. It's not necessary to write long, involved sentences about what you observe. To keep the notes short, invent your own method of shorthand.

- ◆ Maintain a file folder on each student. Store a student's anecdotal record in his or her folder at the end of the day.

- ◆ Record only what you saw and not the subjective reasons you think may have caused the behavior.

- ◆ Plan time at the end of the day to discuss your observations and anecdotes with each identified student. Let the students know what you have observed, and provide them with an opportunity to react and ask pertinent questions.

Expert Opinion _____

Purchase several sheets of self-adhesive mailing labels and a clipboard. Identify the four to five students you will be observing on a particular day, and write each of their names and the date in the corner of separate mailing labels. As you walk around the room during a lesson, jot down observational notes for each student on his or her mailing label (use more than one label if necessary). At the end of the day, remove each student's label and place it on a sheet of paper you then store in the student's folder. This way you can transfer your observations to students' folders quickly and can easily keep track of each student's progress in a chronological fashion.

Checklists

Use of a predesigned checklist enables you to gauge students' progress against a predetermined set of observational criteria. As you watch students participate in a project or activity, you can check off items according to how those students perform or behave. This data is similar in some respects to the information gleaned via anecdotal records; however, it does provide a series of constants against which all students can be assessed.

One form of checklist has students' names listed down the left-hand side of a grid with the specific behaviors or skills listed across the top. As you observe a behavior in each student, you can place a check next to that student's name.

Here's an example of a checklist that could be used as part of an elementary science lesson to assess process skills:

Name	A	B	C	D	E	F	G
1. _____	____	____	____	____	____	____	____
2. _____	____	____	____	____	____	____	____
3. _____	____	____	____	____	____	____	____
4. _____	____	____	____	____	____	____	____
5. _____	____	____	____	____	____	____	____
etc.							

A = Observing   E = Measuring

B = Classifying   F = Predicting

C = Inferring   G = Experimenting

D = Communicating

It's important to remember that the best kind of checklist is one you create specifically for a lesson, a group of students, or a specific set of objectives. Teacher-created checklists are far more useful (and specific) than commercial ones.

Portfolio Assessment

By definition, a portfolio is a coordinated assembly of past and present work that provides the viewer with a definitive and representational look at an artist's work and talent. Through a portfolio, an artist can collect a variety of work to reveal not only the depth of his or her talent but the breadth as well.

Portfolios are useful in the classroom, too. They are more than a haphazard group of papers and tests; instead, they demonstrate the talents and skills of individual students while demonstrating that student's growth record (and resulting progress) over a period of time.

Portfolios can be as simple as a single file folder for each student or as complex as a series of mailbox compartments set up in a corner of the classroom. Included in each portfolio can be the following (this is not an exhaustive list):

- Examples of the student's work in progress

- Dated progress notes written by the teacher

- Dated progress notes written by the student

- Dated progress notes written by the parent(s)

- Work samples selected by the teacher

- Work samples selected by the student

- Self-evaluation forms completed by the student

- Anecdotal and observational records maintained by the teacher

- Photographs/illustrations of completed projects

- Audio- or videotapes of selected work

- Experiment or project logs

- Tests, quizzes, and/or exams

- Written work of any kind

- Lists of books or outside materials read

The advantage of portfolios is that they provide teachers, students, administrators, and parents with a vehicle to document growth and a forum to discuss and share that growth as well as procedures and processes that might stimulate further growth. Although they are useful in terms of parent/teacher conferences, they are more beneficial in terms of teacher/student conferences. In a sense, portfolios personalize the evaluation process, making it dynamic and relevant to the lives of students and useful to the planning and design of successful lessons.

> **Expert Opinion**
>
> The types of items that can be included in a portfolio are limitless, but they should include representative samples of each student's work over time.

Student Self-Evaluation

The effective classroom program involves students in each and every aspect of that program—and that includes evaluation.

Self-evaluation can take many forms. Simplest of all would be in the context of student/teacher discussions. Teacher/student conferences allow you to pose several types of questions that provide opportunities for students to "look inward" and gauge their learning. Here are some examples:

"Tell me about the way you worked."

"Tell me about some discoveries you've made."

"Tell me about some of the things that didn't go well for you."

"Tell me about some of the things that gave you trouble."

"What comments would you like to make about your behavior?"

"What were some things you could do for yourself?"

"What were some things you needed help with?"

> **It's Elementary**
>
> When younger students participate in evaluating their own progress, they begin to develop an internal sense of responsibility, which helps them assume control over their learning.

High-Stakes Testing

Simply stated, high-stakes testing is when students are given a standardized test, the results of which are rewarded in some way. Failing the test might have negative consequences (or rewards), too. For example, in California, students must pass the California High School Exit Examination to graduate. If they don't pass, they don't graduate. Thus, when some sort of reward system is attached to a standardized test, that test becomes a high-stakes test. SATs (Standardized Achievement Test) and ACTs (American College Testing) are good examples of high-stakes testing because the "reward" is often admission into college.

Various types of federal legislation, such as Title I and the No Child Left Behind Act, require states to administer standardized tests to select groups of students. Often students' achievement on these tests determines the amount of funding or financial reimbursement a school, district, or state will receive from the federal government.

As a classroom teacher, you have little control over the use of high-stakes testing. You may be required to administer these tests whether or not you agree with them. In fact, in many districts, these tests are used to evaluate individual teacher performance. Suffice it to say, these tests will impact you and the kind of instruction you provide for a long time to come.

Final Thoughts

Overall, I like to think of evaluation as a process that offers opportunities for growth—teacher growth, student growth, and program growth. It's one thing to assess and evaluate student performance; it's quite another to do something with that information. If all you do is administer an endless bank of tests, checklists, and self-evaluative forms and do nothing with the results, then your evaluation is close to worthless. The data you gather from all forms of evaluation should be used productively to help students develop the skills, processes, and attitudes that help make learning an important part of their lives.

Evaluation is an integral part of the learning process. As such, it must be sensitive to the needs, attitudes, and abilities of individual students as well as the class as a whole. Be careful that you do not over-rely on one or more forms of evaluation just because they are easy or convenient for you. Be aware that evaluation involves some part of a student's self-esteem, and that affective factors are an important ingredient in evaluation. In other words, *what* you evaluate is just as important as *how* you evaluate.

The Least You Need to Know

♦ Assessment and evaluation are both part of the learning/teaching cycle.

♦ It's important to assess both the products of learning as well as the processes of learning.

♦ Evaluation must take place before, during, and after any lesson or instructional activity.

♦ A wide variety of evaluative measures are available for you to use in the classroom.

♦ Assessment and evaluation must be multidisciplinary and multifaceted to be effective.

Part 3

Effective Teaching, Effective Learning

Think about your favorite teacher. Think about how that person made learning exciting; how he or she turned you on to a subject like you've never been turned on before. Remember how that individual "energized" learning so much that you just couldn't wait to get to school each day. Perhaps she or he was the person who influenced you to become a teacher.

What did that teacher do to make learning so magical? What did that teacher do to get you so excited? In Part 3, I discuss all you need to know to be that exciting teacher in the lives of your students. I tell you about all the tricks of the trade, all the inside tips, and all the skills you need to be a dynamic, stimulating, and motivating teacher.

Hartley's First Law: Anyone can lead a horse to water, but if you can get him to float on his back, then you've really got something.

Chapter **10**

The Methods Are the Magic

In This Chapter

- More methodologies than you can shake a stick at

- Knowledge, synthesis, and performance: the Three Musketeers of teaching

- No games, please

- Variety is the spice of … your classroom

It's important to give some thought as to *what* you are going to teach students; however, you must consider the methods of your presentation as well. You have undoubtedly been in a class that consisted of nothing more than dry, stale lectures. Chances are you found the class less than intellectually stimulating. The same fate awaits your students if you concentrate on one type of teaching methodology (only lectures, for example) to the exclusion of others.

The Method Is the Medium

Not all teachers are created equal. Many are stimulating and dynamic. Students learn, and the classroom is filled with enthusiasm and energy. Other teachers are not so exciting. Their classrooms are stale, and their lessons lack vitality and creativity. Learning, if it happens, is minimal or accidental.

Jabberwocky

Methodology is the way(s) in which teachers share information with students. The information itself is known as the *content;* how that content is shared in a classroom is dependent on the teaching methods.

What's the difference? Every teacher has her or his own unique personality, but the factor that often determines the effectiveness of any lesson is the *methodologies* used.

Just as there's a lot of content that you must share with your students, there's also a wide variety of ways you can present that content. The challenge is in knowing *how* to teach as much as it is in knowing *what* to teach.

So Many Ways!

The following chart lists a wide variety of lesson methodologies appropriate for the presentation of material, which I will discuss in this chapter. Notice how these teaching methods move from Least Impact and Involvement (for students) to Greatest Impact and Involvement.

As you look at the chart, you'll notice that lecture, for example, is a way of providing students with basic knowledge. You'll also note that lecture has the least impact on students as well as the lowest level of student involvement. As you move up the scale (from left to right), you'll note how each successive method increases the level of impact and involvement for students. At the top, reflective inquiry has the highest level of student involvement. It also has the greatest impact of all the methods listed.

Jabberwocky

Knowledge is the basic information of a subject; the facts and data of a topic. **Synthesis** is the combination of knowledge elements that form a new whole. **Performance** refers to the ability to effectively use new information in a productive manner.

Across the bottom of the chart are three categories: *knowledge, synthesis,* and *performance.* These refer to the impact of each method in terms of how well students will utilize it. For example, lecture is simply designed to provide students with basic knowledge about a topic. Reflective inquiry, on the other hand, offers opportunities for students to use knowledge in a productive and meaningful way.

Least Impact and Involvement		Greatest Impact and Involvement
		Reflective inquiry
		Skill practice
		Projects
		Simulations
		Modeling
		Role-playing
		Debriefing
		Independent practice
		Buzz sessions
		Problem-solving activities
		Graphic organizers
		Experimenting
		Small group discussions
		Mental imagery
		Brainstorming
		Interviewing
		Round robins
		Field trips
		Observations
		Demonstrations
		Audio-visual presentations
		Reading information
Lectures		
Knowledge	**Synthesis**	**Performance**

Now let's take a look at each of those three major categories and the methodologies that are part of each one.

Knowledge

How do you present basic information to your students? It makes no difference whether you're sharing consonant digraphs with your first-grade students or differential calculus with your twelfth-grade students; you must teach them some basic information. You have several options for sharing that information.

Lecture

Lecture is an arrangement in which teachers share information directly with students, with roots going back to the ancient Greeks. Lecture is a familiar form of information-sharing, but it is not without its drawbacks. It has been overused and abused, and it is often the method used when teachers don't know or aren't familiar with other avenues of presentation. Also, many lecturers might not have been the best teacher role models in school.

Fire Alarm

Often, teachers assume that lecturing is nothing more than speaking to a group of students. Wrong! Good lecturing also demonstrates a respect for the learner, a knowledge of the content, and an awareness of the context in which the material is presented.

Good lectures must be built on three basic principles:

- Knowing and responding to the background knowledge of the learner is necessary for an effective lecture.

- Having a clear understanding of the material is valuable in being able to explain it to others.

- The physical design of the room and the placement of students impact the effectiveness of a lecture.

Lecture is often the method of choice when introducing and explaining new concepts. It can also be used to add insight and expand on previously presented material. Teachers recommend that the number of concepts (within a single lesson) be limited to one or two at the elementary level and three to five at the secondary level.

It's important to keep in mind that lecture need not be a long and drawn-out affair. For example, the 10-2 strategy is an easily used, amazingly effective tool for all grade levels. In this strategy, no more than 10 minutes of lecture should occur before students are allowed 2 minutes for processing. This is also supportive of how the brain learns (see Chapter 2). When 10-2 is used in both elementary and secondary classrooms, the rate of both comprehension and retention of information increases dramatically.

During the 2-minute break, you can ask students several open-ended questions, such as the following:

"What have you learned so far in this lesson?"

"Why is this information important?"

"How does this information relate to any information we have learned previously?"

"How do you feel about your progress so far?"

"How does this data apply to other situations?"

These questions can be answered individually, in small group discussions, or as part of whole class interactions.

The value of the 10-2 strategy is that it can be used with all types of content. Equally important, it has a positive effect on brain growth.

Lectures are information-sharing tools for any classroom teacher. However, it's critically important that you not use lecture as your one and only tool. You must supplement it with other instructional methods to achieve the highest levels of comprehension and utility for your students.

Reading Information

With this method, you assign material from the textbook for students to read independently. You may also choose to have your students read other supplemental materials in addition to the textbook. These may include, but are limited to children's or adolescent literature, brochures, flyers, pamphlets, and information read directly from a selected website.

Audio-Visual Presentation

In this format, you rely exclusively on the use of slides, movies, filmstrips, PowerPoint slides, photographs, illustrations, videos, or overhead transparencies. In contrast to a lecture, most of the information is presented visually, rather than orally.

Demonstration

In this format, students witness a real or simulated activity in which you use materials from the real world. These materials may include artifacts and objects used by individuals in a specific line of work; for example, microscopes (biologists), barometer (meteorologists), transit (surveyors), or word processing program (writers).

Observation

This format allows students to watch an event or occurrence take place firsthand. The only drawback is that sometimes unexpected and unplanned events happen over which you may have little control.

Field Trips

With field trips, you are able to take your students out of the classroom and into a new learning environment (see Chapter 19). This learning environment usually lasts for several hours or an entire school day.

Round Robin

In this setting, each student has an opportunity to share some information or ideas in a small group format. Everyone participates equally and taps into the collective wisdom of the group.

Interviewing

This format may include the personal interview, in which one person talks with another person. It may also involve the group interview, in which several people talk with a single individual.

Brainstorming

Brainstorming can be a valuable instructional tool which you can incorporate into almost any lesson. Simply defined, it is the generation of lots of ideas (without regard for quality) about a single topic. This method is particularly appropriate at the start of a lesson to tap into the background knowledge students may or may not have about a topic.

Effective brainstorming is governed by four basic rules:

- ♦ Generate as many ideas as possible—the more the better.

- ♦ There is no evaluation of any single idea or group of ideas. There is no criticism about whether an idea is good or bad.

- ◆ Zany, wild, and crazy ideas are encouraged and solicited.

- ◆ Individuals are free to build upon the ideas of others.

Mental Imagery

Mental imagery is the creation of pictures in one's mind prior to reading printed material. Mental imagery helps students construct "mind pictures" that aid in comprehension and tie together their background knowledge and textual knowledge. After images are created (and colored by a reader's experiences), they become a permanent part of long-term memory.

Mental imagery works particularly well when the following guidelines are made part of the entire process:

- ◆ Students need to understand that their images are personal and are affected by their own backgrounds and experiences.

- ◆ There is no right or wrong image for any single student.

- ◆ Provide students with sufficient opportunity to create their images prior to any discussion.

- ◆ Provide adequate time for students to discuss the images they develop.

- ◆ Assist students in image development through a series of open-ended questions ("Tell us more about your image." "Can you add some additional details?").

Expert Opinion

Mental imagery is receiving considerable attention by classroom teachers at all levels and in all subjects because of its proven ability to promote positive learning experiences.

Synthesis

One of the objectives of any lesson is to provide opportunities for students to pull together various bits of information to form a new whole or basic understanding of a topic. This process underscores the need for students to actually *do* something with the information they receive.

Small Group Discussions

Here, the class is divided into small groups of two to four students. Each group is assigned a specific task to accomplish. The group works together, and members are responsible for each other (see Chapter 12 for additional information).

Discussions are a useful strategy for stimulating thought as well as providing students with opportunities to defend their position(s). Your role in these discussions is that of a moderator. You can pose an initial question, supplemental questions when the discussion falters, or review questions for a group to consider at the end of a discussion. It's important that you not take an active role in the discussions, but rather serve as a facilitator.

Experimenting

Through experimenting, ideas are proved or disproved, and predictions confirmed or denied. Experimentation involves manipulating data and assessing the results to discover some scientific principle or truth. Students need to understand that they conduct experiments every day, from watching ice cream melt to deciding on what clothes to wear outside based on the temperature. In the classroom, they need additional opportunities to try out their newly learned knowledge in a wide variety of learning tasks.

Graphic Organizers

A graphic organizer is a pictorial representation of the relationships that exist between ideas. It shows how ideas are connected and how ideas are related to each other. It is the basis for all forms of comprehension. By definition, comprehension is an understanding of how ideas or concepts are assembled into groups.

For example, if I asked you to assemble a list of vegetables (vegetables is the group) you might list some of the following: broccoli, squash, beans, peas, corn, pumpkins, etc. Each of these items is a member of the vegetable group. Thus, you comprehend vegetables because you understand how all those individual vegetables are related to each other.

Graphic organizers assist students in categorizing information. Most important, they help students understand the connections between their background knowledge and the knowledge they're learning in class.

One widely used graphic organizer is semantic webbing. Semantic webbing is a visual display of students' words, ideas, and images in concert with textual words, ideas, and images. A semantic web helps students comprehend text by activating their background knowledge, organizing new concepts, and discovering the relationships between the two. A semantic web includes the following steps:

1. A word or phrase central to some material to be read is selected and written on the chalkboard.

2. Students are encouraged to think of as many words as they can that relate to the central word. These can be recorded on separate sheets of paper or on the chalkboard.

3. Students are asked to identify categories that encompass one or more of the recorded words.

4. Category titles are written on the board. Students then share words from their individual lists or the master list appropriate for each category. Words are written under each category title.

5. Students should be encouraged to discuss and defend their word placements. Predictions about story content can also be made.

6. After the material has been read, new words or categories can be added to the web. Other words or categories can be modified or changed, depending on the information gleaned from the story.

Problem-Solving Activities

In this situation, the class, small groups, or individuals are given a problem or series of problems and are directed to find an appropriate solution. It is important to include problems for which the teacher does not have a preordained answer. (See Chapter 13 for additional ideas.)

Buzz Sessions

In this instance, temporary groups are formed for the purpose of discussing a specific topic. The emphasis is on either the background knowledge students bring to a learning task or a summary discussion of important points in a lesson.

Performance

Having a lot of knowledge is one thing. Being able to pull together bits and pieces of knowledge is another thing. But the crux of a good lesson is the opportunities for students to use their knowledge in productive, hands-on learning tasks.

Independent Practice

This method is one in which each student has an opportunity to use previously learned material on a specific academic task. For example, after learning about the short *a* sound, first-grade students might each locate short *a* words in a book they can read on their own. Or after learning about how to determine the square root of a number, students might figure out the square roots of a column of numbers from their math textbook.

Debriefing

Usually conducted at the conclusion of a lesson, debriefing allows students to condense and coalesce their knowledge and information as a group or whole class. It is an active thinking process.

It's Elementary

Role-plays are typically short, lasting for a maximum of 15 minutes. The best ones are those in which two or more students engage in a dialogue about a specific event or circumstance. Keep the directions you provide to a minimum; this is a wonderful opportunity for students to capitalize on their creativity.

Role-Playing

In this event, a student (or students) takes on the role of a specific individual (a historical person, for example) and acts out the actions of that person as though he were actually that person. The intent is to develop a feeling for and an appreciation of the thoughts and actions of an individual.

Modeling

In this method, you model the behavior students are to duplicate within an activity and encourage students to parallel your behavior in their own activity. Students may model appropriate behavior for each other, too.

Simulations

Simulations are activities in which students are given real-life problem situations and asked to work through those situations as though they were actually a part of them.

Every simulation has five basic characteristics:

- They are abstractions of real-life situations. They provide opportunities for you to bring the outside world into the classroom.

- The emphasis is on decision-making. Students have opportunities to make decisions and follow through on those decisions.

- Students have roles that parallel those in real life (mother, father, child).

- The rules are simple, uncomplicated, and few in number.

- A simulation has two or more rounds—opportunities to make decisions more than once.

If you've ever played the games *Monopoly*, *Clue*, or *Life*, you have been part of a simulation. Potential classroom simulations may include some of the following:

- A sixth-grade "family" is sitting around a table deciding how they'll spend their monthly income. How much will be spent on food, the mortgage, medical bills, transportation, etc.? Unexpectedly, the car needs a new transmission. Will the family be able to go to a movie this weekend?

- A third-grade class has been divided into various "neighborhoods." What factors will ensure that everyone's needs are satisfied? What kinds of stores or markets do they need? Where will the schools be located? What are some of the essential services? What are some of the critical transportation issues?

Projects

Students are allowed to create their own original designs, models, or structures to illustrate an important point or content fact. These can take many forms and formats:

mobiles	newspapers	collages
dioramas	brochures	three-dimensional models
shadow boxes	flyers	
posters	letters to the editor	

Skill Practice

Here, you provide students with an opportunity to apply their newly learned skills in a true-to-life experience. The emphasis is on the use of those skills.

Guided Practice

In this event, students are allowed to experience all the events of a learning situation. Usually the work is done individually, although it can be done collectively, too. The teacher is a facilitator and a cheerleader.

Reflective Inquiry

This method is student-initiated and student-controlled. Individual students are encouraged to select a topic they want to investigate further. In so doing, they pose a series of questions that they want to answer on their own. The questions are typically higher-order questions (see Chapter 11) and emphasize a variety of divergent thinking skills.

Vary Your Lessons

If you'd like to make every lesson successful, you must do one thing: include a variety of teaching and learning methodologies in every lesson. If variety is the spice of life, then fill your lessons with lots of spice as you incorporate multiple teaching strategies.

Here's a good rule of thumb: For every lesson, try to include at least one knowledge method, one synthesis method, and one performance method. That way, your students are getting the necessary information; they're pulling together that information into a comprehensible whole; and they're afforded opportunities to use that information in a creative and engaging way.

The Least You Need to Know

- ◆ You have a wide variety of teaching methods available to use in any lesson.
- ◆ Teaching methods fall into one of three basic categories: knowledge, synthesis, and performance.
- ◆ Lessons must include knowledge, an opportunity to understand that knowledge, and ways to use that knowledge productively.
- ◆ Games are not an appropriate instructional strategy.
- ◆ Your most effective lessons will be multimethod lessons.

The Questions Are the Answer

In This Chapter

- Why teachers ask questions
- Levels of questions you can ask your students
- Take advantage of wait time
- Tips and tricks for effective questioning

One of the most used (and most abused) teaching tools is questioning. This teaching tool undoubtedly extends as far back as the dawn of recorded history. Teachers ask *lots* and *lots* of questions during the course of the day.

Unfortunately, most of the questioning that takes place in a classroom is trivial, with the emphasis on memory and information retrieval. Seldom are students given opportunities to think about what they're reading or doing, and rarely are they invited to generate their own questions for discovery.

Yet good questioning is one of the most significant teaching skills you can acquire. And take it from me: it is also one of the most challenging!

A Typical (Read: Boring) Classroom Scene

Here's a scenario that might bring back some memories for you. Picture a ninth-grade science class and the teacher, Mr. Boring, who is continuing a lesson on rocks.

"Who can tell us what a rock is?" Mr. Boring asks.

No response.

"Doesn't anybody remember what we talked about two days ago?" he inquires.

Still no response.

"Once again, what is a rock?" he asks.

By this time, boredom is setting in, even though the lesson is just beginning.

"Okay Jeremy, can you give me an example of an igneous rock?"

"I dunno," Jeremy replied.

"Melissa, what about you?"

"I can't remember," Melissa answered.

"Julio, can you tell us one rock that might be classified as igneous?" Mr. Boring asks.

The question catches Julio unaware, as he is doodling in the margin of his science book. "I don't know," he replies.

"Karen, what about you?"

"Limestone," she guesses.

"No, that's not the correct answer."

This classroom scene might be more prevalent than we like to admit. It depicts a teacher asking inane questions, students with little or no involvement in the lesson, and a kind of verbal ping-pong in which the teacher keeps asking low-level questions of various students until one student "gets" the right answer or until the teacher is forced to "give" the answer to a class of uninterested and uninvolved students.

As you might imagine, no instruction has taken place. The only objective in this scene is to obtain an answer to a predetermined question. It's a guessing game between students and the teacher. Students try to guess at the answers imbedded in the teacher's head. If they get it, the game moves on to the next question; if they don't get it, the teacher keeps asking until someone does or until the teacher gives the correct answer.

Why Ask Questions?

Teachers ask questions for several reasons. They query to tap into background knowledge (to find out what students know before the lesson begins) with questions such as "Before we begin the lesson, why do you think plants are useful to humans?" This is critical because you always want to know both the depth and breadth of background knowledge students bring to a lesson.

Teachers ask questions to evaluate student progress or performance during a lesson with questions such as "How would you summarize what we have discussed so far on the Trojan Wars?" These are often called *criterion checks* and are a way of monitoring how well students are understanding a lesson. Stop every 10 to 15 minutes and ask students a question about how well they comprehend the material.

As a teacher, you need to evaluate student understanding at the end of a lesson with questions such as "What are the three types of rocks?" Unfortunately, this may be the most overused function of questions. Yes, you need to know if students mastered the objectives of the lesson, but to *always* end a lesson with a barrage of short-term memory questions is a sure way to make your lessons dull and boring.

Jabberwocky

A **criterion check** is a point in any lesson where the teacher stops and checks to see if students understand the material up to that point.

Questions should get students involved in the lesson. Use questions such as "Now that we have discussed latitude and longitude, how can we use those terms on this map of the world?" as effective motivational tools to assist students in becoming actively involved in the dynamics of a lesson. Mental engagement can be assured whenever appropriate questions are carefully sprinkled throughout a lesson.

Expert Opinion

Here's a nifty idea shared by Gwyn Loud, a teacher in Wellesley, Massachusetts:

One way to begin a lesson is to ask students to write down as many questions as they can think of about the topic. This process is valuable for several reasons. First, it emphasizes that learning means questioning and being curious. Second, the questions provide important insights about their preconceptions of the topic. Third, when students' questions are discussed and investigated, they have a wonderful sense of "ownership" of the lesson. Their interest is high, and they feel that their questions have value, which helps build their confidence.

Use questions such as "How many different questions can you come up with regarding the destruction of the Amazon rain forest?" to stimulate students to ask their own questions. When students self-generate questions, they will be more inclined to pursue the answers to those questions simply because they own the queries.

Movin' On Up: Levels of Questions

The goal of classroom questioning is not to determine whether students have learned something (as would be the case in tests, quizzes, and exams), but rather to guide students to help them learn necessary information and material. Questions should be used to *teach* students rather than to just *test* students!

Teachers frequently spend a great deal of classroom time testing students through questions. In fact, observations of teachers at all levels of education reveal that most spend more than 90 percent of their instructional time testing students (through questioning). And most of the questions teachers ask are typically factual questions that rely on short-term memory.

Although questions are widely used and serve many functions, teachers tend to overuse factual questions such as "What is the capital of California?" Not surprising, many teachers ask upward of 400 questions each and every school day. And approximately 80 percent of all the questions teachers ask tend to be factual, literal, or knowledge-based questions. The result is a classroom in which there is little creative thinking taking place.

It's been my experience that one all-important factor is key in the successful classroom: *students tend to read and think based on the kinds of questions they anticipate receiving from the teacher.* If students are constantly bombarded with questions that require only low levels of intellectual involvement (or no involvement whatsoever), they will tend to think accordingly. Conversely, students who are given questions based on higher levels of thinking will tend to think more creatively and divergently.

Jabberwocky

Taxonomy is an orderly classification of items according to a systematic relationship (low to high, small to big, simple to complex).

Many years ago, an educator named Benjamin Bloom developed a classification system we now refer to as Bloom's *Taxonomy* to assist teachers in recognizing their various levels of question-asking (among other things). The system contains six levels, which are arranged in hierarchical form, moving from the lowest level of cognition (thinking) to the highest level of cognition (or from the least complex to the most complex):

Knowledge

Comprehension

Application

Analysis

Synthesis

Evaluation

Fire Alarm _____

Observations of both elementary and secondary classrooms has shown that teachers significantly overuse knowledge questions. In fact, during the course of an average day, many teachers will ask upward of 300 or more knowledge-based questions.

Knowledge

This is the lowest level of questions and requires students to recall information. Knowledge questions usually require students to identify information in basically the same form it was presented. Some examples of knowledge questions include …

"What is the biggest city in Japan?"

"Who wrote *War and Peace?*"

"How many ounces in a pound?"

Words often used in knowledge questions include *know, who, define, what, name, where, list*, and *when*.

Comprehension

Simply stated, comprehension is the way in which ideas are organized into categories. Comprehension questions are those that ask students to take several bits of information and put them into a single category or grouping. These questions go beyond simple recall and require students to combine data together. Some examples of comprehension questions include …

"How would you illustrate the water cycle?"

"What is the main idea of this story?"

"If I put these three blocks together, what shape do they form?"

Words often used in comprehension questions include *describe, use your own words, outline, explain, discuss,* and *compare*.

Application

At this level, teachers ask students to take information they already know and apply it to a new situation. In other words, they must use their knowledge to determine a correct response. Some examples of application questions include …

"How would you use your knowledge of latitude and longitude to locate Greenland?"

"What happens when you multiply each of these numbers by nine?"

"If you had eight inches of water in your basement and a hose, how would you use the hose to get the water out?"

Words often used in application questions include *apply, manipulate, put to use, employ, dramatize, demonstrate, interpret,* and *choose.*

Expert Opinion

Never end a presentation by asking, "Are there any questions?" This is the surest way to turn off students. Instead, say something like, "Take five minutes and write down two questions you have about the lesson. Share those questions and discuss possible answers with a partner."

Analysis

An analysis question is one that asks a student to break down something into its component parts. To analyze requires students to identify reasons, causes, or motives and reach conclusions or generalizations. Some examples of analysis questions include …

"What are some of the factors that cause rust?"

"Why did the United States go to war with England?"

"Why do we call all these animals mammals?"

Words often used in analysis questions include *analyze, why, take apart, diagram, draw conclusions, simplify, distinguish,* and *survey.*

Jabberwocky

In **analysis**, you move from the whole to the parts. In **synthesis**, you move from the parts to the whole.

Synthesis

Synthesis questions challenge students to engage in creative and original thinking. These questions invite students to produce original ideas and solve problems. There's always a variety of potential responses to synthesis questions. Some examples of synthesis questions include …

"How would you assemble these items to create a windmill?"

"How would your life be different if you could breathe under water?"

"Construct a tower one foot tall using only four blocks."

"Put these words together to form a complete sentence."

Words often used in synthesis questions include *compose, construct, design, revise, create, formulate, produce,* and *plan.*

Evaluation

Evaluation requires an individual to make a judgment about something. We are asked to judge the value of an idea, a candidate, a work of art, or a solution to a problem. When students are engaged in decision making and problem-solving, they should be thinking at this level. Evaluation questions do not have single right answers. Some examples of evaluation questions include …

"What do you think about your work so far?"

"What story did you like the best?"

"Do you think that the pioneers did the right thing?"

"Why do you think Benjamin Franklin is so famous?"

Words often used in evaluation questions include *judge, rate, assess, evaluate, What is the best …, value, criticize,* and *compare.*

What does all this mean? Several things, actually! It means you can ask your students several different kinds of questions. If you only focus on one type of question, your students might not be exposed to higher levels of thinking necessary to a complete understanding of a topic. If, for example, you only ask students knowledge-based questions, then your students might think that learning (a specific topic) is nothing more than the ability to memorize a select number of facts.

You can use this taxonomy to help craft a wide range of questions—from low-level thinking questions to high-level thinking questions. If variety is the spice of life, you should sprinkle a variety of question types throughout every lesson, regardless of the topic or the grade level you teach.

Bloom's Taxonomy is not grade-specific. That is, it does not begin at the lower grades (kindergarten, first, second) with knowledge and comprehension questions and move upward to the higher grades (tenth, eleventh, twelfth) with synthesis and evaluation questions. The six levels of questions are appropriate for *all* grade levels.

Perhaps most important, *students tend to read and think based on the types of questions they anticipate receiving from the teacher.* In other words, students will tend to approach any subject as a knowledge-based subject if they are presented with an overabundance of knowledge-level questions throughout a lesson. On the other hand, students will tend to approach a topic at higher levels of thinking if they are presented with an abundance of questions at higher levels of thinking.

Your Secret Weapon: Wait Time

Listen in on many classrooms at all levels, and you'll probably hear teachers asking question after question. With so many questions coming at them, students have little time to think. Looking at it another way: the more questions that are asked, the less thinking occurs. Classroom observations reveal that teachers typically wait less than 1 second for students to respond to a question. Teachers often conclude that students don't know the answer to a question if they don't respond quickly. And when they do respond, they usually use knowledge-level responses.

Classroom observations also reveal that if a student manages to get a response in, most teachers tend to ask another question within an average time span of $\%_{10}$ second!

A Most Interesting Solution

Is this a problem? Yes! But here's an interesting solution: increase the time between asking a question and having students respond to that question from the typical 1 second to 5 seconds. This is known as *wait time*. Believe it or not, this simple act produces significant and profound changes in the classroom, including:

◆ The length of student responses increases 400 to 800 percent.

◆ The number of unsolicited but appropriate responses increases.

◆ Failure to respond decreases.

- Student confidence increases.

- Students ask more questions.

- Student achievement increases significantly.

Here's a tip: when you ask a question, don't preface it with a student's name, for example, "Marsha, what are some of the reasons why Leonardo da Vinci is considered a genius?" As soon as you say one student's name, all the other brains in the room immediately shut down. Often, the other students will be saying to themselves, *We don't have to think now because Marsha is going to answer the question.*

Jabberwocky

Wait time is the period of silence between the time a question is asked and the time when one or more students respond to that question.

Instead, ask the question, wait, and then ask for a response. Interestingly, you'll discover a heightened level of involvement. Everyone has to think about a response because nobody knows who will be called on to respond. And, the responses you receive will be considerably better and there will be more group thinking.

Like Good Coffee, You Need Percolation Time

Wait time provides students time to percolate a question down through their brain cells and create an appropriate response. After you ask a question, let it percolate in students' heads for a while. And after a student responds, let the response percolate as well. Believe me, you'll wind up with a much better brew in your classroom.

Adding wait time to your teaching repertoire will, perhaps more than any other teaching strategy, have the greatest impact on student performance. However, it's only fair to tell you that it looks simpler than it is. It may be for you, as it has always been for me, one of the greatest teaching challenges you will ever face simply because teachers are uncomfortable with classroom silence. We tend to abhor it, often believing that learning can't really be going on in a quiet classroom. But with practice, you'll begin to see the incredible benefits of wait time!

Questioning Tips and Tricks

Asking good questions at the right time and in the right place is a learned skill—one that will require time and attention throughout your teaching career. Here are some tips and ideas that will help you make your classroom (or any subject you may teach) dynamic and intellectually stimulating.

Back and Forth

Remember Mr. Boring from the beginning of the chapter? Mr. Boring and thousands of other teachers engage in a practice that I refer to as verbal ping-pong: the teacher asks a question; a student responds. The teacher asks a question; another student responds. The teacher asks a question; another student responds, etc.

Sounds pretty exciting, doesn't it? But it happens all the time. When a student answers a question, there's absolutely no response from a teacher. Most teachers tend to accept student answers without praise, encouragement, criticism, or remediation. One educator refers to this as the "okay classroom"—one in which the teacher is nonresponsive and nonencouraging.

Students need specific feedback to understand what is expected of them, correct errors, and get help in improving their performance (see Chapter 2). If all we do after getting an answer to a question is mumble "Uh-huh" or "Okay," our students are not getting any specific feedback. Equally important, this nonresponsiveness from the teacher tends to inhibit both the quality of responses as well as higher-level thinking abilities.

When you ask a question and get a response from a student, be sure to always give some kind of response to that student. The response should be one of four kinds:

- ◆ **Praise.** "Congratulations, you're on the right track!"

- ◆ **Encouragement.** "Hernando, I really liked how you pulled together all the information about Saturn into your answer."

- ◆ **Criticism.** "No, that's not correct. You forgot to carry the two."

- ◆ *Remediation.* "Sarah, your answer wasn't quite right. Think about how Sylvester felt when he was a rock."

Jabberwocky

Remediation is a teacher comment that helps students reach a more accurate or higher-level response.

Using Student Responses

Although most teachers typically respond to student answers with an "Okay" or "Uh-huh," and some may even respond with a "Good," "Nice job," "Great," "Cool," or perhaps an occasional "Wow!", a more powerful response is to use the student's answer as part of a follow-up question. Here's a scenario:

Teacher: How are these insects able to walk on the surface of the water?

Student: They use surface tension.

Teacher: So you think they use the natural surface tension of water to stay on top?

Student: Yeah. You know we learned that the water molecules at the surface of water form a strong attraction.

Teacher: Are you saying, then, that the insects use that attraction to walk on the water?

Student: Yes, but the insect has to be a certain weight or it will fall through.

Notice what happened here. For each response the student provided, the teacher used some of the student's words to craft a follow-up response or question. This process accomplished several things:

- It recognized that the teacher was actually listening to the student.

- It provided the teacher with an opportunity for the student to clarify her or his thinking.

- It provided a motivation to keep the conversation going.

- It celebrated the student's participation in the lesson.

The Least You Need to Know

- The types of questions you ask will influence how your students think.

- Use questions to help your students comprehend a topic, rather than to simply test them on it.

- Good questions can engage and involve students in the learning process.

- Good question-asking is a lifelong teaching skill and takes constant practice.

- Questions are important at every level, from kindergarten to twelfth grade, and for every student, from the high achievers to the low achievers.

Chapter 12

Cooperative Learning: Effective Group Work

In This Chapter

- ◆ The definition of cooperative learning
- ◆ The benefits of cooperative learning for your students
- ◆ The essential elements of cooperative learning
- ◆ Strategies you can use to teach with cooperative learning

In the business world, employers state that the most significant skill or attribute they look for in a potential employee is her or his ability to work well with others. Companies need and want individuals who can work effectively in a cooperative environment, an area where ideas are freely shared and personalities are respected.

The same holds true in a classroom environment. When students are presented with opportunities to share in an atmosphere of mutual trust and respect, learning can mushroom significantly. But cooperative learning is not simply the act of assigning kids to a group and giving them a common assignment to complete. It involves planning and coordination to make it work.

What Is Cooperative Learning, and What Does It Do?

Cooperative learning is a successful teaching strategy in which small teams, each with students of different ability levels, use a variety of learning activities to improve their understanding of a subject. Each member of a team is responsible, not only for learning what is taught, but also for helping his or her teammates learn—thus creating an atmosphere of achievement.

Jabberwocky

Cooperative learning is the instructional practice of placing students into small groups and having them work together toward a common goal. Each group member learns new material *and* helps other group members learn important information.

Although cooperative learning is specifically targeted for students in grades 2 through 12, it is equally successful for any subject, topic, or level. It can be effectively used for third-grade math, ninth-grade social studies, fifth-grade language arts, or twelfth-grade physics.

The success of cooperative learning is based on three interrelated factors:

◆ **Group goals.** Cooperative learning teams work to earn recognition for the improvement of each member of a group.

◆ **Individual accountability.** Each member of a team is assessed individually. Teammates work together, but the learning gains of individuals form the basis of a team score.

◆ **Equal opportunities for success.** Individual improvement over prior performance is more important than reaching a pre-established score (90 percent on a test, for example). A student who moves from 60 percent on a test one week to 68 percent (8 percent improvement) the next week contributes just as much to a group as a student who moves from 82 percent to 90 percent (also 8 percent improvement).

However, the ultimate success of cooperative learning is based on a single and very important principle: students must be *taught* how to participate in a group situation. Teachers cannot assume that students know how to behave in a group setting.

What's in It for My Students?

Based on the experiences of thousands of classroom teachers, these are the benefits of cooperative learning:

- ◆ **Student achievement.** The effects on student achievement are positive and long-lasting, regardless of grade level or subject matter.

- ◆ **Student retention.** Students are more apt to stay in school and not drop out because their contributions are solicited, respected, and celebrated.

- ◆ **Improved relations.** One of the most positive benefits is that students who cooperate with each other also tend to understand and like each other more. This is particularly true for members of different ethnic groups. Relationships between students with learning disabilities and other students in the class improve dramatically as well.

- ◆ **Improved critical thinking skills.** More opportunities for critical thinking skills are provided, and students show a significant improvement in those thinking skills.

- ◆ **Oral communication improvement.** Students improve in their oral communication skills with members of their peer group.

- ◆ **Promoted social skills.** Students' social skills are enhanced.

- ◆ **Heightened self-esteem.** When students' work is valued by team members, their individual self-esteem and respect escalate dramatically.

Fire Alarm _____

Ability grouping is when all the "low-ability" students are placed in one group, all the "high-ability" students are placed in another group, and all the "medium-ability" students are placed in a third group (for years elementary teachers would put students into three reading groups—the "Bluebirds," the "Redbirds," and the "Blackbirds," for example). Today, we know that such grouping practices promote inequality and are counterproductive to the learning process.

The Basic Elements of Cooperative Learning

As you have probably gathered by now, cooperative learning is much more than tossing a bunch of students together into a group and asking them to answer all the odd-numbered questions at the end of Chapter 12 in the textbook. The effectiveness of cooperative learning is predicated on several essential elements. Include these suggestions in your classroom, and you'll see more student achievement, less discipline problems, and increased levels of student understanding:

◆ **Positive interdependence.** It's important that you structure learning tasks so students come to believe they sink or swim together. Students need to know that each group member's efforts are required for group success and that each group member has a unique contribution to make to the joint effort.

◆ **Face-to-face interaction.** Arrange students so that they face each other for direct eye-to-eye contact. Invite students to connect the present (material currently being learned) with the past (previously learned information). Every so often, encourage them to orally explain how to solve problems.

Expert Opinion

Teachers have discovered that "low-ability" students actually perform better when they're placed in heterogeneous groups (mixed-ability groups) than when they're in homogeneous groups (all students of low ability).

Fire Alarm

Teachers have discovered that many of the positive affective, social, attitudinal, and academic benefits of cooperative learning tend to emerge and be retained only after students have spent 4 or more weeks together in the same heterogeneous group.

◆ **Heterogeneous groups.** Groups should be comprised of three, four, or five members. Mix the membership within a group according to academic abilities, ethnic backgrounds, race, and gender. It's also important that groups not be arranged according to friendships or cliques.

◆ **Clear directions and/or instructions.** Be sure to state the directions or instructions in clear, precise terms. Let your students know exactly what they are to do. When appropriate, inform them what they are to generate as evidence of their mastery of the material. You must share these directions with students before they engage in cooperative learning activities.

◆ **Equal opportunity for success.** Be sure every student knows that she or he has an equal chance of learning the material. Inform every student that she or he can help the group earn rewards for academic success. Be sure students understand that there's absolutely no academic penalty for being placed in a particular group.

◆ **A clear set of learning objectives.** You must describe exactly what students are expected to learn. Let students know that cooperative learning groups are a means to an end rather than an end in itself. Do not use ambiguous language; describe precisely what students will learn or the knowledge they will gain.

◆ **Individual and group accountability.** Give an individual test to each student or randomly examine students orally. Plan time to observe a group, and record the frequency with which each member contributes to the group's work. Invite students to teach what they learn to someone else. Ask group members to discuss how well they're achieving their goals or how they're maintaining effective working relationships. Help students make decisions about what behaviors to continue, what to change, and what to eliminate.

♦ **Sufficient time.** Be sure you have sufficient time to learn the targeted information. Groups should stay together until the designated subject matter is learned.

Strategies for Your Classroom

To help your students master essential material, you must provide a range of classroom possibilities. You can do this by using this collection of specific cooperative learning activities in your classroom. Of course, you're not going to use all these at the same time, nor are you going to use any one of these over and over and over again. (Remember, variety is the spice of life.) And keep in mind that these activities are part of larger lessons—any one of these could be part of the "Procedures" section of a lesson plan (see Chapter 5):

♦ **Jigsaw.** Set up groups of four, five, or six students. Divide the material to be learned into four, five, or six sections. Then assign each team member to one of the subsections of material. She or he should work on that material and how it will be learned. Each of these subgroups is known as an "expert" group. After students have mastered the material in their expert group, they each return to their original groups. Each expert then teaches the information he or she has learned to the other members of the group.

♦ **STAD (student teams—achievement divisions).** Assign students to four-person teams, mixing each team according to ability, gender, race, and ethnicity. After the presentation of a teacher-directed lesson, have students work in teams to master the material. Buddy work, group quizzes, or focused study questions may be part of a group's efforts. Give a quiz to all group members. Assign improvement scores to each individual as well as the entire team as a whole.

♦ **TGT (teams-games-tournament).** This strategy is an extension of STAD. Each week, group together students with comparable levels of previous achievement for a competition. Ask members of each of these groups questions and earn points for correct answers. Teammates help one another prepare for the tournaments through instruction, sharing, and coaching techniques.

- **Think-pair-share.** This cooperative learning activity involves a three-step structure. In the first step, ask students a question and have them think silently about it. Pair up individuals during the second step so they can exchange thoughts. During the third step, have the pairs share their responses with other pairs, other teams, or the entire group.

- **Numbered heads.** Divide the class into teams of four students each. Give each member of the team a number: 1, 2, 3, or 4. Ask questions of the entire class, and have the groups work together to answer the question so all the groups can verbally respond to the question. Then call out a number ("3"); each "number 3" will give the answer.

- **Three-step interview.** Have each member of a team choose another member to be a partner. During the first step, have individuals interview their partners by asking clarifying questions. During the second step, have partners reverse the roles. In the final step, have members share their partner's response with the team.

- **Reader's roundtable.** Divide the class is into several small groups. Assign all the groups the same piece of reading (a book, a textbook, an article). Each group is responsible for dividing the reading into several parts—one part for each member of the group. Each member reads her or his assigned section and explains it to the team. Then, each team share an overall interpretation with the entire class. In this activity, it would be important to discuss the differences in interpretation with class members.

- **Three-minute review.** Occasionally during a lecture or discussion, stop and give teams 3 minutes to review what's been said and ask clarifying questions. Invite each team to arrive at a summary statement (a main idea) of what was presented, then write these on the chalkboard. Take time to discuss any differences among teams. At the end of the lesson, invite teams to review the summary statements and to arrive at the most appropriate ones for sections of the lesson or the entire lesson all together.

- **Partners.** Divide the class into teams of four. Have each team move to a different location in the room. Give half of each four-person team an assignment to master to be able to teach the other half. Have partners work to learn and consult with other partners working on the same material. After a sufficient length of time, regroup all the teams with each set of partners teaching and quizzing their teammates. Have each team take time to review how well they learned and how they might improve the learning process.

As you become more familiar with cooperative learning, you might want to create your own learning activities. Even better, challenge your students to invent and design variations of these suggestions for use in the classroom.

Teaching With Cooperative Learning

The effective use of cooperative learning in the classroom is often built upon a four-step process. Consider the following four elements as you begin to design and implement cooperative learning into your teaching routines:

◆ **Presentation of content.** In Chapter 10, I talked about the ways in which you can present information to your students. These instructional activities *must* be done prior to any cooperative learning activity. Cooperative learning is *not* a self-instruction model, but rather a way for students to "mess around" with previously presented material. In short, cooperative learning comes *after* you've taught something to your students.

◆ **Teamwork.** This is the time—after you've taught the new material—when students are engaged in a cooperative learning activity. The cooperative learning strategy (Jigsaw, STAD, Think-pair-share, Numbered heads) is selected and explained to the entire class. Students are divided into various teams (using the criteria previously explained) and provided sufficient time to complete their assigned duties.

◆ **Individual assessment.** In cooperative learning, the objective is not the production of a single set of correct answers for the entire group but rather the development and enhancement of each member's achievement. Although members of the team work together to master information, each individual member must be assessed in relation to her or his mastery of the content. In short, everybody is tested in line with her or his achievement potential.

◆ **Team recognition.** It's most appropriate to recognize and celebrate the efforts of the team as a whole. It's equally important to celebrate the efforts of the team to assist individual members in learning a specific body of knowledge. These ceremonies can be either public or private. Teachers have rewarded teams with an extra recess, a "homework pass," a snack, a certificate or award, or some other appropriate reward. In many cases, the reward can be as simple as a classroom cheer or extended series of high fives.

Expert Opinion

For variety, consider three types of cooperative learning groups:

Informal: ad hoc groups that last from a few minutes to a class period

Formal: lasting from several days to several weeks—they offer the time necessary to completely understand an assignment

Long-term: groups that last for a semester or the entire year and provide students with sustained support over a long period of time

A Sample Lesson

Here's a lesson using the Jigsaw cooperative learning strategy:

Malinda Coons thoroughly enjoys teaching social studies to her third-grade students in San Diego. One of the topics she covers each year focuses on specific geographical regions of the United States, and she has prepared a unit on North American deserts. This year she's using the Jigsaw cooperative learning strategy as part of her lesson plan on the Sonoran Desert of the American Southwest.

♦ **Presentation of content.** Melinda's students are asked to read the chapter in the social studies textbook about the Sonoran Desert. Afterward, Malinda reads students the children's book *Around One Cactus: Owls, Bats and Leaping Rats* by Anthony D. Fredericks (a story about the animals that live around a Saguaro cactus—particularly nocturnal animals). Her students are excited about the strange and wonderful animals that live in the desert. Finally, Malinda shows a video about desert life that was filmed by a friend who lives in Tucson, Arizona.

♦ **Teamwork.** Melinda divides her class into five separate groups of five students. Each member of a group is given a different assignment; for example, in the first group, Tyrone is responsible for researching the animals of the desert; Elena is charged with learning about the plant life of the desert; Ramon is responsible for checking out the climate of the Sonoran desert; Sarah is assigned the Native American cultures that live in the desert; and Clarice will read about important desert towns and cities.

Each person goes off to do her or his individual research. To help this process, each student also meets with students who have the identical assignment (one from each jigsaw group). For example, students assigned to the "Animals of the Desert" group meet as a team of specialists, gathering information, becoming experts on their topic, and rehearsing their presentations (this is an "expert" group).

After each student has completed her or his research, she or he comes back to the original jigsaw group. Each person presents a report to the group. For example, the "Animal Expert" (Tyrone) in each group teaches the other group members about desert animals. The "Climate Expert" (Ramon) shares what he has learned with the entire team. Each student in each group educates the whole group about her or his specialty. Each person in the group listens carefully to the information presented by a teammate, asking questions for clarification.

- **Individual assessment.** Upon the completion of the cooperative learning activity, Malinda gives each student a quiz on the desert. Students know ahead of time the components of that quiz because they were the same components they studied in their cooperative learning groups (animals, plants, climate, Native American cultures, and towns and cities).

- **Team recognition.** Every individual in the class makes significant achievement on the quiz. Malinda takes time to acknowledge the work and effort of all five teams in helping their individual members improve. The entire class is rewarded with an extra 15-minute recess period.

Cooperative learning can be a teaching tool that helps you have a positive impact on your students' comprehension of important information. In fact, it might well be one of the most flexible and powerful strategies you can use.

The Least You Need to Know

- Cooperative learning is the practice of breaking students into small groups and having them work toward a common goal.

- Cooperative learning has been used successfully across grades 2 through 12 and in every subject area.

- Several elements must be in place for cooperative learning to be successful.

- Teachers can use a variety of cooperative learning strategies—or enlist their students to help create their own.

- The effective use of cooperative learning follows a four-step process: presentation of content, teamwork, individual assessment, and team recognition.

Think About It: Using Thinking Skills in the Classroom

In This Chapter

- ◆ Learning from students' perspective

- ◆ Reasons why hypotheses and predictions are important

- ◆ Using problem-solving in your classroom

- ◆ Ways to foster creative thinking for every student

Try solving these problems:

- ◆ What day follows the day before yesterday if two days from now will be Sunday?

- ◆ In the following line of letters, cross out five letters so that the remaining letters, without changing their order, will spell a familiar English word.

    T F I E V E A L E C T H T E I R N S G

- ◆ You walk into a room to find John and Mary lying dead on the floor. There is broken glass and water all around them. How did they die?

How did you do? Were you able to arrive at some answers very quickly? Did you need to use a pencil and paper and map out a plan of attack? Or did you give up altogether? When college students were asked problems like these, most students did not know how to proceed to figure out the appropriate answers. They either guessed or gave up. (The answers to these questions are at the end of the chapter.)

Remember, knowledge is never stagnant nor are the ways we have in presenting it. What is important is that learning involves much more than an accumulation of factual information. What is done with that information is what makes learning meaningful, relevant, and purposeful.

What Students Think About Learning

John Barrel, an educator in New Jersey, outlines a series of expectations that students have about how classrooms are run and what students do in those classrooms. See if these sound familiar:

- The teacher "teaches" and the students "sit and listen" or "learn" passively.

- There is one "right answer" to any question, and it is in the textbook or the teacher's head.

- The answer to most questions can be given in one or two words, and the teacher won't challenge you to go much deeper.

- Books and teachers are always "right," and we learn only from them, not any other resource in the room, such as classmates.

- "Thinking" is not something we talk about.

- If I memorize enough stuff, I can get a good grade.

Barrel calls these conditions the "hidden curriculum"—or that set of assumptions and expectations students traditionally have about education. As you look over these statements, you'll quickly notice that they are, for the most part, indicative of passive classrooms. By that I mean they are the result of teacher-directed learning environments in which students have little input, little involvement, and little engagement.

In Chapter 10, I talked about the various ways you have of sharing information with your students. When students become more actively engaged in the dynamics of learning, that learning becomes more personal and meaningful for them.

What results is not a hidden curriculum but rather a completely new set of expectations—one in which student participation is active, sustained, and deliberate. In short, student assumptions about their role in the learning process is one in which they generate hypotheses, solve problems, and think creatively.

Guess What?: Generating Hypotheses and Predictions

Generating *hypotheses*, or making predictions, is one of the most powerful instructional tools you have as a teacher. Some teachers refer to it as a process of making "educated guesses" because there are two elements involved. One, we need some background knowledge or prior experiences (the "educated") to make a prediction. Second, we need to use that knowledge in an active way (the "guess").

Making hypotheses is something we do quite naturally. For example, we make educated guesses about the weather when we walk outside each day. We watch weather people on the TV use the most sophisticated scientific equipment to help them in making their educated guesses about tomorrow's weather. And we observe the tracking of Caribbean hurricanes on various Internet sites as meteorologists try to predict where and when they will make landfall in the United States.

Jabberwocky

A hypothesis is an assumption, interpretation, or guess based on currently available information. It is always subject to refinement as new data becomes available.

Deductive and Inductive Thinking

Generating hypotheses involves two types of thinking. The first, *deductive* thinking, is the process of using a general rule to make a prediction about a future event or occurrence. For example, while reading a story that takes place in Minnesota in December, you would predict that there would be snow on the ground and that the temperature would be cold.

Inductive thinking, on the other hand, is the process of drawing new conclusions based on information we already know and are taught. For example, if you were reading a story about a shark that attacked a surfer off the coast of southern California, you might induce that all southern California sharks attack people.

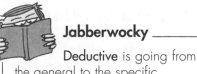

Jabberwocky

Deductive is going from the general to the specific. **Inductive** is going from the specific to the general.

Explanations and Conclusions

Although the act of generating hypotheses is a powerful activity in any type of classroom instruction, it is equally important for students to defend or explain their predictions. Encourage students to "look inside their heads" and describe the thought processes that led them to a specific conclusion.

Interestingly, the process of defending their educated guesses is equally important for young students as it is for older ones. You can help in this process by modeling those types of thinking behaviors for your students. In essence, you serve as a model of good thinking—demonstrating for students the thought processes and mental activities you use.

Do this by selecting a book or chapter in a textbook and thinking out loud—verbalizing what is going on in your head as you read:

"From this title, I predict that this story will be about a missing ring and a haunted house."

"Based on what I read in chapter three, I think that in the next chapter we'll find out how the two twins were able to sail to the other side of the lake."

"By looking at this illustration, I predict that the next section of this chapter will describe Columbus's first meeting with the Indians."

Because students cannot observe your thinking processes firsthand, your verbalization enables them to get a sense of good thinking as practiced by an accomplished reader—you.

Demonstrate this type of modeling for your students in several different types of reading materials (books, textbooks, handouts, brochures, flyers, etc.). As you read and model, allow students opportunities to interject their thoughts about what may be going on in their heads as they listen to the selection. Your goal, obviously, will be to have students internalize this process and be able to do it on their own.

Anticipation Guide: A Hypothesis-Generating Strategy

Anticipation guides alert students to some of the major concepts in textual material before it's read, which gives students an opportunity to share ideas and opinions as well as activate their prior knowledge about a topic before they read about that subject. It's also a helpful technique for eliciting students' misconceptions about a subject. Students become actively involved in the dynamics of reading a specified selection because they have an opportunity to talk about the topic before reading about it. Here's how to use it:

1. Read the story or selection, and attempt to select the major concepts, ideas, or facts in the text. For example, in a selection on "Weather," the following concepts could be identified:

   ◆ Many different types of clouds exist.

   ◆ Different examples of severe weather include tornadoes, hurricanes, and thunderstorms.

   ◆ Precipitation occurs in the form of rain, snow, sleet, and hailstones.

   ◆ Many types of weather occur along fronts.

2. Create 5 to 10 statements (not questions) that reflect common misconceptions about the subject, are ambiguous, or are indicative of students' prior knowledge. Write statements on the chalkboard, or photocopy and distribute them.

3. Give students plenty of opportunities to agree or disagree with each statement. Whole group or paired discussions would be appropriate. After discussions, let each student record a positive or negative response to each statement. Initiate discussions focusing on reasons for individual responses.

4. Invite students to read the text, keeping in mind the statements and their individual or group reactions to those statements.

5. After reading the selection, engage the group in a discussion on how the textual information may have changed their opinions. Provide students with an opportunity to record their reactions to each statement based upon what they have read in the text.

Expert Opinion

When using anticipation guides, it's not important that students reach a consensus nor that they agree with everything the author states. It's more important for them to engage in an active dialogue that allows them to react to the relationships between prior knowledge and current knowledge.

Anticipation guides are appropriate for use with any subject area (reading, English, language arts, science, social studies, math) and at all grade levels. They encourage and stimulate hypothesis formation and open new avenues of learning for students.

I Have a Problem: Problem-Solving

Problem-solving is a process—an ongoing activity in which we take what we know to discover what we don't know. It involves overcoming obstacles by generating hypotheses, testing those predictions, and arriving at satisfactory solutions.

Jabberwocky ⎯⎯⎯⎯

Problem-solving is the ability to identify and solve problems by applying appropriate skills systematically.

Problem-solving involves three basic functions:

1. Seeking information

2. Generating new knowledge

3. Making decisions

Problem-solving is, and should be, a very real part of the curriculum. It presupposes that students can take on some of the responsibility for their own learning and can take personal action to solve problems, resolve conflicts, discuss alternatives, and focus on thinking as a vital element of the curriculum. It provides students with opportunities to use their newly acquired knowledge in meaningful, real-life activities and assists them in working at higher levels of thinking (see Chapter 11).

Here is a five-stage model that most students can easily memorize and put into action and which has direct applications to many areas of the curriculum as well as everyday life:

1. **Understand the problem.** It's important that students understand the nature of a problem and its related goals. Encourage students to frame a problem in their own words.

Expert Opinion ⎯⎯⎯⎯⎯⎯⎯⎯⎯⎯⎯⎯⎯⎯⎯⎯⎯⎯⎯⎯

Here are some techniques that will help students understand the nature of a problem and the conditions that surround it:

- ◆ List all related relevant facts.
- ◆ Make a list of all the given information.
- ◆ Restate the problem in their own words.
- ◆ List the conditions that surround a problem.
- ◆ Describe related known problems.

2. **Describe any barriers.** Students need to be aware of any barriers or constraints that may be preventing them from achieving their goal. In short, what is creating the problem? Encouraging students to verbalize these impediments is always an important step.

3. **Identify various solutions.** After the nature and parameters of a problem are understood, students will need to select one or more appropriate strategies to help resolve the problem. Students need to understand that they have many strategies available to them and that no single strategy will work for all problems. Here are some problem-solving possibilities:

   ◆ *Create visual images.* Many problem-solvers find it useful to create "mind pictures" of a problem and its potential solutions prior to working on the problem. Mental imaging allows the problem-solvers to map out many dimensions of a problem and "see" it clearly.

   ◆ *Guesstimate.* Give students opportunities to engage in some trial-and-error approaches to problem-solving. It should be understood, however, that this is not a singular approach to problem-solving but rather an attempt to gather some preliminary data.

   ◆ *Create a table.* A table is an orderly arrangement of data. When students have opportunities to design and create tables of information, they begin to understand that they can group and organize most data relative to a problem.

   ◆ *Use manipulatives.* By moving objects around on a table or desk, students can develop patterns and organize elements of a problem into recognizable and visually satisfying components.

   ◆ *Work backward.* It's frequently helpful for students to take the data presented at the end of a problem and use a series of computations to arrive at the data presented at the beginning of the problem.

   ◆ *Look for a pattern.* Looking for patterns is an important problem-solving strategy because many problems are similar and fall into predictable patterns. A pattern, by definition, is a regular, systematic repetition and may be numerical, visual, or behavioral.

   ◆ *Create a systematic list.* Recording information in list form is a process used quite frequently to map out a plan of attack for defining and solving problems. Encourage students to record their ideas in lists to determine regularities, patterns, or similarities between problem elements.

4. **Try out a solution.** When working through a strategy or combination of strategies, it will be important for students to …

   ♦ *Keep accurate and up-to-date records of their thoughts, proceedings, and procedures.* Recording the data collected, the predictions made, and the strategies used is an important part of the problem solving process.

   ♦ *Try to work through a selected strategy or combination of strategies until it becomes evident that it's not working, it needs to be modified, or it is yielding inappropriate data.* As students become more proficient problem-solvers, they should feel comfortable rejecting potential strategies at any time during their quest for solutions.

   ♦ *Monitor with great care the steps undertaken as part of a solution.* Although it might be a natural tendency for students to "rush" through a strategy to arrive at a quick answer, encourage them to carefully assess and monitor their progress.

   ♦ *Feel comfortable putting a problem aside for a period of time and tackling it at a later time.* For example, scientists rarely come up with a solution the first time they approach a problem. Students should also feel comfortable letting a problem rest for a while and returning to it later.

It's Elementary

For younger students, illustrations are helpful in organizing data, manipulating information, and outlining the limits of a problem and its possible solution(s). Students can use drawings to help them look at a problem from many different perspectives.

5. **Evaluate the results.** It's vitally important that students have multiple opportunities to assess their own problem-solving skills and the solutions they generate from using those skills. Frequently, students are overly dependent upon teachers to evaluate their performance in the classroom. The process of self-assessment is not easy, however. It involves risk-taking, self-assurance, and a certain level of independence. But it can be effectively promoted by asking students questions such as "How do you feel about your progress so far?" "Are you satisfied with the results you obtained?" and "Why do you believe this is an appropriate response to the problem?"

Creative Thinking

Creative thinking, or divergent thinking, promotes the idea that students can "move beyond" right answers and begin thinking independently. It's thinking without limits and without boundaries. Creative thinking requires an attitude or outlook that allows you to search for ideas and manipulate knowledge and experience.

However, before we launch into some strategies that will help you promote creative thinking in your classroom or in any subject area, let's take a look at some of the factors that tend to inhibit creative thought.

Secondary Thoughts

Because they have been condi-tioned by an educational sys-tem traditionally built on rote memorization and low-level thinking skills, many older stu-dents believe they are not or can-not become creative. Students often have the mistaken impres-sions that success in school is built upon the ability to memorize bits of information and regurgitate that data on paper-and-pencil tests.

Enhancers of Creative Thinking

Teachers sometimes make the mistake of assuming that exercises and activities designed to strengthen creative thinking muscles are appropriate only for gifted or creative students. Nothing could be further from the truth. In fact, creative thinking should be promoted in any subject area and for all students.

Here are four creative thinking strategies—all of which can be incorporated into any subject area:

- **Fluency.** This is the ability to create a potpourri of ideas or lists of ideas. It involves the generation of many thoughts without regard to quality—otherwise known as brainstorming. Brainstorming is designed to produce many ideas and can be used in small or large groups of students. However, it should not be con-sidered an end in itself but rather a prelude to further investigation and discov-ery. To be effective, brainstorming should adhere to the following guidelines:

  - *No negative criticism.* Defer judgment until a large number of alternatives has been produced.

  - *Freewheeling is desired.* Encourage wild, off-beat, and unusual ideas.

- *Quantity is stressed.* Include the small, obvious alternatives as well as the wild, unusual, and clever ones.

- *Stress a continuous flow of ideas.* Permit no value-judging or evaluation of ideas during brainstorming.

- **Flexibility.** This skill involves drawing relationships between seemingly unrelated ideas; for example, "How is a rubber band like a dictionary?" Locating common elements between items helps students look for many possible answers to a problem.

- **Originality.** This refers to the creation of ideas that are singular and unique—those that are different from any other. It involves the willingness to take risks, to be unconventional, and to deviate from common patterns. The original thinker is able to analyze known information, to manipulate and transform it so that new and different relationships are discovered, and to recognize and decide which ideas are the most original.

- **Elaboration.** This is the process individuals go through to expand an idea—to enlarge it until it is workable or feasible. It is a process of multiplication or addition that builds and "inflates" ideas into an expanded final form.

A Sample Lesson in Creative Thinking

Here is a portion of a sample lesson that Sarah McNamara, a seventh-grade teacher in New Hampshire used to help her students focus on the elements of characterization in a story. Her intent was not to have everyone arrive at the same answers but rather to stimulate their creative thinking so they could begin looking at story characters from many different points of view.

Fluency

Make a list of 10 things the main character might say.

Make a list of classmates who share personality features of the main character.

Make a list of 20 adjectives that describe the main character.

Flexibility

Illustrate some of the similarities between two or more characters.

Make a three-dimensional model of one of the characters in the story.

Cut out pictures of several people from old magazines. Using a combination of body types, faces, and so on, construct a character similar to the one in the story.

Originality

Make a sock puppet or stick figure of the main character, and act out a portion of the story.

Make a cartoon strip using some of the characters from the story.

Make a dictionary of descriptive words that you could use for each of the characters. Use words and phrases cut out of old magazines.

Elaboration

If you were the author of the story, in what further episodes, events, or discoveries would you have the characters participate?

Develop a radio show using some of the characters from the story.

Write a letter to the author of the story from the viewpoint of one of the characters.

Asking Divergent Questions

Selected use of the following questions can help students appreciate the diversity of observations and responses they can make to all types of educational materials. Use these questions to enhance the creative thinking abilities of your students with both verbal and written information.

List all the words you can think of to describe _____.

What are all the possible solutions for _____?

List as many _____ as you can think of.

How would _____ view this?

What would _____ mean from the viewpoint of _____?

How would a _____ describe _____?

How would you feel if you were _____?

What would _____ do?

You are a _____. Describe your feelings.

How is _____ like _____?

I only know about _____. Explain _____ to me.

What ideas from _____ are like _____?

What _____ is most like a _____?

What would happen if there were more _____?

Suppose _____ happened. What would be the results?

Imagine if _____ and _____ were reversed. What would happen?

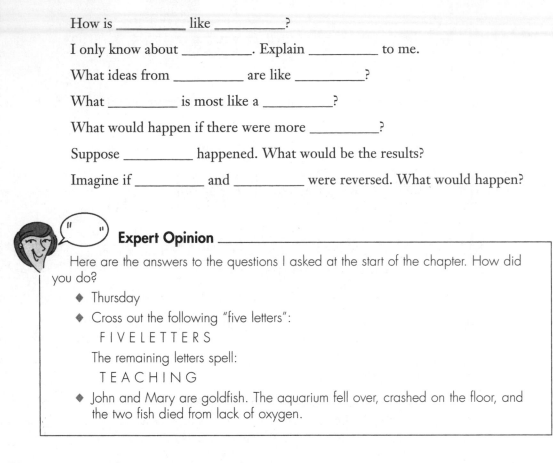

Expert Opinion _____

Here are the answers to the questions I asked at the start of the chapter. How did you do?

- ◆ Thursday
- ◆ Cross out the following "five letters":

    F I V E L E T T E R S

    The remaining letters spell:

    T E A C H I N G

- ◆ John and Mary are goldfish. The aquarium fell over, crashed on the floor, and the two fish died from lack of oxygen.

The Least You Need to Know

- ◆ Students often have some preconceived notions about teaching and learning.

- ◆ Helping students make predictions and generate hypotheses is one of the most powerful instructional tools you have.

- ◆ Teachers can use problem-solving activities in any grade and in any subject area.

- ◆ Creative thinking encourages students to think beyond right answers and interpret information in many ways.

Motivation: The Little Engine That Could

In This Chapter

- ◆ Common misperceptions about motivation
- ◆ Tips for motivating students
- ◆ Locus of control
- ◆ Praise and encouragement
- ◆ Pros and cons of rewards

Teachers often ask the wrong kind of question about motivation. They ask, "How can I motivate my students?" That kind of question implies that motivation is something *done to* or *created for* students. That kind of thinking is dangerous.

True, we all have unmotivated students in our classrooms. Perhaps, at some time in our educational career, we were unmotivated as well. We may have been uninterested in a subject, uninspired to do the work, or uncaring about the topic or the way in which it was presented. Make no mistake about it: motivation is a critical factor in how students learn. But to be successful, we need to look at motivation from the other side, from the students' side. In this chapter, I'll show you how to do that.

Understanding Motivation

Teachers (and lots of other people, too) often have some preconceived notions about what *motivation* is and how it's manifested in students. As teachers, we need to deal with those perceptions first before we can discuss the ways in which we can enhance students' motivation.

Common Motivation Misconceptions

Here are a few misconceptions about motivation:

- People are either motivated or they're not—in all tasks, assignments, or learning situations.

Jabberwocky

Motivation is defined as an emotion, desire, or psychological need that incites a person to do something. The word *motive* comes from a Latin root meaning "to move."

- Motivation is a constant, stable condition like the number of fingers on your hand or the color of your skin.

- We can enhance motivation for a learning task through rewards (or punishment).

- There are two types of students—those who are motivated (they will learn) and those who are not motivated (they will not learn).

As you look at these misconceptions, you might notice that most are couched in terms that imply that motivation is something controlled or managed from the *outside*. That is to say, motivated students are those who have been inspired by dedicated teachers and supportive parents.

Often, when teachers talk about motivation, they talk about what *they* do to interest students in a topic or encourage them to participate willingly in the dynamics of a lesson. The assumption is twofold: teachers create motivational conditions in the classroom and students come to class motivated or unmotivated to work. Those assumptions imply that motivation is an external event or condition. That view often causes anxiety and frustration for many teachers.

The Biggest Misconception of All

Perhaps the biggest misconception about motivation many new or experienced teachers have is that you can motivate your students by *making learning fun*. Teachers often define their colleagues' skill as educators in terms of their ability to make learning enjoyable and entertaining.

Unfortunately, the *motivation = fun stuff* equation is one of the most common teaching myths. You probably remember fun and enjoyable activities or situations when you were in school; perhaps you learned something, too. But learning doesn't have to be fun to be motivational.

Teachers who strive to make every classroom activity fun are looking at motivation as an externally controlled condition. That sends the wrong message to students. Yes, learning can be amusing and enjoyable, but it doesn't need to be fun to be effective. *Fun* is a byproduct of learning, not a purpose for learning.

Three Elements of Motivation

At its simplest, motivation is comprised of three critical elements:

1. Expecting success

2. Developing a community of learners

3. Placing a value on learning

Your awareness of these three factors and your willingness to address these issues in your classroom will determine, to a large extent, how well your students will be motivated. These factors are equally important for elementary students as they are for secondary students.

Expectations of Success

Whether you're teaching kindergarten students about the letter B or you're teaching adolescents about the social ramifications of Salvador Dali's painting *The Persistence of Memory*, you must provide instruction that will ensure a measure of success for every student. Each student must know that she or he can achieve a degree of success with an assignment or academic task.

Often, people don't try new things because they're afraid of failure. This fear of failure begins early in our academic careers and carries forward into our adult lives. As classroom teachers, we must establish and promote conditions that will emphasize and support an expectation of success for each student. Try these ideas:

- Offer *differentiated instruction.* Be aware that you'll have students of differing abilities in your classroom. Don't make the mistake of crafting a single lesson for everybody—without taking into consideration the different ability levels.

- **Provide feedback promptly, frequently, and efficiently.** Students must be able to see a direct connection between any effort or completed task (such as homework) and a response from you. Here are some suggestions for providing successful feedback:

  - Make feedback immediate. ("I'm returning the social studies test you took yesterday.")

  - Never be sarcastic when giving feedback. ("Everybody must have had a 'brain freeze' when you did this assignment!")

  - Allow students to revise their incorrect responses. ("I'm not sure that's correct. Is there another way we could do this?")

  - Use verbal as well as written feedback. ("You must feel pretty good when you do work like this.")

  - Allow students to control some feedback. ("How do you think you did on the scooter test?")

  - Make comments specific, and suggest corrections. ("You provided a good rationale for Wilson's League of Nations, but you might want to look further into Congress's response.")

  - Offer feedback in terms of a student's pro-gress, not her or his comparison with others. ("Look how you moved from 14 correct on the spelling test to 17 correct this week.")

Jabberwocky

Differentiated instruction is a respect for the different ability levels in your classroom and, therefore, a respect for each student's ability to succeed. You might provide one type of learning task for struggling students and another for independent students. You might need to adjust the time available for completion of an assignment or offer additional assistance for another.

- **Students should have multiple opportunities to set their own academic goals.** Invite them to establish obtainable goals for a lesson, a unit, or even for the whole year. Ask them what they would like to learn about a topic and what they think they must do to learn that material. Psychologists tell us that the goals we set for ourselves (as opposed to the goals others set for us) are intrinsically more motivational. We're more inclined to pursue those goals and relish in the success that comes about when we achieve them.

◆ **Help students see the connection between effort and result.** Let students know that the work they put into an assignment will result in the completion of a task or some new material learned. It's important that students understand that learning is work and that the more they work, the more they can learn.

A Community of Learners

Human beings have basic needs such as water, air, and food. But we also need a feeling of belongingness—a knowledge that we are part of a group and are recognized by that group.

Psychologists tell us that children are no different. Take a look at the following chart, which outlines some of the needs of students at various levels.

Grades, Ages	Needs
Elementary, 5 to 11	Warmth, support, assurance, participation, acceptance
Middle school, 11 to 14	Group membership, peer acceptance, admiration
High school, 14 to 18	Acceptance, respect, peer group conformation

Note that at all ages and at all levels, students want and need to be respected members of a group. Effective group membership is essential to establishing positive learning environments where collaboration, meaningful student interaction, class cohesion, and individual motivation are valued.

I refer to this as a *community of learners*—a classroom that celebrates all its members and provides a supportive, inspirational, and motivational environment. Composed of four elements, a community of learners …

◆ Celebrates student events and accomplishments.

◆ Provides success for all.

◆ Celebrates humor.

◆ Has a fair, purposeful classroom structure.

A community of learners can be established in any classroom. Here are some ideas for turning your classroom into a community of learners:

- ◆ **Take time for student interaction.** Student interaction and sharing enhances instructional time and prepares students to function more effectively as a body of learners. We must recognize the importance of these dynamics and find ways to celebrate student life.

- ◆ **Spend time at the beginning of the year talking about guidelines students find in their homes.** Draw parallels from the home as a learning environment to being a family of learners in the classroom.

- ◆ **Celebrate the accomplishments that make a group cohesive.** Recognize the work of cooperative groups, inform the class about its accomplishments over time, and inform students about the goals they're attaining.

- ◆ **Use a morning meeting to foster an atmosphere of trust and respect.** A meeting in which students feel safe to take risks necessary for learning. During these morning meetings, students and the teacher gather in a circle for 10 to 15 minutes and greet one another in a personal way, listen and respond to one another's news, practice academic and social skills, and share appropriate news and announcements.

- ◆ **Provide numerous opportunities for students to share their accomplishments with the class and the class to share their achievements with the larger school community.** Use skits, plays, readers theater productions, library displays, bulletin boards, a class newspaper or newsletter, or other media to promote the efforts of the whole classroom.

A Value on Learning

The third element that contributes to the motivation of students is whether or not students see a value in what they're learning. The predominant question in the back of every learner's mind is, *What's in it for me?* Learning something is one thing, but knowing *why* you need to learn something is quite another.

For motivation to occur, students must know the reasons, rationale, and whys of any learning task. Your students will be more engaged and more motivated when you provide them with specific reasons for learning something. To do that, relate the learning directly to their lives. When students see a connection between what they learn in the classroom and their lives outside the classroom, they'll be motivated to actively participate in the learning process.

Try the following suggestions:

> "Let's take a look at how this idea of friction might affect our performance on a skateboard."

> "We know Andrew likes to collect baseball cards. If he wanted to add 25 new cards to his collection and each one was priced at $1.79 each, how much money would he need?"

> "Remember the fight on the playground last week? How was that confrontation similar to or different from the conflict between the North and the South?"

> "I know you're all familiar with this rap song. I wonder if we can take the 'food pyramid' and turn it into our own rap song."

It's also important that you provide your students with opportunities to make their own choices. Making personal choices helps develop a sense of ownership and can be a powerful motivational strategy. Students can select various ways to complete an assignment, the due date of an assignment, or the complexity of a learning task. These kinds of decisions offer students a measure of control over their academic lives. More control = more motivation.

Motivated students are active students. As we discussed in Chapter 10, active students are engaged students. Too often students see school as a passive environment—one in which there is little involvement. By utilizing a variety of instructional methodologies, we can provide conditions that will involve and motivate students to take an active role in their own learning.

Provide opportunities for students to create tangible or finished products. Completing a worksheet of addition facts is not a tangible product; answering all the odd-numbered questions after Chapter 11 in the history textbook is not a tangible product. For learning to be meaningful, students must create meaningful products. Here are just a few examples.

Subject	Elementary	Secondary
Writing	Take on the role of a character and write a journal entry.	Write a letter of protest to a magazine editor.
Math	Set up a student store to buy and sell pencils.	Compute the various angles on the face of an office building.
Science	Identify the types of creatures found under a single rock.	Create a three-dimensional model of the constellation Orion.

Locus of Control

How can we provide the conditions that will stimulate students to be more motivated to learn? Many educators say it comes down to a question of *locus of control*.

It's important to view the concept of locus of control as a continuum. That is, people aren't 100 percent *external* or 100 percent *internal*; they fall somewhere along a continuum line, with a predisposition to one side or the other. Here's what it looks like:

External . . . . Internal

Interestingly, internal students demonstrate higher levels of academic achievement. External students tend to exhibit lower levels of academic achievement.

It stands to reason that if we can help students achieve a more internal locus of control, we can assist them in achieving higher levels of scholastic achievement. One of the ways teachers do this is through the use of praise and encouragement.

Jabberwocky

Locus of control refers to the degree to which individuals perceive they are in control of the factors that affect their lives. **External** individuals feel they are strongly influenced by others (parents, teachers, peers). **Internal** individuals feel they are primarily responsible for the events that happen to them.

Praise and Encouragement

Consider for a moment these two pieces of information. What do they tell you about a classroom atmosphere?

♦ About 90 percent of the positive things students do in a classroom go unrecognized.

♦ On average, only about 2 percent of a teacher's day is devoted to any kind of praise.

Expert Opinion

Positive recognition should be done in a casual manner, should require no more than 8 to 10 words, and last no longer than 3 to 5 seconds.

It is quite obvious that we often don't take the time to recognize and celebrate the work or efforts of our students. When we don't recognize our students, we deprive them of a powerful motivational incentive for any and all learning tasks.

But praise and encouragement are also at two ends of the locus of control continuum. Praise fosters an external locus of control, and encouragement fosters an internal locus of control. Here's how they're classified:

Praise:

- ◆ Recognizes the doer. ("You got an A on the test.")

- ◆ Is control from the outside. ("You are good when you follow all the class rules.")

- ◆ Is evaluation by others. ("You pleased me when you picked up all the pencils.")

- ◆ Focuses on the finished, well-done task. ("You are worthwhile because you did the job well.")

- ◆ Emphasizes personal gains. ("You came in first; therefore, you are good.")

Encouragement:

- ◆ Recognizes the effort of the doer. ("You worked really hard to get your grade.")

- ◆ Is faith that the individual can control self. ("You are a responsible person.")

- ◆ Promotes self-evaluation. ("How do you feel about your work so far?")

- ◆ Emphasizes effort and progress of a task. ("Look at all the improvement you have made.")

- ◆ Emphasizes appreciation of contributions and assets. ("Your efforts helped us have a good science fair.")

This is not to say we should eliminate all praise and concentrate solely on encouragement. Rather, we need to emphasize more encouragement than praise to help students achieve a more internal locus of control.

We also need to take time regularly and consistently to recognize our student's effort or work. No one likes to do work without recognition—you don't, I don't, and your students don't.

Praise and Encouragement Considerations

Praise and encouragement, in large quantities, can be powerful elements in any successful teacher's classroom. But you must remember some major considerations if your verbal comments are to be effective:

- ◆ **You must use the praise or encouragement consistently.** It cannot be used every once in a while or randomly. And it cannot be used just for the good students and not the underachieving students. It must be a regular element for every student in every learning activity.

It's Elementary

It's generally acceptable to praise or encourage students in front of other students.

Secondary Thoughts

At the middle school and high school level, praise and encourage individuals privately. Save the public praise for groups.

♦ **You must be honest with the praise or encouragement.** It must acknowledge the learner's true achievement, rather than any fake or made-up accomplishments.

♦ **You must be specific with the praise or encouragement.** General statements such as "Good," "Great," or "Cool" are too general to have any meaning. Provide a very specific reference for a student. ("You must feel very proud about the work you did on your Civil War project.")

♦ **You must give immediate feedback.** It has to occur soon after the event or task is completed, or it will be meaningless.

To Reward or Not To Reward?

Some teachers use tangible rewards to motivate their students. They may give stickers, smiley faces, coupons, patches, gold stars, and the like as motivational tools. The practice of providing these tangible rewards has been a consistent one in education.

But there are some controversies surrounding the use of tangible rewards:

♦ They are a form of external control; one person controls the behavior of another.

♦ They do not foster an internal locus of control.

♦ They are a form of bribery or coercion.

♦ The more rewards teachers give, the more rewards students come to expect.

♦ Students often do work for the rewards rather than for the learning that may occur.

♦ Some experts see rewards as a way of manipulating and controlling people. They equate it with the way we train animals—do a trick and get a treat.

Early in my teaching career, I used to give lots of gold stars and smelly stickers. Over the years, I've rethought the value of those external rewards and have talked with many teachers. I've reached some new conclusions I'd like to share with you:

- Emphasize encouragement more than praise. But if you have to, emphasize praise more than rewards.

- Don't make rewards a regular condition of learning. Make it an unexpected part of tasks that students find unattractive or boring.

- If you decide to use rewards, use them for the completion of a task not for a student's participation in that task.

Think carefully about the value of rewards in your classroom. Are there other ways of motivating students that do not involve tangible items? Rewards are often based on criteria established by teachers, not students. The best motivation comes from an internal source, and in a classroom, that encourages responsibility and self-determination.

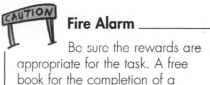

Fire Alarm _____

Be sure the rewards are appropriate for the task. A free book for the completion of a math worksheet might be a little over the top.

But They're Not Motivated!

Every teacher gets them; you will, too. They are the unmotivated students, those who could care less about the lesson, class, or school in general. How do you deal with the unmotivated?

First, consider the elements presented earlier in this chapter. That type of motivational classroom might be just the incentive for your unmotivated students (who may be reacting to their previous expectations of how teachers act or how classrooms are run) to make changes in their own behavior. You might also consider these additional ideas:

- Create an atmosphere of puzzlement and novelty in your teaching. Tap into students' natural curiosity with unusual events. ("Has anyone ever seen a creature covered in slime? I have one right here in this box.")

- Use a combination of both individual and group projects. Provide opportunities for students to share and discuss in groups as well as opportunities to work on their own.

- Periodically invite students to meet and discuss any barriers to their learning (time, textbook, teacher, rules, etc.).

- Ensure numerous opportunities for students to set their own goals. Keep those goals realistic, and be sure to start with tiny steps before moving to larger goals.

- Be especially vigilant for opportunities to encourage (more so than praise) learning accomplishments.

- Model your enthusiasm for learning. Let students see your excitement for a task or assignment.

- It's critical that students know you're working for their benefit, not for a paycheck. Be encouraging and supportive in all your contacts with an unmotivated student. As soon as you give up, so will the student.

- Variety is the spice of life. Use different strategies, various techniques, and a potpourri of methods.

- Provide frequent offers of help ("I don't know; let's see what we can discover together").

- Be willing to accept (and celebrate) different viewpoints. ("That's not what I had in mind; could you please explain your position?")

- Students who are turned off to learning are often turned off to authority. Don't be dictatorial or authoritative. Create an invitational, cooperative climate in your classroom, one without intimidation or threats.

> **Expert Opinion**
>
> Relate academic tasks to students' lives. They might never ask you why they have to learn something, but you should always give them the answer.

The Least You Need to Know

- Teachers often view motivation as an external force rather than an internal one.

- To be motivated, students must have an expectation of success, feel part of a community of learners, and know why they are learning something.

- Internally motivated students achieve more.

- Praise and encouragement are at opposite ends of the motivation continuum.

- Rewards are frequently misused and might not be motivational.

Part 4

Management Tools (or How to Maintain Your Sanity and Keep Your Job)

It's just you and your students. The classroom door is closed. The day is about to begin. And you're wondering to yourself, *Now, what the heck do I do?* Part 4 has the answers you're looking for.

The chapters in this part give you the guidance you need to effectively manage your classroom. You learn how to create an exciting learning environment, how to deal with the homework issue, ways to teach your special needs students, and how to create some special projects and events you don't want to miss. Of course, one of your biggest concerns is how you're going to deal with discipline in your classroom. I provide you with strategies and techniques that will make your classroom the envy of the school—a place where good behavior flourishes alongside outstanding teaching.

Ferguson's Precept: A crisis is when you can't say, "Let's forget the whole thing."

Chapter 15

Creating a Learning Environment

In This Chapter

- The influence of your classroom
- It's a physical world!
- Soft spaces and hard places
- Take this desk and …
- Ways to store and use materials
- How you can pull it all together

Learning does not take place in a vacuum. You might be an excellent teacher and have exciting lesson plans filled with valuable resources. You might even have motivated students. Still, the environment or classroom in which all that is to take place will determine, to a large extent, how successful you will be as a teacher.

Classrooms devoid of interest, lacking in intellectual stimulation, or absent in social engagement are classrooms that often have a negative impact on students' ability to learn. How you set up your classroom will be a major influence on how your students will succeed both academically and personally.

Save the Environment!

Have you ever been in a cheap motel room? You know, the kind that has a single bed in the middle of the room, a lack of wall decorations (other than one dusty print of a colorless bowl of flowers), ancient and well-worn furniture, a tattered rug, and a closet with a single hanger in it. The bathroom is often small, cramped, and musty. You're just there for one night, but you can't wait to get out.

Unfortunately, many classrooms are the same way. They look like they were designed with the motto, "Keep it simple, keep it old, keep it dull, and keep it cheap," in mind.

Effective teaching is dependent upon environmental factors just as much as it is dependent on psychological, social, and personal factors. The way you lay out your classroom and the ways your students perceive your classroom will have a major impact on their level of comfort, their willingness to participate in learning activities, and most important, their behavior. Your classroom design will send one of two messages to your students:

- This is a comfortable place that supports my needs, both physical and psychological, and one in which I feel secure and respected. I enjoy being here.

- This is an environment devoid of feeling, social opportunities, and intellectual stimulation. It is a place I *have* to be in, not a place I *want* to be in.

Where students learn is just as important as *what* students learn. What you put into your classroom is as significant as what you put into every lesson.

Making a Good First Impression

When you visit someone's home for the first time, what's one of the first things you do? You probably look around at the furniture, it's arrangement, the décor, the interior decorating, and a dozen other things. You try to get a sense of this new environment. In short, even before you sit down in the living room or wander out to the deck, you have a pretty good idea of the personality of your hosts as well as their decoration philosophy.

The same is true for students. As soon as they enter your classroom, they'll get an initial impression of you and the classroom in which they will be spending the next nine months of their lives. It's been said that first impressions are often lasting impressions, and no where is that more true than on the first day of class. Students, from kindergarten to twelfth grade, will be able to determine …

- ◆ Your organization skills (orderly/sequential; random/haphazard).

- ◆ Your personality (fun/exciting; dull/drab).

- ◆ Your creative skills (prepackaged posters, banners, bulletin boards; original art work, decorations, displays).

- ◆ Your classroom management plan (detailed/specific; loose/unstructured).

- ◆ Your instructional preferences (multitasking; singular activities).

Let's Get Physical!

If you've ever been in a classroom in which all the desks were in straight rows and straight lines, you might have gotten the impression that it was an orderly classroom run by an orderly teacher and a place not subject to change, modification, or variation. Such classrooms can be sterile and predictable—and not much fun!

Arranging the furniture may be the most important thing you can do before students arrive on that all-important first day. Use a piece of graph paper and draw your current classroom arrangement, including all the tables, desks, windows, doors, bookcases, cabinets, electrical outlets, bulletin boards, and even the wastepaper basket and pencil sharpener. I like to cut out small pieces of paper in the shape and scaled dimensions of all these items so I can move them around on the graph paper. Use this model to make decisions on the preferred placement of furniture in your room.

The arrangement of furniture in a classroom is an important decision to make before students arrive on the first day. However, you should feel comfortable changing the arrangement several times throughout the year. Modifying and adjusting the configuration of students' desks (and yours) is just as natural as changing the location of the sofa, love seat, TV, coffee table, and lamps in your living room at home.

 Expert Opinion

When designing your classroom, remember that furniture directs the flow of traffic within the classroom environment and defines the instructional activities that can take place within that classroom.

Let's look at some possible room arrangements:

♦ Horseshoe configuration. One of the most versatile designs for any classroom is the horseshoe pattern. You can set up two or three large semicircles of student desks facing the chalkboard or front of the room. Or scatter mini-horseshoe patterns of a few desks each about the classroom. This pattern opens up the center front of the room for oral presentations, skits, or small group work on the floor.

A variation of the horseshoe pattern is the "U" or three-sided arrangement of desks. Two or three desks form each of the two sides, and two or three desks form the bottom of the pattern.

♦ Clusters. Another popular way of arranging student desks is in clusters or small groupings of four or five student desks together. In a classroom of 25 students, you might have 5 clusters of 5 desks each. Separate each cluster with sufficient space for student movement. Clusters enhance social interactions among students and provide for easy access by the teacher.

♦ Pairs or triads. A variation on the cluster approach is the arrangement of student desks into small groups of two or three. Students create mini-groups of study buddies and can work together for extended periods of time on selected projects and activities.

♦ Rows and lines. You might want to consider rows or lines as an initial arrangement at the beginning of the year. By assigning students to specific desks, you can learn their names and get a sense of the different personalities and instructional needs quicker. Later, you can arrange the classroom in other configurations based on the needs and abilities of students.

Expert Opinion

After you arrange the furniture in your classroom, take time to sit at each student's desk. Determine if you have a clear line of sight to the chalkboard. Is the chalkboard easy to read?

♦ Combination approach. You might want to use a combination of several arrangements. A combination approach allows you several instructional options and signals to students that both you and your classroom are flexible. You might invite students to suggest a variety of flexible options according to planned units of study or personal preferences. By allowing students to make some choices in the physical design of the classroom, you're providing them with an important sense of ownership in the classroom.

The most important consideration in any arrangement of desks and other furniture in your classroom is that students must always have a clear and unobstructed view of all instruction. Whether you lecture, show a video, conduct a scientific experiment, invite a guest speaker, or use the chalkboard, it's important that every student, no matter their physical placement, be able to see and hear what is going on.

Soften It Up!

Remember that motel room I talked about earlier in the chapter? If you picture that room in your mind, one of the distinctive things you might notice is all the straight lines and sharp angles. All the furniture is square or rectangular, and all the features are equally square and rectangular. All that "squareness" is psychologically inhibiting.

Some classrooms are like motel rooms, cold and uninviting because they're composed of straight lines and sharp angles. You can soften this "hardness" in a number of ways:

- Use lots of throw rugs or carpets squares throughout the room.

- Include lots of pillows, bean bag chairs, old sofas, and other soft furniture.

- Use a variety of fabrics (wool, burlap, cotton) in the room decorations.

- Include items children might find at home, such as photographs, aquariums, standing lamps, padded chairs, posters, and personal artifacts.

- Add a variety of plants—real or artificial; they are one of the most important "softening" elements in any classroom.

- Be creative! A friend of mine brought an old bathtub into his classroom, tossed in some pillows, and turned it into a reading center for his third graders. What a great idea!

- Use cardboard or large appliance boxes to create private spaces or student study areas.

- Elementary teachers and secondary science teachers should consider the addition of classroom pets such as small mammals (hamsters, guinea pigs, mice), reptiles (snakes, lizards, turtle), birds (canaries, parakeets), and fish (guppies, goldfish).

Expert Opinion

Students need to know that your classroom is a psychologically safe environment. Many youngsters come from homes that are not psychologically secure or safe. Your classroom might be the only secure and comfortable environment in their lives. Rounded edges, lines, and corners suggest psychological safety and comfort—more so than straight lines and angles.

Fire Alarm

Don't make your room too busy. A room filled with too many stations, bulletin boards, artifacts, and displays can lead to visual overload. For some students, this can be disruptive and visually confusing. The key is to create interest and calm.

My Space, My Place

Students of any age need to know that a classroom is their place; that it's not just the teacher's place into which they have been temporarily invited. If students have the impression that a classroom is "owned" by the teacher, they will be less likely to make an investment in learning. Classrooms that invite student engagement and celebrate the work of students are classrooms in which the best instruction takes place.

What is usually any child's favorite room in the house? For most kids it's his or her bedroom. Why? Because their bedroom is usually the one room in the house they get to decorate, arrange, or design. It's *their* room! A classroom should be no different. Students will feel most comfortable when they can personalize the classroom and when their contributions are valued.

Here are some suggested strategies:

- ◆ Provide plenty of spaces for students to post their work. This can include bulletin boards, walls, the classroom door, cabinet doors, lines down from the ceiling, or other special locations.

- ◆ Invite students to suggest desk arrangements, furniture placements, color schemes, decorations, and the like.

- ◆ As appropriate, invite students to bring in personal items from home to use in the classroom.

- ◆ Celebrate your students' different cultures and countries of origin by decorating with artifacts from those countries or cultures. These can include masks, posters, costumes, pictures, photos, murals, quilts, maps, trinkets, souvenirs, etc.

It's Elementary

As an elementary teacher, I would invite students to each lay down on a sheet of newsprint. I would trace their body outline with a pencil and then ask each student to cut out and then color his or her outline. I would then post the outlines along the classroom walls and invite each student to think of one or two sentences describing themselves to go inside dialogue balloons (just like in comic strips) posted over each child's body outline. These would remain posted for several weeks. This was a great way for students to get to know each other at the start of the year.

Talk to Me

When you begin to arrange your classroom space, consider how you want students to interact with each other and how you want to interact with your students. The answers to those questions will play a major role in the design of your classroom.

You know that the best kind of teaching and the best kind of learning take place in a social environment. Students must have opportunities to discuss, share, and converse with each other in productive conversations. You need to consider how you might arrange desks and other furniture to facilitate that process. Obviously, the traditional rows and lines of desks do not stimulate group interaction.

Also as you consider how you want to work with and interact with your students, keep these considerations in mind:

- In classrooms where desks are arranged in rows, teachers tend to call on students in the front center area of the room more than students in other areas.

- Passageways and desk arrangements should allow you to reach every student with a minimum of steps.

- You need to physically move around the room at regular intervals. Students see teachers who "post" themselves in the front of the room for an entire period as dictatorial and disconnected. You need to have a close presence with students regularly throughout a lesson.

- Make regular and close eye contact with each student. When talking with a student, remember the 4-6 rule: stand no more than 4 to 6 feet away from that individual. Design your classroom so you can reach this distance with every student in a minimal amount of time.

Your Space, Your Desk

The first object you see when you walk into any classroom is probably the teacher's desk. In many classrooms, the teacher's desk is a focal point—a place where students deposit homework; a place for student-teacher conferences; a place from which a teacher lectures; and a place where papers are read, graded, and filed.

But a teacher's desk can also be a psychological deterrent to learning. A desk, whether in a classroom, office, or executive suite, is a symbol of power. Its placement within a room says a lot about the person who occupies it. If it's placed in the front of the room, it says that the occupant wants others to know she or he is in charge, that he or she is the authority figure.

That often causes discomfort and anxiety for many students. Rather than place your desk front and center in the classroom (the traditional way), try turning your desk around so it faces a wall, preferably in a corner and preferably in the back of the room. Then you'll send your students the message that your desk is just another piece of furniture, not a place of power.

Secondary Thoughts

Don't conduct your lessons from your desk. Move away from your desk, and use a small table, a lectern, or some other minor piece of furniture to hold your notes and other instructional materials.

I know some of you might be saying that you worked long and hard to earn that teacher's desk. You're right, but it's far more important how students perceive you as an instructor than it is for you to exert some artificial power over them by parking yourself behind a large piece of furniture.

It's a Material World

With everything you need to teach and with the limited amount of space you might have in your classroom, it might seem as though there's never enough room to keep all the equipment, supplies, and materials at the ready for any and all parts of your instructional program. In deciding how and where to store your instructional materials, keep some things in mind.

Materials must be readily accessible by you and your students. Students need to know exactly where all materials are kept and that they will be able to obtain those materials on their own. You might want to use a special check-out system so students can obtain materials on their own without your intervention.

Materials and equipment that require safety precautions (hot plates and other electrical devises, slides, crockery, etc.) must be kept in a location out of the reach of youngsters. Provide any necessary instructions and precautions to students early in the school year.

Materials and equipment kept in containers, storage cabinets, or lockers must be labeled on the outside for easy and quick identification. For younger students or those lacking adequate reading abilities, have an illustration or photograph of the object(s) on the outside of the container.

Supplies and materials should be kept in a variety of locations in the classroom so they're readily accessible at all times and are evenly distributed throughout the room.

Some supplies will be in constant use and need to be obtained quickly and easily. Paper towels, scissors, pens, chalk, pens and pencils, and string are items used fairly often and should be supplied in several locations throughout the room.

Designing Your Classroom

After reading this chapter, you might be wondering how you'll ever be able to design your instructional environment—your classroom. Remember that a well-designed classroom is in a state of constant evolution—it is always subject to change and modification depending on the students who occupy it as well as the instructional activities you have planned for those students.

As you think about how to create the best possible learning environment for your grade or subject area, you might want to keep these things in mind.

Traffic Patterns

Is there room to move around the room? Take a look at how students will move into the room, to their desks, and between activities or locations within the room. You need to be sure students with physical challenges can safely negotiate the room. Traffic routes to and from frequently used places also need to be clear, unobstructed, and easy. Consider the following routes for each student in the room:

- From a desk to the pencil sharpener
- From a desk to the wastebasket
- From a desk to the water fountain or sink
- From a desk to you
- From a desk to the bathroom (in the classroom or outside the classroom)
- From a desk to the door and vice versa
- From a desk to a center activity or small group location

Fire Alarm _____

Keep large objects and furniture away from your classroom door. Students will need space to enter the classroom (often in small groups) as well as exit (often in large groups).

Not only must you consider the traffic patterns for individual students but also for larger groups as well. The class will need to exit the classroom en mass at the end of a period, for recess, lunch, their specials (art, music, P.E., library), and end-of-day dismissal. Plan for an efficient flow of lots of bodies through your room.

Different Activity Areas

In most classrooms, there will be a variety of activities and activity areas for students. You need to carefully plan these so they don't interfere with each other or with other instructional tasks that take place during the course of the day. You don't want a messy area near the computer(s). You don't want a noisy area near a quiet reading area. And you don't want a small group area near the front of the classroom where most instruction takes place.

The Least You Need to Know

- ◆ Your classroom environment will have a direct impact on how well your students will learn.

- ◆ You can arrange your classroom furniture in a variety of ways—and then change it when you or your students need something else.

- ◆ Soft classrooms produce higher levels of achievement than hard classrooms do.

- ◆ Your students will need a sense of ownership in the classroom.

- ◆ Your desk doesn't have to be front and center in the classroom—move it!

- ◆ Well-designed classrooms have well-designed traffic patterns.

Positive Discipline, Positive Behavior

In This Chapter

You've probably seen classrooms in which students were orderly, work was productive, and a sense of purpose and direction filled the room. You might also have seen classrooms that were chaotic, disruptive, and seemingly out of control. Maybe you were even a student in one or both of those classrooms at some time in your educational career.

What's the difference? Is it a teacher who has a loud voice and a commanding presence in the classroom? Is it a teacher who has a large wooden paddle hanging in the front of the room and a list of rules several pages long? Or is it a teacher who has explicit expectations for students and ways of making those expectations absolutely clear to students? As you might expect, the latter choice is the method advocated by most educators. Let's take a look at how you can create a classroom that is disciplined, orderly, and clearly focused on the task of learning.

The Facts of Life: Kids Misbehave

For more than 30 years, the general public has ranked classroom discipline at or near the top of their major concerns about American education. Teachers, too, have cited discipline problems or misbehavior as the predominant concern of their professional lives. Everyone realizes that there's a significant relationship between how well students behave and how well those same students learn.

Disruptive behavior comes in many forms and in many ways:

- Talking out of turn

- Tardiness

- Moving around the room without permission

- Wasting time

- Physical contact with another student

- Interrupting

- Inattention

- Ignoring rules

- Obtaining materials without permission

- Goofing off

Jabberwocky

Disruptive behavior is any behavior that interferes with or impedes the teacher's ability to teach and students' abilities to learn.

For the most part, much of disruptive behavior is insignificant *by itself*. However, when there's an accumulation of several disruptive incidents during a lesson, a day, or perhaps even an entire year, it can have negative consequences, both minor and major, for any classroom.

Misbehavior adds to the stress levels of both students and teachers. When we are negatively stressed, we are not at our best; our concentration is diverted and our focus is shifted away from our primary task.

Misbehavior in the classroom also diverts us from our primary responsibility—that is, teaching. With only about 50 percent of our instructional time spent on instructional matters, that means we're only giving our students half of their education.

Disruptive behavior creates a classroom climate that is not respectful of other individuals, fosters poor human relations, and tears down any trust that might be established between you and your students. Over time, this creates a classroom climate that's more destructive than constructive. Many students might even be fearful about attending school as a result.

Constant disruptive behavior will sap your energy as well as the energy levels of your students. You'll have less motivation to teach, and they'll have less motivation to learn. Disruptive behavior tears you away from your primal responsibility and distracts students from theirs.

> **CAUTION**
>
> **Fire Alarm**
>
> According to research from several observers, teachers in a typical classroom lose about 50 percent of their teaching time because of students' disruptive behavior.

Are Teachers the Culprit?

Many interesting observations have been made about classroom behavior, and what we're seeing is that the teacher's behavior often contributes to a climate that inadvertently fosters and creates discipline problems through certain types of management procedures.

How many of the following selected teacher behaviors that create management problems—rather than solve them—have you experienced or seen:

- **Extreme negativity.** The teacher's comments to the class are frequently couched in negative and/or highly authoritative terms. ("It's obvious that nobody knows what a theorem is. It looks like many of you will fail the test on Friday.")

- **Excessive authoritarian climate.** These teachers desire to be the absolute and complete authority figure in the classroom. All decisions are theirs. ("It's my way or the highway!")

- **Overreacting.** This teacher creates mountains out of molehills by escalating minor disturbances into major ones. ("I'm tired of your tardiness. I want all of you to write one hundred times, 'I will not be late to Mrs. Northwing's class.'")

◆ **Mass punishment.** These teachers hope peer pressure will result in a change of behavior for a few select students. ("It's obvious that Robert and Edwardo can't behave, so we just won't celebrate Linda's birthday today.")

◆ **Blaming.** This teacher often picks out two or three students and consistently blames them for every little infraction that may occur. ("Alright, who made that noise? Was it you again, LaToya?")

◆ **Lack of instructional goals.** Often teachers will engage students without a clearly defined or clearly understood (by students) goal for the lesson. ("Okay, is there anything anyone wants to talk about before we begin?")

◆ **Repeating or reviewing already understood material.** In an effort to make sure students are exposed to important material, teachers might constantly repeat material over and over again in the same way. There is no challenge. ("All right, I want you to look up the definitions for these 20 words, write them in your notebook, and then write them again on this chart.")

◆ **Dealing with a single student at length.** This teacher often disrupts his own instructional rhythm by spending an inordinate amount of time on one student. ("I can't believe you are still talking, Sierra. I've told you over and over and over again about talking in class." [Five minutes of lecture ensue.])

◆ **Not recognizing students' ability levels.** This teacher plans a lesson that is often over the heads of many students in the class. A single lesson is much easier to prepare than multiple mini-lessons. ("This is material everybody should know, so I want everyone to listen carefully so you can all do well on the exam.")

Expert Opinion

Always admonish behaviors rather than personalities:

Wrong: "I've had it with you, Carla. You're always late!"

Better: "Carla, your tardiness disrupts the class and makes it difficult for me to begin a lesson."

A combination of these teacher behaviors can create and promote significant discipline problems in any classroom. Be aware that avoiding these behaviors will go a long way toward creating a climate of trust and caring that will significantly reduce and quite possibly eliminate misbehavior.

The Rule of Rules

Most classroom teachers have a set of rules for their students to follow. Often, these rules inform students about what they can or can't do in a classroom. The intent is to create a sense of order and comfort so teaching and learning can take place.

But for classroom rules to be effective, you should create or base them on a few simple principles.

Students Should Have a Sense of Ownership of the Rules

Invite students to contribute a set of expectations about behavior. Take time at the beginning of the school year to solicit their input.

Most often you'll discover that the classroom rules students suggest fall into several specific categories. In a classroom meeting, for example, second-graders might say that there should be no kicking, no hitting, no pinching, no poking, etc. All those behaviors fall into the category of "personal space."

As you brainstorm with students, look for groupings or clusters of ideas. Take time to talk with students about how they can combine their ideas and suggestions into the following categories such as honoring personal space, respecting property, considering the feelings of others, paying attention, and using appropriate movements.

The final list you create will be a personal one for students because they helped create it. They will have that all-important sense of ownership and will be more inclined to follow the rules they helped create.

Expert Opinion

Frame rules in positive terms. Instead of "Don't hit people," say "Respect other people." Instead of "No talking when someone else is talking," say "Take turns talking."

Remember the Rule of Five

The best set of classroom rules is one students can remember and use every day. When a list of rules becomes long and exhaustive, students will never be able to remember, much less conform to, those rules.

The Rule of Five says there should be no more than five basic rules in any classroom. The clustering activity mentioned in the preceding section will help you cluster student suggestions into a manageable list of rules.

Secondary Thoughts

When crafting rules for secondary students, try not to create rules with absolutes. Words like *never* and *always* don't give you or your students any latitude when unexpected events happen. Allow yourself some flexibility within the context of any rule. This also humanizes any rules you create.

The Rules Should Be Appropriate to the Grade Level

"Absolutely no talking" would be a very difficult rule to enforce in a kindergarten class where students are very verbal and very social. Making sure the rules are appropriate for your grade level also means you need to be sensitive to potential exceptions. Creating a rule for your high school social studies class such as, "All homework must be turned in on time—no exceptions" does not allow for the inevitable unplanned events that often impact an adolescent's life (sports, jobs, social life).

Be Sure All Students Understand the Classroom Rules

You might have a rule posted in the classroom such as "Respect other people." It's important that you clearly spell out examples of that rule in practice for students. For example, you might say, "Always listen when someone else is talking," or "Be sure to share any games with your classmates."

It's valuable for students to know the specific types of behaviors expected of them. It's equally important that you describe those behaviors in terms and examples that are concrete and specific for the grade level you're teaching. For every rule, you must communicate in clearly defined terms and language students will understand, give the specific rationale or reason for a rule, and offer concrete examples of the rule as you want it to be practiced.

Do the Classroom Rules Enhance or Hinder Learning?

Hindering rules are often *too* specific: "All homework must be turned in to the blue box on my desk by 2:55 each day." Compare that rule with "All homework should be turned in on time." The latter rule allows some flexibility and doesn't cause unnecessary stress for students. The first rule places more emphasis on the time of delivery than it does on the actual homework assignment.

Be Sure Your Classroom Rules Are Consistent with School Rules

Although you might think it would be nice to have your students take responsibility for using the restroom on their own and want to establish that as one of your classroom rules, the school might have a policy that every student must have a bathroom or office pass to leave the classroom. Be sure any rule in your classroom doesn't contradict a school rule.

Tips for Achieving and Maintaining Discipline

Discipline is not about getting kids to do what you want them to do. That's what dictators do, and you're not a dictator—you're an educator. Discipline is providing an environment in which positive teaching and positive learning can occur simultaneously. Discipline is not control from the outside; it's order from within.

In conversations with teachers, I've discovered some practical and universal ideas that will help you achieve discipline in your classroom. Tap into the experience of these pros, and turn your classroom into a place where students learn and enjoy the process.

- ◆ **Greet students at the door.** Interact with your students on a personal level every day. Greet them by name, interject a positive comment or observation, shake their hand, and welcome them into the classroom. This sets a positive tone for a lesson or for the day.

- ◆ **Get students focused before you begin any lesson.** Be sure you have their attention before you begin. Don't try to talk over students; you'll be initiating a competition to see who can speak louder and also let them know it's okay to talk while you are talking.

- ◆ **Use positive presence.** Don't park yourself in the front of the classroom. Move around the room continuously, and get in and around your students. Make frequent eye contact, and smile with students. Monitor students with your physical presence.

Fire Alarm _____

Teachers often make the mistake of using "stop" messages rather than a "start" message. For example, "Stop talking. We need to get started." A better message is "Get out your math books, and turn to page 44." The effect is tremendous. It establishes a productive, businesslike tone for the lesson. The focus is not on the (negative) behavior, but the importance of the lesson.

◆ **Model the behavior you want students to produce.** If you exhibit respectful-ness, trust, enthusiasm, interest, and courtesy in your everyday dealings with students, they will return the favor in kind. Remember the saying, "Values are caught, not taught."

◆ **Use low-profile intervention.** When you see a student who is misbehaving, be sure your intervention is quiet, calm, and inconspicuous. Use the student's name in part of your presentation, for example, "As an example, let's measure Michael's height in centimeters." Michael, who has been whispering to his neighbor, hears his name and is drawn back into the lesson with no disruption of the class.

◆ **Send positive "I" messages.** Thomas Gordon, creator of Teacher Effectiveness Training, under-scores the importance of "I" messages as a powerful way of humanizing the classroom and ensuring positive discipline. An I-message is composed of three parts:

1. Include a description of the student's behavior. ("When you talk while I talk …")

2. Relate the effect this behavior has on you, the teacher. ("I have to stop my teaching …")

3. Let the student know the feeling it generates in you. ("which frustrates me")

◆ **Verbal reprimands should be private, brief, and as immediate as possible.** The more private a reprimand, the less likely you will be challenged. The more immediate the reprimand, the less likely the student will feel you condone her or his behavior. And keep reprimands brief. The more you talk, the more you distract from the lesson and the more you "reward" a student for inappropriate behavior.

◆ **Provide lots of positive feedback.** Many veteran teachers will tell you, "10 percent of the students will give you 90 percent of your headaches!" But what about the 90 percent of those other students in your classroom? Don't forget them; recognize their contributions and behavior:

◆ Acknowledge positive student behavior when it is not expected.

◆ Acknowledge compliance with requests.

◆ Acknowledge hard work, kindness, and dependability.

◆ **Be consistent!** Although this is easier said than done, the key to an effective discipline policy in any classroom is consistency. Make these principles part of your classroom action plan:

  ◆ If you have a rule, enforce that rule.

  ◆ Don't hand out lots of warnings without following through on consequences. Lots of warnings tell students that you won't enforce a rule.

  ◆ Be fair and impartial. The rules are there for everyone, and that includes girls as well as boys, tall people and short people, students with freckles and students without freckles, and special needs kids as well as gifted kids.

Watch Out!

If you're anything like me and a couple million other teachers in the world, you will undoubtedly make a few mistakes regarding an appropriate discipline policy for your classroom. Watch out for these.

◆ Teach students to listen. We sometimes make the mistake of repeating the same instructions several times. When we do that, we teach students not to listen. Give a request only twice, and let students know that after two times they will be on their own.

◆ Don't be their friend. It's your nature to be caring, considerate, outgoing, and sensitive. After all, you're a teacher! But when you become your students' friend, you lose their respect. Yes, it's important that you be a role model and someone they can look up to and trust. It's important that you care about them. But don't ever try to be their friend.

◆ Keep your administrator informed. As you craft your classroom discipline policy, be sure you run it by your principal first. Get her or him involved, and let that individual know what your rules are, how you plan to enforce them, and how your classroom rules are in line with any rules and regulations of the school.

◆ Keep parents informed, too. Good classroom discipline does not exist in isolation from the discipline practiced at home or in the local community. Inform parents of your expectations for students though newsletters, phone calls, parent-teacher conferences, or other means of communication. When parents know what you expect, they will be more supportive of your actions.

◆ Watch out for an excess of negative comments. Frame your comments, suggestions, and behavior modification in positive terms, such as, "Let's walk silently down the right side of the hallway," or "I really like when you come into the room ready to work."

◆ Teach your students proper discipline. During the first week of school, establish a set of expectations, the specific details of those expectations, and the consequences if those expectations are not followed. Nothing is more important than a well-crafted and well-articulated discipline policy. If it's true that "an ounce of prevention is worth a pound of cure," the time you take at the start of the school year will pay enormous dividends throughout the rest of the school year.

The Least You Need to Know

◆ Disruptive behavior has consequences for students as well as teachers.

◆ Teachers often create situations that lead to misbehavior.

◆ Classroom rules should be brief, to the point, and explicit.

◆ Teachers can use several practical strategies every day to ensure good discipline.

◆ Teachers need to be aware of personal behaviors that promote good classroom discipline.

Homework: Yes? No?

In This Chapter

- ◆ How much homework is enough?
- ◆ Should parents help with homework?
- ◆ The feedback factor
- ◆ Ways to make homework relevant
- ◆ Tips for every teacher

When you were in school, do you remember hearing something like this: "For homework tonight, class, I want you to read Chapter 9 in the text-book and answer all the odd-numbered questions." For some students (perhaps you), those kinds of after-school assignments might have struck fear into your heart or might have been just another reason for disliking that particular subject or teacher.

Homework has been a staple of classroom life ever since the one-room schoolhouse. For many, it is viewed as a natural and logical extension of the instruction that takes place in the classroom. For others, it is boring, meaningless, and perhaps even ridiculous. So let's discuss the value of homework to help you make decisions about its utility for your classroom.

The Question of Homework

Mention the word *homework* to most students, and you'll probably get a series of groans, yawns, and other verbal reactions—most of which I can't print in the pages of this book. It seems as though homework is something done *to* students for reasons that may range from reinforcement of classroom concepts to punishment. Ask the average teacher why he or she assigns homework, and you may hear, "It's required by the administration," "I've always done it, " or "It's good for the students—it teaches them responsibility and discipline."

How Much Is Enough?

From studies of effective teaching, we know there is a positive correlation between homework as a learning tool and student achievement in the classroom. Some educators argue that homework does not have as much of an effect on the scholastic achievement of elementary students as it does on secondary students. Nevertheless, we know there are measurable gains at both levels. That statement comes with a caveat; that is, the amount of homework assigned needs to be tailored to the students' age and grade level.

Expert Opinion

Teachers often report that the value of homework is threefold: (1) It helps develop good study habits. (2) It fosters positive attitudes toward school. (3) It communicates to students that learning happens in places outside of school as well as in school.

The burning question is: how much homework should teachers assign to students? There is no clear answer to that query, but I'd like to offer the following simple formula, which has been suggested by many teachers:

$$\text{Homework} = \text{Grade level} \times 10$$

This means that the amount of after-school homework (in minutes) is equivalent to the grade you teach times 10. For example, if you teach fifth grade, you would assign 50 minutes of homework per evening (5th grade × 10 = 50). Here's a sampling:

Grade Level	×	Minutes of Homework per Evening
2	10	20
4	10	40
6	10	60
8	10	80
10	10	100

The "Homework = Grade level × 10" formula refers to the *total* amount of homework per student—not the amount of homework per *subject*. Consequently, if you follow this formula, you will need to coordinate your homework assignments with other secondary teachers so you don't overload your students.

It's Elementary

Students in kindergarten and first grade should not receive any homework. No research suggests that homework at these levels is necessary or productive.

How Involved Should Parents Be?

The question of parent involvement in the completion of homework is often one of those black or white issues for teachers. Teachers are either very supportive of the notion of parents helping children or they are dead set against it.

Some schools and many districts have written policies regarding the degree of involvement parents should have in their children's homework. Based on a review of many of those documents, I'd like to offer the following suggestions regarding the role of parents in homework:

◆ Keep parents regularly informed about the amount of homework assigned to their children. (Check out www.schoolnotes.com as a way for parents *and* students to keep track of homework assignments in your class on a daily basis.)

◆ Parents should facilitate the completion of homework assignments. They should not do assignments for students; rather, they should provide the atmosphere and support system that will increase the likelihood of student completion (e.g., a quiet place to study, encouragement, and praise).

◆ Parents should have active and regular conversations with their children about homework assignments, concerns, and issues. A solid interest in homework helps support the completion of that homework.

Expert Opinion

In my classroom, we had a "Homework Council" composed of several parent volunteers. We would meet periodically throughout the year and establish policies and practices regarding homework assignments. Decisions included how much homework, what subjects to emphasize, grading practices, and other similar issues. As a result, parents had a sense of ownership and were highly supportive of any assignments made.

◆ Be sure parents understand the purposes of homework, the amount of homework assigned, consequences for noncompletion of homework, and a list of the types of suggested or acceptable parent involvement.

What's the Purpose of Homework?

Teachers will say that homework, if it is to be effective, must serve one of two purposes. The first is for the general purpose of practice. Homework cannot be used to introduce a new concept; it should be used to provide students with necessary practice to help them master a concept presented in the classroom.

Although practice is both important and necessary, I'd like to suggest that the practice has to be realistic. For example, assigning students 100 2-digit addition problems as a homework assignment may be overdoing it. There's nothing to suggest that 100 is any better than 20 (for example). If 20 gives your students the necessary practice time, why extend it even further?

The second general purpose of homework would be to prepare students for a forthcoming presentation or new topic. For example, before you introduce the topic of desert animals to your third-grade students, you may ask them to read the children's book *Around One Cactus: Owls, Bats and Leaping Rats* (by Anthony D. Fredericks) as a homework assignment the night before. Or before you lecture your eleventh-grade students about small-business economics, you might want them to interview one or more small business owners in the local community beforehand about the challenges they face with supply and demand issues.

Secondary Thoughts

Many students at the secondary level hold part-time jobs and are involved in after-school sports or a variety of extracurricular activities. All these compete for a student's time. Be sensitive to all the outside influences in students' lives, and adjust your homework assignments accordingly.

What's the Response to Homework?

Doing a homework assignment and turning it in without receiving any feedback is nonproductive as well as demoralizing. My own experience, as well as those of teachers at all grade levels, has shown that the impact of a homework assignment is directly proportional to the immediacy and nature of any resulting feedback.

Here's the bottom line: if you assign homework, grade it, comment on it, and get it back to students as quickly as you can. Timely, frequent, and specific feedback to students has been proven to be the most powerful academic motivator (for the completion of that homework) and has a greater impact on learning.

Two Key Words: *Interesting* and *Relevant*

"This is boring!"

Have you ever heard a student use that comment in reference to a homework assignment? Have *you* ever used that comment in reference to a homework assignment? Many students define homework in terms of punishment or redundancy. They will often ask, "What does this have to do with anything?"

Although there is a need for practice and reinforcement in some homework assignments, it is not necessary (and may even be counterproductive) to fill every homework assignment with lots of skill-and-drill practice. Instead, spice up those assignments with some creative and unique learning opportunities that help students connect with the real world.

Reading and Language Arts

These suggested homework activities provide opportunities for students to enhance their developing reading and language arts abilities:

◆ Write a one-paragraph summary of a TV program you watch this evening.

◆ Alphabetize all the ingredients on a box of cereal.

◆ Create a reader's theater script for a book you just completed.

◆ Make a crossword puzzle using the names, places, and events from a book.

Mathematics

Students frequently think math assignments are the most uncreative of the entire curriculum. Consider these suggestions as ways of changing that perception:

◆ Find 15 items in your house that are rectangles.

◆ Select one of your mother's favorite recipes and double it.

◆ Use a menu from a local restaurant and plan a meal for four people within a budget of $50.

◆ Locate a chart or graph in the local newspaper. Explain what it means in words.

Science and Health

Science is a process of asking questions and then seeking the answers to those questions. Scientists do it all the time. Your students can do it as well, in these creative homework assignments:

◆ Organize everything you had for dinner on the food pyramid.

◆ Write to an environmental group and ask for their policy statement on an environmental issue.

◆ Locate all the products in your kitchen that come from the rainforest.

◆ Collect specimens of rocks, leaves, and soil.

Social Studies

Social studies and all its attendant disciplines—anthropology, sociology, political science, economics, geography, and history—can be enhanced through a creative array of assignments. Here are a few examples:

◆ Write a Bill of Rights for the new moon colony you just established.

◆ Interview several people in your neighborhood about the local issue of ….

◆ Create a neighborhood map.

◆ Create a travel brochure for a specific section of the country.

◆ Interview an older person about a historical event (national or local).

It's Elementary

Obtain a large wall calendar (with large boxes). Inform students that this is the "Homework Calendar." Write each homework assignment in the appropriate date. Post the calendar in a special location. Absent students can check for missed assignments immediately upon their return.

Music and Art

Provide opportunities for your students to use and appreciate the arts in their everyday lives with a few of these suggested homework assignments:

◆ Create a television public service announcement (PSA) that encourages people to visit the community art museum or music festival.

◆ Make a colorful poster that advertises a forthcoming book or textbook chapter.

- Listen to a piece of classical music, and identify four different instruments.

- Write a letter to an artist whose work you admire. Explain what you enjoy about that work.

Sounds Good ... Now What?

These suggested homework assignments include both short-term as well as long-term assignments. Most important, they let students know that homework doesn't have to be dry and pedantic but can be filled with all sorts of learning possibilities—possibilities that stimulate students in applying what they learn in your classroom to the world outside the classroom.

In Chapter 13, I talked about ways you can enhance the thinking that takes place in your classroom. You can use four of those thinking strategies to create dynamic and engaging homework assignments. For example, here are some homework suggestions for a lesson on tide pools:

- **Fluency.** Make a list of all the words you can think of that describe a tide pool.

- **Flexibility.** Describe a tide pool through a seagull's eyes. Or describe how a sea star might see that same tide pool.

- **Originality.** You are a sea urchin. Describe your feelings about the rise and fall of tides.

- **Elaboration.** Imagine that you had to live in a tide pool for the next year. What habits would you need to change?

Some Practices to Practice

Students either like homework or they don't. And guess what. Teachers either like homework or they don't! I've talked to and visited lots of classroom teachers at both the elementary and secondary levels; here are some suggestions they'd like to pass along to you.

The End Product

Students will often ask, "Why do we gotta do this stuff?" The question they are asking is one of purpose. Students at any age need to know the "why" of a homework assignment. If the response is, "It's for your own good," the assignment will be less than meaningful for them.

Be sure you provide your students with a valid reason and rationale for any homework assignment. Attach the assignment to their real and immediate world. State clearly the purpose for any assignment. A *wise* assignment is one that includes the "*whys*."

Shifting Perspective

Often students feel as though homework is assigned strictly for the benefit of the classroom teacher. Provide your students with alternate audiences for their homework assignments, and you will increase the interest level significantly.

For example, as part of a social studies lesson on communities, invite students to create a brochure of historical sites in your community for members of a local senior citizen center. Here are a few other audiences:

- Parents

- Members of their peer group

- Community members

- Other school personnel

- Siblings and other family members

- Another class or section

It's Your Choice

As appropriate, offer students several choices within a homework assignment. Of course, not every assignment will lend itself to choice-making. However, when the teacher gives students the option of making some choices, they will be more motivated to complete those assignments. Here are a few possibilities:

- Do the even-numbered or odd-numbered problems.

- Select any four of the following nine questions.

- Select any two of the following eight multiple intelligence activities.

- Work alone or work with a buddy.

- Select an appropriate due date from one of the following.

By providing students with choices, you are also providing them with a sense of owner-ship in their homework assignments. As a result, they will be more invested in those tasks.

Expert Opinion

Many teachers give homework passes. Students earn these special certificates after accomplishing certain tasks in the classroom. Students can then use these passes to opt out of homework for a day or several days. I don't like these simply because they tend to diminish the value of homework. The message is that homework isn't very important. Instead, use a "Homework Extension Card." Students can earn and use this certificate to extend the deadline for a specific homework assignment by one, two, or three days and still receive full credit.

Give Them a Break

Students have other obligations in their lives besides school. For that reason, I'm a firm believer in not assigning any homework over the weekend. Students need oppor-tunities to be with their families, play, or just "chill out" from all the demands of the academic world. Scheduling a homework assignment to be due on Monday morning puts an additional burden on students that just isn't fair or necessary. Let kids be kids on the weekends—there's plenty to do from Monday through Friday.

The same rule holds true for holidays and vacation periods. These are times away from the academic rigors of classroom life. Let your students enjoy these breaks free of the anxiety of an impending assignment or fast-approaching due date. You'll see higher levels of motivation as a result.

Final Tips

Here's an assembly of tips and suggestions from teachers who have wrestled with the homework issue for years. Tap into their expertise, and incorporate some of these ideas into your classroom routines.

◆ At the beginning of the year, assign each student a "Homework Buddy." If one partner is absent, the other can gather assignments and call or visit her or his buddy to let them know what was missed.

◆ Give students a second (or third) chance. Remember, very few of us mastered the art of walking the first time we tried it. Most authors (this one included) need multiple drafts before a book is finished. In both cases, many attempts were necessary. Give your students the same option.

◆ Be sure to share any homework assignments in both verbal and written form. For each subject or class, post the homework assignments on individual clipboards attached to the wall. Consider tape-recording assignments for physically challenged students in your class.

◆ Always put a date on every homework assignment. That way, students who are absent for extended periods of time can retrieve the necessary assignments by date.

Secondary Thoughts

Keep a homework notebook, with a separate section for each class. Each day, record the homework assignment with any necessary directions. Include copies of any handouts. When students return from an absence, they are responsible for checking the notebook and obtaining the necessary information.

The Least You Need to Know

◆ Tailor the amount of homework you assign to the grade level you teach.

◆ Parents, if properly and consistently informed, can be valuable allies.

◆ Students need immediate feedback for a homework assignment to be meaningful.

◆ Homework must be relevant to the lives of students outside the classroom.

◆ Provide students with a sense of ownership in all their homework assignments, and motivation levels will skyrocket.

Teaching Special Needs Students

In This Chapter

- A brief legislative history of teaching special needs students
- Categories of exceptionalities in the classroom
- Teaching strategies for special needs students
- Working with ADHD students

For many years, teachers and administrators provided for special needs children by removing them from the regular classroom and isolating them in classrooms staffed by one or more specialists. These students were all grouped together in one classroom and provided with instructional procedures and materials that could be similar to, or completely different from, those used in the regular classrooms. This pull-out, or tutorial, approach to education was deemed educationally sound because the specialist teacher could meet the special needs of the students on an individual basis.

As a classroom teacher, you will have a wide diversity of children exhibiting various talents, skills, emotions, physical and mental attributes, languages, and perceptions. Although all this diversity may, on the surface, seem overwhelming to you, it needn't be. I believe this variety offers some unique opportunities for every class you teach.

A Quick History Lesson

In the latter half of the twentieth century, a number of court cases and legal challenges were held regarding educational issues. Then, in 1975, Congress passed the Education of All Handicapped Children—PL 94-142 law. This law provided for inclusion of all students in "the least restrictive environment." This environment included "the use of supplementary aids and services."

In 1990, the original law and its amendments merged into the Individuals with Disabilities Education Act (IDEA), which was reauthorized in 1997. Sometimes called the mainstreaming law, the IDEA "requires students with disabilities to be educated with their nondisabled peers to the maximum extend appropriate, with the supplemental aids and services needed to help them achieve." The law also requires schools to have alternative placements available (special classroom, residential institution, etc.) if selected students cannot be educated in the general education setting.

The IDEA defines disabilities as follows:

- Mental retardation
- A hearing impairment including deafness
- Serious emotional disturbance
- An orthopedic impairment
- Autism
- Traumatic brain injury
- Other health impairment (limited strength or vitality due to chronic or acute health problems such as asthma or diabetes)
- A specific learning disability
- Deaf-blindness
- Multiple disabilities

One of the provisions of PL 94-142 (reauthorized in 1986 as P.L. 99-457) is that an *Individualized Education Plan* (often referred to as an *IEP*) be developed for each and every special needs student. This plan is written in consultation with administrators, teachers, special education specialists, school counselors, and parents.

It is quite common, therefore, to find many classrooms with students of all ability levels working and learning together. The notion that special needs children, whenever and wherever possible, should be included in all activities and functions of the regular classroom is known as *inclusion*.

Inclusion also means that students of all abilities, talents, and skills are offered learning opportunities that can only accrue between and among different individuals.

Jabberwocky _____

An **Individualized Education Plan (IEP)** outlines the specific learning objectives for a student and how they will be carried out over the course of the school year. Each IEP is reviewed and updated (as needed) on an annual basis.

Inclusion is involving all students in the educational setting that best meets their needs, regardless of background, creed, or level of ability. It also means that significant efforts are made to include special needs students in regular public school classrooms to the fullest extent possible.

We Are All Exceptional!

Educators at all levels refer to special needs students as those with exceptionalities. In general, exceptionalities fall in six broad categories:

- **Intellectual.** This includes students who have superior intelligence as well as those who are slow to learn.

- **Communicative.** These students have special learning disabilities or speech or language impairments.

- **Sensory.** Sensory-grouped students have auditory or visual disabilities.

- **Behavioral.** These students are emotionally disturbed or socially maladjusted.

- **Physical.** This includes students with orthopedic or mobility disabilities.

- **Multiple.** These students have a combination of conditions, such as orthopedically challenged *and* visually impaired.

Fire Alarm _____

Most educators prefer not to use the term *handicapped* because of its negative implications. You'll more often see terms like *challenged* and *exceptionality*—both of which have more positive implications.

Although statistics are difficult to obtain, it has been estimated that between 10 and 13 percent of the school-age population has exceptionalities. Thus, in an average-size classroom of 25 students, it is conceivable that 3 or 4 individuals will exhibit one or more exceptionalities.

Tips For Working With Exceptionalities

It is quite likely that you will have a diversity of students in your classroom—representing a variety of talents and abilities. With this in mind, I suggest some generalized strategies for you to consider as you work with all special needs students:

◆ Be aware that special needs students may not want to be singled out for any special treatment. To do so may identify their disability for other students and cause them to receive some form of attention they may not be able to handle.

◆ Ensure that your attitude and responses to special needs students are identical to those to other students. View all students as contributing students.

◆ Consider learning over a long period of time. Special needs students may require extended periods of time to master a concept or learn a specific skill. You may need to repeat information several times and reinforce it in many ways.

◆ It is quite easy to fall into the trap of focusing on the weaknesses of special needs students. Yet it is vitally important that you be aware of and seek to identify the individual strengths of each and every student in your classroom.

◆ Help students understand that grading, evaluation, and assessment is based on identifiable objectives in accordance with individual potential. Evaluation should not be coupled with the limitations of students but rather to their expectations.

◆ Provide significant opportunities for students of all abilities to learn from each other. Structure a variety of learning activities in which the social climate of the classroom is both promoted and enhanced. It is important that everyone feels like he or she is contributing.

Expert Opinion

Students (and even some teachers) may view the extra attention special needs students receive as unfair. However, according to long-time special education teacher Deb Watkins, "Fairness isn't about treating everyone the same; it's giving everyone what they need."

◆ Do not make inappropriate assumptions based on students' exceptionalities. For example, don't assume that a student who is confined to a wheelchair is an unhappy child. Don't assume that a learning disabled student is not gifted in the visual arts. Also, don't assume that children with disabilities are disabled in *all* areas.

Students Who Have Special Needs

It is inevitable that you will have the opportunity (and pleasure) of working with special needs students in your classroom. You may need to make *accommodations* for some and *modifications* for others. Providing for the needs of special education students will certainly be one of your greatest challenges as a professional educator. Consider these tips and strategies.

Students with Learning Disabilities

Learning disabled students are those who demonstrate a significant discrepancy, which is not the result of some other handicap, between academic achievement and intellectual abilities in one or more of the areas of oral expression, listening comprehension, written expression, basic reading skills, reading comprehension, mathematical calculation, mathematics reasoning, or spelling.

Jabberwocky

When working with special needs students, two terms you are sure to encounter are **accommodation** and **modification**. An accommodation is a device, material, or support process that will enable a student to accomplish a task more efficiently. Modification refers to changes to the instructional outcomes; a change or decrease in the course content or outcome.

Following is a list of some of the common indicators of learning disabled students. These traits are usually not isolated ones; rather, they appear in varying degrees and amounts in most learning disabled students. A leaning disabled student ...

- Has poor auditory memory—both short term and long term.

- Has a low tolerance level and a high frustration level.

- Has a weak or poor self-esteem.

- Is easily distractible.

- Finds it difficult, if not impossible, to stay on task for extended periods of time.

- Is spontaneous in expression; often cannot control emotions.

- Is easily confused.

- Is verbally demanding.

- Has some difficulty in working with others in small or large group settings.

- Has difficulty in following complicated directions or remembering directions for extended periods of time.

- Has coordination problems with both large and small muscle groups.

- Has inflexibility of thought; is difficult to persuade otherwise.

- Has poor handwriting skills.

- Has a poor concept of time.

Teaching learning disabled youngsters will present you with some unique and distinctive challenges. Not only will these students demand more of your time and patience; so, too, will they require specialized instructional strategies in a structured environment that supports and enhances their learning potential. It is important to remember that learning disabled students are not students who are incapacitated or unable to learn; rather, they need differentiated instruction tailored to their distinctive learning abilities. Use these appropriate strategies with learning disabled students:

- Provide oral instruction for students with reading disabilities. Present tests and reading materials in an oral format so the assessment is not unduly influenced by lack of reading ability.

- Provide learning disabled students with frequent progress checks. Let them know how well they are progressing toward an individual or class goal.

- Give immediate feedback to learning disabled students. They need to see quickly the relationship between what was taught and what was learned.

- Make activities concise and short, whenever possible. Long, drawn-out projects are particularly frustrating for a learning disabled child.

- Learning disabled youngsters have difficulty learning abstract terms and concepts. Whenever possible, provide them with concrete objects and events—items they can touch, hear, smell, etc.

- Learning disabled students need and should get lots of specific praise. Instead of just saying, "You did well," or "I like your work," be sure you provide specific praising comments that link the activity directly with the recognition; for example, "I was particularly pleased by the way in which you organized the rock collection for Karin and Miranda."

- When necessary, plan to repeat instructions or offer information in both written and verbal formats. Again, it is vitally necessary that learning disabled children utilize as many of their sensory modalities as possible.

◆ Encourage cooperative learning
activities (see Chapter 12) when possible. Invite students of varying abilities to work together on a specific
project or toward a common goal.
Create an atmosphere in which a
true "community of learners" is facilitated and enhanced.

It's Elementary

Offer learning disabled students
a multisensory approach to
learning. Take advantage of all
the senses in helping these students enjoy, appreciate, and
learn.

For additional information on teaching learning disabled students, contact the
Learning Disabilities Association of America at 4156 Library Road, Pittsburgh, PA
15234; 412-341-1515; www.ldanatl.org.

Students Who Have Higher Ability

Students of high ability, often referred to as gifted students, present a unique challenge to teachers. They are often the first ones done with an assignment or those who
continually ask for more creative and interesting work. They need exciting activities
and energizing projects that offer a creative curriculum within the framework of the
regular classroom program.

Characteristics of Gifted Students

Gifted students exhibit several common characteristics, as outlined in the following
list. As in the case of learning disabled students, giftedness usually means a combination of factors in varying degrees and amounts. A gifted student …

◆ Has a high level of curiosity.

◆ Has a well-developed imagination.

◆ Often gives uncommon responses to common queries.

◆ Can remember and retain a great deal of information.

◆ Can not only pose original solutions to common problems but can also pose
original problems, too.

◆ Has the ability to concentrate on a problem or issue for extended periods of time.

◆ Is capable of comprehending complex concepts.

◆ Is well organized.

- Is excited about learning new facts and concepts.

- Is often an independent learner.

Teaching Gifted Students

If there's one constant about gifted students it's the fact that they're full of questions (and full of answers). They're also imbued with a sense of inquisitiveness. Providing for their instructional needs is not an easy task and will certainly extend you to the full limits of your own creativity and inventiveness. Keep some of these instructional strategies in mind:

- Allow gifted students to design and follow through on self-initiated projects. Have them pursue questions of their own choosing.

- Provide gifted students with lots of open-ended activities—activities for which there are no right or wrong answers or any preconceived notions.

- Keep the emphasis on divergent thinking—helping gifted students focus on many possibilities rather than any set of predetermined answers.

- Provide opportunities for gifted youngsters to engage in active problem-solving. Be sure the problems assigned are not those for which you have already established appropriate answers but rather those that will allow gifted students to arrive at their own conclusions.

- Encourage gifted students to take on leadership roles that enhance portions of the classroom program (Note: gifted students are often socially immature.)

- Provide numerous opportunities for gifted students to read extensively about subjects that interest them. Work closely with the school librarian and public librarian to select and provide trade books in keeping with students' interests.

- Provide numerous long-term and ex-tended activities that allow gifted students the opportunity to engage in a learning project over an extended period of time.

To obtain additional information on teaching gifted students, contact the National Association for Gifted Children at 1707 L Street N.W., Suite 550, Washington, D.C. 20036; 202-785-4268; www.nagc.org.

Students Who Have Hearing Impairments

Hearing impairment may range from mildly impaired to total deafness. Although it is unlikely that you will have any deaf students in your classroom, it is quite possible that you will have one or more who will need to wear one or two hearing aids. Here are some teaching strategies:

- ◆ Provide written or pictorial directions.

- ◆ Physically act out the steps for an activity. You or one of the other students in the class can do this.

Secondary Thoughts _____

Other students can be responsible for taking notes (on a rotating basis) for a hearing impaired student.

- ◆ Seat a hearing impaired child in the front of the classroom and in a place where he or she has a good field of vision of both you and the chalkboard.

- ◆ Many hearing impaired youngsters have been taught to read lips. When addressing the class, be sure to enunciate your words (but don't overdo it) and look directly at the hearing impaired student or in his or her general direction.

- ◆ Provide a variety of multisensory experiences for students. Allow students to capitalize on their other learning modalities.

- ◆ It may be necessary to wait longer than usual for a response from a hearing impaired student. Be patient.

- ◆ Whenever possible, use lots of concrete objects such as models, diagrams, realia, samples, and the like. Try to demonstrate what you are saying by using touchable items.

Students Who Have Visual Impairments

All students exhibit different levels of visual acuity. However, it is quite likely that you will have students whose vision is severely hampered or restricted. These students may need to wear special glasses and require the use of special equipment. Although it is unlikely that you will have a blind student in your classroom, it is conceivable that you will need to provide a modified instructional plan for visually limited students. Consider these tips:

- ◆ Tape-record portions of textbooks, trade books, and other printed materials so students can listen (with earphones) to an oral presentation of necessary material.

- ◆ When using the chalkboard, use white chalk and bold lines. Also, be sure to say out loud whatever you write on the chalkboard.

- ◆ As with hearing impaired student, it is important to seat the visually impaired student close to the main instructional area.

- ◆ Provide clear oral instructions.

- ◆ Be aware of any terminology you may use that would demand visual acuity the student is not capable of. For example, phrases such as "over there" and "like that one" would be inappropriate.

- ◆ Partner the student with other students who can assist or help.

Students Who Have Physical Impairments

Physically challenged students include those who require the aid of a wheelchair, canes, walkers, braces, crutches, or other physical aids for getting around. As with other impairments, these youngsters' exceptionalities may range from severe to mild and may be the result of one or more factors. What is of primary importance is the fact that these students are no different intellectually than the more mobile students in your classroom. Here are some techniques to remember:

- ◆ Be sure there is adequate access to all parts of the classroom. Keep aisles between desks clear, and provide sufficient space around demonstration tables and other apparatus for physically disabled students to maneuver.

- ◆ Encourage students to participate in all activities to the fullest extent possible.

- ◆ Establish a rotating series of "helpers" to assist any physically disabled students in moving about the room. Students often enjoy this responsibility and the opportunity to assist whenever necessary.

- ◆ Focus on the intellectual investment in an activity. That is, help the child use his or her problem-solving abilities and thinking skills in completing an assignment without regard to his or her ability to get to an area that requires object manipulation.

- ◆ When designing an activity or constructing necessary equipment, be on the lookout for alternative methods of display, manipulation, or presentation.

◆ Physically impaired students will, quite naturally, be frustrated at not being able to do everything the other students can accomplish. Be sure to take some time periodically to talk with those students and help them get their feelings and/or frustrations out in the open. Help the child understand that those feelings are natural but also that they need to be discussed periodically.

Students Who Have Emotional Problems

Students with emotional problems are those who demonstrate an inability to build or maintain satisfactory interpersonal relationships, develop physical symptoms or fears associated with personal or school problems, exhibit a pervasive mood of unhappiness under normal circumstances, or show inappropriate types of behavior under normal circumstances.

Although you will certainly not be expected to remediate all the emotional difficulties of students, you need to understand that you can and do have a positive impact on students' ability to seek solutions and work in concert with those trying to help them. Here are some guidelines for your classroom:

◆ Whenever possible, give the student a sense of responsibility. Put the student in charge of something (operating an overhead projector, cleaning the classroom aquarium, re-potting a plant), and be sure to recognize the effort the student put into completing the assigned task.

◆ Provide opportunities for the student to self-select an activity or two he or she would like to pursue independently. Invite the student to share his or her findings or discoveries with the rest of the class.

◆ Get the student involved in activities with other students—particularly those students who can serve as good role models for the child. It is important that the emotionally disturbed child has opportunities to interact with fellow students who can provide appropriate behavioral guidelines through their actions.

◆ Discuss appropriate classroom behavior at frequent intervals. Don't expect students to remember in May all the classroom rules that were established in September. Provide "refresher courses" on expected behavior throughout the year.

◆ Emotionally disabled students benefit from a highly structured program—one in which the sequence of activities and procedures is constant and stable. You will certainly want to consider a varied academic program for all your students, but you will also want to think about an internal structure that provides the support emotionally impaired youngsters need.

◆ Be sure to seat an emotionally impaired child away from any distractions (highly verbal students, equipment, tools, etc.).

◆ Whenever possible, keep the activities short and quick. Provide immediate feedback, reinforcement, and a sufficient amount of praise.

Students Who Have ADHD

Students with Attention-Deficit/Hyperactivity Disorder (ADHD) offer significant and often perplexing challenges for many teachers. However, it is interesting to note that the IDEA's definition of students with disabilities does not include students with ADHD. For this reason, ADHD students are not eligible for services under IDEA unless they fall into other disability categories (hearing impairment, learning disability, etc.). However, they can receive services under *Section 504 of the Rehabilitation Act of 1973.*

ADHD students comprise approximately 3 to 5 percent of the school-age population. This may be as many as 35 million children under the age of 18. Significantly more boys than girls are affected, although reasons for this difference are not yet clear. Students with ADHD generally have difficulties with attention, hyperactivity, impulse control, emotional stability, or a combination of those factors.

As you consider this list of signs of ADHD, know that several of these traits must be present in combination before a diagnosis of ADHD can be made. A student who has ADHD …

Jabberwocky

Section 504 of the Rehabilitation Act of 1973 is a civil rights law requiring that institutions not discriminate against people with disabilities in any way if they want to receive federal funds. It requires that a school create a special plan to accommodate students' learning needs. However, the law provides no funding to do so.

◆ Has difficulty following directions.

◆ Has difficulty playing quietly.

◆ Talks excessively.

◆ Fidgets or squirms when sitting.

◆ Blurts out things.

◆ Is easily distracted.

◆ Often engages in dangerous play without thinking about the consequences.

◆ Has difficulty awaiting turns.

◆ Interrupts or intrudes.

- ◆ Doesn't seem to listen.

- ◆ Has difficulty paying attention.

- ◆ Has difficulty remaining seated.

- ◆ Often shifts from one activity to another.

When working with ADHD students in your classroom, keep the following in mind:

- ◆ Make your instructions brief and clear, and teach one step at a time.

- ◆ Be sure to make behavioral expectations clear.

- ◆ Carefully monitor work, especially when students move from one activity to another.

- ◆ Make frequent eye contact. Interestingly, students in the second row are more focused then those in the first.

- ◆ Adjust work time so it matches attention spans. Provide frequent breaks as necessary.

- ◆ Provide a quiet work area where students can move for better concentration.

- ◆ Establish and use a secret signal to let students know when they are off task or misbehaving.

- ◆ Use physical contact (a hand on the shoulder) to focus attention.

- ◆ Combine both visual and auditory information when giving directions.

- ◆ Ease transitions by providing cues and warnings.

- ◆ Teach relaxation techniques for longer work periods or tests.

- ◆ Each day be sure students have one task they can complete successfully.

- ◆ Limit the amount of homework.

- ◆ Whenever possible, break an assignment into manageable segments.

You are not alone when you're working with special needs students. Often specialists, clinicians, and other experts are available in the school as part of an educational team. Included on the team may be special education teachers, diagnosticians, parents, social workers, representatives from community agencies, administrators, and other teachers. By working in concert and sharing ideas, you can provide a purposeful education plan for each special needs student.

The Least You Need to Know

- ◆ Several laws have been passed that protect the rights of special needs students.

- ◆ There are six broad categories of special needs students: intellectual, communicative, sensory, behavioral, physical, and multiple.

- ◆ Teaching special needs students requires compassion as well as knowledge of their specific instructional needs.

- ◆ Each exceptionality requires its own special teaching behaviors and practices.

- ◆ ADHD students can become fully functioning members of any classroom.

Special Projects, Special Events

In This Chapter

- ◆ Guest speakers in your classroom
- ◆ Field trips
- ◆ Learning centers

Are you beginning to feel like the guy in the circus who juggles a bowling ball, a chain saw, a small dog, and a flaming torch—all at the same time? Well, guess what? In real life, that guy is actually a teacher! How is he able to do it so well? Because he does it every day—in the classroom!

By now, you probably have the idea that you, too, will be a juggler. Well, it's true! You have so many resources available to coordinate, including not only tangible classroom materials (textbooks, computers, etc.), but also intangible "goods," too.

In fact, you can enhance any classroom program by integrating selected projects and events into the overall curriculum. These may include guest speakers, field trips, learning centers, and current events. Many teachers have discovered that the use of these resources can add both depth and breath to any curriculum.

Talk to Us!

People in the local community can add immeasurably to your classroom program. Besides bringing in a wealth of experiences to share with students, people in your community can demonstrate to students that education is an everyday part of their lives or occupations and that learning can be shared and enjoyed by all.

The following list provides you with some possibilities for potential guest presenters to incorporate into your everyday curriculum:

4-H club leader

architect

artist

astronomer

auto mechanic

baker

biologist

butcher

carpenter

chef

college professor

college student

commercial pilot

community worker

computer operator

construction worker

cook

county agent

dietician

doctor

early community inhabitant

ecologist

electrician

engineer

environmental group leader

environmentalist

exchange student

factory worker

farmer

gardener

high school science teacher

high school students

landscaper

local author

local industry representative

mason

medical laboratory worker

musician

newspaper reporter

nurse

park ranger

person with unusual hobbies

pet store owner

pharmacist

plumber

restaurateur

roofer

sanitation worker

shop/store owner

train conductor

traveler

tree surgeon

TV weatherperson

veterinarian

weaver

zoologist

As you can see, the possible "experts" you can bring into your classroom are nearly limitless. Each of the people listed here, as well as others from your own community, can add substantially to your teaching effectiveness. It is important, however, that both the guest presenter and the class be sufficiently prepared prior to any visit. Consider the following items when inviting any speaker to your classroom:

◆ Be sure the people you invite are not only knowledgeable about their subject matter but are also able to present it in an interesting and informative manner. Outside speakers sometimes get caught up in their own jargon, not realizing that their level of vocabulary might not be understood by students at your grade level.

◆ It is important that whomever you invite addresses a topic relevant to a concept or issue currently being discussed in class. Inviting an amateur pilot in to discuss wind and weather three months before the topic is addressed in class may have little carryover effect for students. Be sure you clearly communicate the objective to the speaker when you invite him.

◆ Plan to meet with any speaker in advance of his or her presentation. This will ensure that the speaker is aware of the presentation objectives and how it should relate to the topic(s) being presented in class.

◆ Always confirm the date and time of a speaker's visit several days in advance. A phone call or short note would be most appropriate. Also, it is advisable to let any speaker know about any time limits or the classroom schedule.

◆ The speaker will need to know about the format of any presentation. Is it going to be a lecture, a demonstration, an informal discussion, or a question-and-answer session? Consider bringing in more than one speaker for a panel discussion. Some individuals are more comfortable speaking with others than they are as a solo presenter.

◆ Be sure to provide any speaker with information about your class or your students. What is the age or grade of the students? Are there any learning disabled students, and if so, how should they be dealt with? Are there any potential discipline problems, and if so, how should those be addressed?

◆ Prepare students in advance, too. Ask students to suggest a list of possible questions they could ask the speaker either during or immediately after the presentation. List and duplicate these questions on a sheet of paper for all students. Also provide students with some background data on a visiting speaker prior to the visit, such as the speaker's occupation, background, experiences, and topic of presentation.

Here's a tip for finding speakers: keep a recipe box on your desk. In the box, add tabbed dividers, and write the chapter titles from the textbook or various topic areas on separate tabs. As you read your local newspaper and come across the name of an individual in your community, write his or her name and contact information on an index card and file the card in the appropriate section of the box. Then, in advance of that chapter in your textbook or topic in the curriculum, you can contact that individual as a possible speaker. Keep the card file up to date, and over the years you will build up a valuable resource file of community "experts" for many parts of your classroom program.

Field Trips: Into the Void

Remember field trips when you were a student? Ahhh, the joys of piling into a school bus, the thrill of bouncing along (forever, it seemed) to travel to some distant place, the euphoria of listening to someone lecture about an historical site or collection of artifacts, and the delight of wolfing down a stale peanut butter and jelly sandwich! It does bring back fond memories, doesn't it?

Although some schools and districts are eliminating field trips due to budgetary issues, they are still an important part of the learning landscape. An effective field trip is a combination of planning, preparation, and appropriate follow-through. It also involves coordination between the host site, school, and chaperones. These tried-and-true suggestions will help make your first (or your next) field trip worthwhile.

Before the Trip

The first element of a successful field trip occurs before you go anywhere—deciding on the purpose for the field trip:

- Let students know how the planned trip relates to information discussed in class or their personal lives.

- Invite students to review websites specific to the area they will visit.

- Encourage students to read brochures and flyers about the area.

- Ask students to generate questions they would like to explore at the site.

- Invite students to put together a potential schedule of activities for the day.

Expert Opinion

It's important to discuss with students the reasons for a specific field trip, what they can expect to discover, and any potential highlights.

After choosing a site to visit, research the spot; if possible, visit the site in advance. Talk with locals about the best days and times to go. Try to obtain a map (or create your own) of the site to locate restrooms, water fountains, eating facilities, potential hazards, and a first-aid area (if available).

Depending on how far away you are from the site and the age of your students, decide how long to stay and where to have lunch. For elementary grades, I recommend staying for half a day and eating lunch back at the school. Older students can stay longer and have lunch on-site.

In class, begin preparing for the field trip by talking with students about the reasons for the trip, what they can expect to discover, and any highlights. Let students know how the planned trip correlates with information or concepts discussed in class.

Provide students with resources and information, including related literature and websites, about the site in advance of the field trip. This information can provide students with necessary background information to fully understand and appreciate what they will see and do on their field trip.

Check on medications. Which students will need to bring along any pills, ointments, or medications? Also, be aware of any potential allergies (food items, bee stings, contaminants) students may have. Also, plan how you will accommodate students with specific disabilities (physical, visual, tactile, auditory, or learning) at the site?

With the site selected and researched, begin recruiting parent volunteers and gathering equipment, including a portable first-aid kit, sun block, bug spray, and other appropriate items. Send a letter home to parents and invite them to complete any required permission slips. Also, be sure to provide parents with a required "equipment list" for students.

You can enhance any field trip by inviting students to prepare a guidebook beforehand. This guidebook should not only detail relevant information about the site but also allow students to record impressions gathered during the trip. Individual students or small groups can develop the guidebook well in advance of the field trip. Consider including the following items in a guidebook:

- Photocopies of brochures or other printed materials available from the field trip site (write in advance for these).

- A brief written or pictorial description of the site and the reasons for visiting that place.

- Student-generated questions about the site and what they might see (have students provide space under the questions for responses).

Fire Alarm

Meet with parent volunteers in advance to go over procedures for the day. Communicate the important role they have in the success of the field trip. Make it clear that they are there to monitor and supervise children, keep them safe, and ensure that the group stays together at all times.

- A list of safety rules and expected form of behavior during the trip.

- Articles about current events at the site.

- Blank pages for students to record observations and illustrations of significant details or observations.

- A summary page for students to write a brief wrap-up of the trip.

- Space for photographs and/or illustrations.

A guidebook becomes a valuable record that both the teacher and students can refer to and utilize in subsequent lessons.

Field Trip Day!

On the day of the trip, remind students to bring their guidebooks and writing tools on the bus. Chaperones should meet at the school, where you will introduce them to their students. Once at the site, students should remain in their chaperone groups and always travel with their buddies.

Ask students some of the questions they generated before the trip. Provide opportunities for them to alter and expand their original questions now that they are at the study site. Be sure they understand the relevance of the site to the information they are studying in class.

Provide directed opportunities for students to record their impressions, thoughts, and questions in their guidebooks. Stop every so often to review what they have seen and allow students to make notations about new information. This data becomes invaluable later when summarizing the important points of the trip. For example, students will be able to compare their pretrip predictions with actual observations after the trip.

Before boarding the bus to return to school, plan a 10-minute summary session. Go over important points, and ask students to review any impressive information they have learned. You might want to pose questions such as, "What did you discover that you didn't know before?" "How are your observations similar to the information we learned in the textbook?" or "What was your most amazing discovery?" Encourage students to write summary statements as well as questions they would like to find the answers to in their guidebooks to review later in class.

After the Trip

Your field trip is not over when students return to school. Students need a "debriefing" session in which you discuss important points, clear up misconceptions, explore new questions, and draw relationships between the outside world and the classroom curriculum.

Provide students with an opportunity to share their perceptions of the trip and how specific features related to their background knowledge or to any textbook discussions. Encourage students to create models, dioramas, or some other artistic display of the information they learned during the trip.

Have students record their experiences on the class website. They may also wish to reinvestigate websites they examined prior to the trip to compare their actual discoveries with the data they obtained before the trip (How accurate was the information on that website?).

Review the purposes for the trip, and ask students to decide if those purposes were met. Ask students such questions as, "Did we learn anything new that we didn't know before the trip?" and "If we were to take the trip again, what do you think we should do differently?"

Secrets of Field Trip Success

A successful field trip is predicated on several interrelated factors. Consider the following in planning your trip:

- ◆ Work with students to establish a shared purpose for the trip. Invite students to propose a relationship between classroom lessons and field trip experiences.

- ◆ Have a back-up plan in the event of rain, bad weather, injury, etc.

- ◆ Discuss any trepidations ahead of time. These may include fears related to heights, movements, certain animals, or closed spaces, among others.

- ◆ Be sure to select a field trip site and a day/time when it is less crowded.

- ◆ Only allow parents who are designated/trained chaperones to accompany you on your trip. One chaperone for every five students is an appropriate ratio.

- ◆ Incorporate conservation messages—pack in and out all litter.

Learning Centers

A *learning center* is a space set aside in the classroom that allows easy access to a variety of learning materials in an interesting and productive manner. Learning centers are usually designed to offer a variety of materials, designs, and media through which students can work by themselves or with others to operationalize the information learned in the classroom. Centers are designed to enhance the learning of concepts, skills, themes, or topics. This learning can take place after a topic is presented to students, during the course of presenting important concepts, or as an initial introduction to material in the text.

Jabberwocky

A **learning center** is a self-contained section of the classroom in which students engage in independent and self-directed learning activities.

Learning centers can have any number of designs, each limited only by your creativity and imagination. Feel free to work with your students in creating a center they will want to use. Such shared responsibility assures that students have a sense of ownership in the center and will be more willing to engage in the resultant activities.

Most teachers will agree that there are three different types of learning centers: enrichment centers, skill centers, and interest and exploratory centers.

Enrichment Centers

Enrichment centers are designed to offer students a variety of learning alternatives as an adjunct to a common unit of instruction. These centers are typically used after the presentation of important materials or concepts and are designed to provide students with opportunities to enrich and enhance their appreciation and understanding of the topics through individual experiences in the center. For example, after you have presented a lesson on the life cycle of plants, you might assign individual students to a center with the following components:

- Construction of a terrarium using soil, several plants, rocks, etc.

- Observing several plants under the microscope

- Designing an individual observation kit for use in the field

- Preparation of several foods using different types of common plants

- Exploring various news articles on plants in our daily lives

- Creative writing on the uses and misuses of plants in modern society

- ◆ Watching a filmstrip on the ecological implications of acid rain on plant life

- ◆ Painting a mural on the stages of plant growth

Enrichment centers require you to be aware of your students' learning styles (see Chapter 2) as well as their knowledge about a topic. The enrichment center can provide individual students with varied activities or combination of activities that differ from those pursued by other students. As such, the center becomes an individualized approach to the promotion of the topic.

Skill Centers

Skill centers are similar to enrichment centers in that they are used after the initial teaching of a concept or skill. Their difference lies in the fact that students are assigned particular areas in the center as opposed to having free choice of the topics they want to pursue. Thus, after introductory instruction on a particular concept has taken place, you can assign students to various parts of the center to help reinforce the information presented. You must be aware of the various skill needs of your students to effectively assign individuals to the areas in the center through which they can strengthen and enhance these skills.

It's Elementary

Skill centers are typically used at the elementary level, more so than at the secondary level. Students may work on math facts, phonics elements, or other tasks requiring memorization and/or repetition.

Interest and Exploratory Centers

Interest and exploratory centers differ from enrichment and skill development centers in that they are designed to capitalize on the interests of students. They may not necessarily match the content of the textbook or the curriculum; instead they provide students with hands-on experiences they can pursue at their own pace and level of curiosity. These types of centers can be set up throughout the classroom, with students engaging in their own selection of activities during free time, upon arrival in the morning, as a "free-choice" activity during the day, or just prior to dismissal. These centers allow students to engage in meaningful discoveries that match their individual interests.

The success of this form of learning center depends on your knowledge of your students' interests. You might want to use student interests that will help pinpoint the specific areas you can use in the design of relevant centers. A paper-and-pencil inventory can provide you with important information about their interests.

Parts of a Learning Center

The following ideas provide you with any number of options to include or consider for a center. It is important to understand that no two centers will ever be or look the same. Centers can range from elaborate displays to a card table set in the back of a room. Establish learning centers as formally or informally as you want—the primary criterion is that they match student interests with curricular needs. Here are some suggestions to get you started:

- **Title.** Provide an interesting title that identifies the center as separate from other classroom activities.

- **Furniture.** Arrange necessary furniture in a pleasing and productive manner. Decide how you will set up chairs, tables, storage facilities, and the like.

- **Storage.** Keep materials in a safe place where they are easily accessible by students.

- **Space.** Consider the use of space within the center. Where will the activities take place? Is there a need for independent study? Will large- or small-group instruction take place within the center?

- **Materials.** Determine how you will obtain materials. You might be able to obtain materials from parents or the school. You may also want to consider other sources such as local businesses, catalog supply houses, or community agencies.

- **Location.** Consider the physical placement and arrangement of centers in your room. Students need to be able to move to and among centers with minimal disruption and time.

- **Responsibility.** An important consideration in the development of any center pertains to the responsibilities of students and teacher to the center. For example, students need to know who is responsible for cleaning up, who will be sure there's an adequate supply of consumable materials (paper, paint, soil, water, etc.), who will be in charge of evaluation, and so on.

- **Learning alternatives.** Include a variety of learning alternatives within any center. For example, include a variety of tasks ranging from difficult to easy. Also include activities that relate to various students' interests.

- ◆ **Instructions.** Post a set of directions in each center. Plan time to share and discuss each set of directions and/or routines with students as part of one or more introductory lessons.

- ◆ **Sequence of activities.** It may be important to consider how activities within a center will be sequenced. That is, will students need to complete one or more specific activities before moving on to more complex activities later?

- ◆ **Number of centers.** You will need to decide on the number of centers you want to establish in your classroom. Base your decision on your management skills as well as the needs of your students. You might want to start with a single center and, as you and your students gain more competence in designing and using the center, develop additional centers later in the school year.

- ◆ **Assignment.** Consider assigning students to selected centers as well as offering students opportunities to select centers on their own.

- ◆ **Duration of centers.** Decide how long a center or group of centers will remain in existence. As a rule of thumb, keep a center in operation only as long as students' interests are high and it meets your program's instructional goals.

- ◆ **Management system.** You can assure the success of your centers by teaching your students familiar routines (how to move between centers, how to work cooperatively). Devote several weeks at the beginning of the year to teach these routines.

- ◆ **Time.** Talk with students about the amount of time necessary to engage in or complete the activities within a center. It is not critical for students to complete all the activities within a center.

- ◆ **Help!** Establish a procedure or routine that will allow students to signal when they are having difficulty with a specific center activity.

- ◆ **Assessment.** Decide on the nature and form of assessment for the center(s). Will assessment be the responsibility of the students or the teacher? How will it be accomplished—informally (discussions, observations) or formally (skills test, chapter exam)?

Suggested Learning Centers

Here is a partial list of suggested learning centers you might want to consider for your classroom:

Elementary	Middle School/Secondary
ABC/Spelling Center	Listening Center
Art Center	Writing Center
Pocket Chart Center	Readers Theatre Center
Free Reading Center	Free Reading Center
Storytelling Center	Drama Center
Big Book Center	Poetry Center
Numbers Center	Map and Chart Center
Puzzles/Blocks Center	Invention Center
Science Center	Biography Center
Water Center	Weather Center

As you can see, there is no limit on the type and number of centers possible for your classroom. Take advantage of this instructional tool, and watch students' interest increase.

The Least You Need to Know

- Guest speakers can be a positive addition to any subject area or any classroom topic.

- To be successful, field trips must be well-planned—before, during, and after the event.

- Learning centers provide a variety of hands-on learning opportunities for students.

Part 5

Different Folks, Different Strokes

Although some people might think teachers operate in a vacuum, in reality, teaching is one of the most social occupations ever. As teachers, we need to work with our students, our colleagues, our administrators, parents, and a host of other individuals. In Part 5, I introduce you to some of the people who will most affect your growth and development as a teacher and show you how these folks can have a positive impact on your success.

I also look at the most important person in the entire teaching spectrum—you! I give you practical ideas on how you can take care of yourself now and take care of yourself in the future (without losing your mind!).

Berra's First Law: You can observe a lot just by watching.

Fredericks's Corollary: You can teach a lot just by learning.

20

Teddy Bears and *Harry Potter* (Elementary Education)

In This Chapter

- How to teach reading
- Teaching all the language arts
- Making math meaningful
- Science is fun!
- Making social studies real

Remember your kindergarten teacher? Or how about that really pretty (or perhaps really handsome) teacher you had in third grade? What about that teacher who took the time to teach you the multiplication table or the one who posted your story about a lost dog on the bulletin board for everyone to admire?

Yes, we all have memories of our elementary school teachers. Often our inspiration for becoming a teacher is due to the influence we received from a teacher in those formative years. I know it was for me!

Elementary Teaching: Knowing Everything at Once

It's often been said that elementary teachers are jacks-of-all-trades. They must be able to teach reading, language arts, math, science, social studies, music, art, and physical education—all with the same degree of competence and enthusiasm. If you are preparing to become an elementary teacher, you are about to enter a field full of possibilities and a plethora of discoveries.

Let's look at each of the elementary subjects in a little more detail.

Book It!: Teaching Reading

I recently asked a group of first-grade students to define the word *reading*. Here are some of their definitions:

> Reading is your imagination because you think.
>
> Reading is a good way to learn more.
>
> Reading is snuggling up to my mom.
>
> Reading is a neat way to get more knowledge.
>
> Reading is something to do at night in bed.

It's obvious that these kids have some pretty good ideas about what reading is. Their responses also tell us something about the experiences they have had with printed materials such as books.

Five for Five

There are five primary components of reading instruction. Depending on the grade you teach, you will emphasize some of them more than others. These elements are arranged in the order in which they are typically introduced to students:

- **Phonemic awareness.** A recognition that spoken words are composed of several individual sounds. The focus is on sound units or what we call phonemes.

    What is the first sound you hear in the word *boat?*

    Add "m" to *ice* to make the word _____.

◆ **Phonics.** A recognition of sound-spelling relationships in printed words. Phonics is the association of sounds (phonemes) to written symbols (graphemes).

> What is the consonant at the end of the word *cool?*

> How many syllables are in the word *butter?*

◆ **Vocabulary.** Vocabulary is an under-standing of words—their definitions as well as how those words are used to compose sentences.

> How are these words similar— *apple, plum, cherry?*

> What is a synonym for the word *said?*

It's Elementary

Research on the value of phonemic awareness clearly demonstrates that children who receive phonemic awareness training in preschool, kinder-garten, and first grade do signifi-cantly better on *all* measures of formal reading achievement when compared with children who do not.

◆ **Fluency.** Fluency is the ability of a reader to read in a clear, fluid style, either silently or out loud. It is reading without hesitations.

> I'd like to read to you this story about Orville and Wilber Wright.

> Jessica, will you please read the second paragraph out loud for us?

◆ **Comprehension.** Comprehension is the ability to construct meaning by inter-acting with written material. It is an understanding of an author's message in concert with information a reader brings to that material.

> What background information do you think we need before we read the book *Under One Rock: Bugs, Slugs and Other Ughs* by Anthony D. Fredericks?

> What do you think the author's message was in this book?

Are You Well Balanced?

Many elementary teachers recognize the importance of a balanced reading program. A balanced reading program is one in which the following elements are shared with students:

◆ **Reading aloud to children.** At the very heart of any classroom reading pro-gram are the daily opportunities for teachers to read aloud to their students.

◆ **Shared book experience.** The shared book experience involves the teacher and the entire class. It is a cooperative learning activity in which a favorite book is read by the teacher and reread independently by students.

◆ **Guided reading.** Guided reading involves a teacher and a small group of students who read a book together for a specific purpose. The book selected is geared for the approximate instructional level of students, and they are challenged to think about the reading material through specific reading strategies.

◆ **Individualized reading.** Individualized reading emanates from guided reading. Each student is matched with an appropriate book and is invited to work at her or his own pace on material suited to his or her individual needs.

◆ **Paired reading.** Paired reading allows children the opportunity to work with a partner or buddy. Each pair of students can read the same book together and share appropriate reading strategies and/or interpretations.

◆ **Sustained silent reading.** Sustained silent reading is that time of the instructional day when everyone—including the teacher—simply reads for an extended period of time. Materials are selected by each individual according to personal interests or needs.

◆ **Language exploration.** Language exploration encourages children to become involved in a wide range of extensions related to a book. These extensions may include discussions, writing, art, music, drama, cross-curricular, and other "hands-on, minds-on" activities that promote and elaborate the ideas in text.

◆ **Reading and writing.** Reading and writing are natural partners. As children listen and respond to a wide variety of literature, they are provided with models of efficient writing. These models serve as springboards for the writing students can do in the classroom as a logical and natural extension of book-related activities.

Write On!: Teaching Language Arts

Four language arts are taught in the elementary grades: reading, writing, listening, and speaking. Teaching the language arts helps students build bridges and establish connections between subject areas. Students who are exposed to all the language arts begin to understand the importance of communication. Communication may be expressive (writing and speaking), or it may be receptive (listening and reading).

Most elementary teachers will teach the language arts in an integrated fashion. Reading, writing, speaking, and listening are combined into a variety of activities and learning experiences. Those language arts are integrated into other parts of the elementary program, too. Let's take a look at each one individually.

The Need to Read

Reading is the way we help students obtain meaning from print. Many practices and many strategies assist students in becoming accomplished and successful readers. Most classroom teachers practice a balanced reading program, as described earlier. Other practices you should include in your classroom reading program include the following:

- Encourage students to self-select reading materials.

- Expose children to a wide range of literature.

- Focus on comprehension development (even in the primary grades).

- Help students use their background knowledge.

- Model good reading behaviors.

Write Away!

Many people have unfavorable memories of writing in school, maybe because the traditional focus of writing in the past was on the final product—the paper that was turned in for a grade. Today, the emphasis is on the *processes* of writing rather than the products. By showing students the stages of writing all writers (this author included) use, students develop a better appreciation for the role of writing in their lives. The emphasis is a shift away from something produced for an outside evaluator (the teacher) to something created by and for the individual (the student).

Process writing occurs in six basic stages:

- **Prewriting.** This is the brainstorming stage, when students generate a wide variety of topics and subject about which they can write.

- **Drafting.** Then students select one of the topics on the brainstormed list and develop it into words, sentences, and paragraphs. The first draft is often referred to as the "sloppy copy."

- **Revising.** Now writers begin to clean up their original draft. It may also mean the production of multiple drafts—each one an improvement on the previous.

Jabberwocky

Writing **mini-lessons** are brief lessons (10 to 15 minutes) that the teacher may insert at any place in the writing process. The intent of the lesson is to help students with a specific problem, issue, or challenge to their writing (for example, prefixes, capitalization of proper nouns, using adverbs).

◆ **Sharing.** After revision, writers share their work with one or two other individuals for feedback and suggestions for improvement.

◆ **Editing.** In this second-to-last stage, writers deal with all the necessary grammar, punctuation, capitalization, and spelling. This stage may be proceeded by a *writing mini-lesson* on a specific grammatical or mechanical skill.

◆ **Publishing.** To finish, writers select the final form of their writing. This may include a booklet, a self-made book, posting on a bulletin board, a diary, or another similar way of sharing their writing with an audience.

Hear, Here!

Listening is much more complex than hearing. Listening involves hearing, but it also involves thinking as well as comprehension. Students must not only be able to hear the sounds of language but also be able to do something with (or process) those sounds for listening to occur.

Fire Alarm

Listening is not often taught. According to some educational researchers, the average child will have received approximately 1,274 hours of reading instruction by the time she or he graduates from high school. During that same time, the student will have only received 6 hours of listening instruction.

You can help your students become good listeners when you include the following guidelines in your classroom activities:

◆ **State the purpose for listening.** Invite students to listen for specific information—listening for a main idea, differentiating fact from opinion, or responding to vivid language: "Let's listen for information on the three types of rocks."

◆ **Set the stage for listening.** Provide interesting lead-up activities for any classroom task in addition to creating a listening atmosphere: "Listen closely and learn about some bloodsucking creatures in your own home."

◆ **Use follow-up listening activities for any assignments or tasks.** Let students know that you will be asking them questions: "What was the most important thing you heard in the lesson?" "Did what you heard in the lesson change your mind about what you read?"

◆ **Invite students to summarize comments or information shared by fellow classmates.** Let students know that you will be asking them to summarize or detail information presented by their peers on a regular basis. This can be a powerful listening strategy: "Heather, will you please summarize what Fernando just shared with us?"

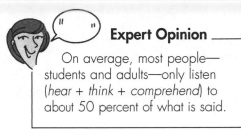

Expert Opinion

On average, most people—students and adults—only listen (*hear* + *think* + *comprehend*) to about 50 percent of what is said.

You can use these further strategies to foster good listening skills in your classroom:

◆ Storytelling by you or the students

◆ Reading aloud to students

◆ Encouraging parents to read to their children regularly

◆ Listening to tape-recorded stories

◆ Inviting guest speakers

◆ Encouraging students to create mind pictures while listening

◆ Encouraging students to make predictions while listening

Speak Up!

Most children discover that speaking is not only a method of communicating with others but also a way in which they can express their emotions and desires. Some important research suggests that adequate speaking opportunities, both in and out of the classroom, form the foundation upon which successful learning rests. It is important to note that competence in speaking translates into competence in reading, writing, and listening.

You can use numerous speaking opportunities in your classroom:

◆ **Informal talk activities.** Weave planned opportunities for students to engage in the exchange of information throughout the school day.

- **Interpretive talk activities.** With your students, take books and stories and re-create them into other formats such as a play or skit.

- **Formal talk activities.** Individual students research, assemble, and present information to their classmates.

- **Dramatic activities.** Drama provides opportunities for students to use language in a meaningful context. These are opportunities for students to put language "into action."

Other speaking activities include the following:

- Show and tell

- Creative dramatics (both formal and informal)

- Puppetry

- Pantomime

- Fingerplays

- Readers theater

It All Adds Up: Teaching Math

You may remember doing endless workbook pages of math facts when you were in school. Or perhaps you recall manipulating objects on your desk to form patterns or sets of similar objects. However you were taught math, it is important to note that the field of mathematics education has changed dramatically over the last few years. The publication of the National Council of Teachers of Mathematics (NCTM) Standards caused a significant change in mathematics education.

Hey, Gimme Five!

The NCTM standards revolve around five content strands that are appropriate for all the grades—pre-kindergarten through twelfth grade. They include number and operations, algebra, geometry, measurement, and data analysis and probability.

The five standards apply across all the grades; however, each one has a different emphasis depending on the grade level. Number and operations, which deals with the development of a sense of whole numbers, receives a greater emphasis in the primary grades than it does in the intermediate grades. Data analysis and probability, which involves an analysis of mathematical information, is more heavily emphasized in the intermediate grades than in the primary grades.

Compute This!

You may be wondering about the skills you need to make math instruction successful in your classroom. Here are some ideas culled from many elementary teachers:

◆ **Make math relevant.** One of the questions in the back of every student's mind is, "Why do I have to know this stuff?" Showing students how they use math (or the concepts in a specific math lesson) in their everyday lives will be a powerful motivating force in your classroom.

◆ **Math should be active.** Too often, math has been nothing more than a series of workbook pages or skill practice done over and over again. Provide your students with opportunities to move objects or *manipulatives* around, engage in physical activities, or participate in real hands-on explorations.

◆ **Good math instruction is inquiry-based.** It allows students to generate their own questions and pursue the answers to their own self-initiated queries. It is a student-driven curriculum that engages students in a search for solutions.

Jabberwocky

Manipulatives are physical materials such as cubes, squares, balls, or other three-dimensional objects that model or simulate mathematical concepts.

◆ **Effective math programs are based on cooperative learning.** In Chapter 12, I discussed the value and advantages of cooperative learning in any classroom. Students who have the encouragement and support of their peers do much better mathematically.

◆ **Promote the use of models.** Models help students make sense of math ideas. For example, "Using the ones, tens, and hundreds cubes, see how many different ways you can come up with to represent the number 234."

◆ **Integrate math with the other subjects.** It's easy to divorce math from reading, social studies, and art because it is numerically based rather than language based. But good teachers know that students can discuss math concepts and write in journals about those ideas. Students can examine the history of mathematical ideas in social studies, the necessity of math for accurate measurements in science, and the art of geometrical shapes and patterns.

◆ **Ask students to describe the processes or thinking they used to arrive at an answer.** Inviting students to justify their solutions is a powerful teaching tool that will endure long after a lesson is over. It helps make math more student-centered and less teacher-directed.

◆ **Design math instruction to help students think and reason.** It should not be based on the memorization of principles, but rather on how to use those principles in everyday life.

It's Moving: Teaching Science

Science is fun! Science is exploring the unknown and discovering the world around us. For students, science should be a dynamic and interactive discipline. It should allow students to examine new ideas, play around with concepts, and discover that knowledge is always changing. It also means that elementary teachers give students a multitude of opportunities to probe, poke, and peek into the mysteries of the universe—whether that universe is a child's own backyard or a galaxy far away.

Expert Opinion

According to the eminent child psychologist Jean Piaget, knowledge is a *process* rather than a state. Thus, a process approach to science education emphasizes the *doing* of science, more so than learning the products or facts of science. In short, a person constructs knowledge instead of accumulates it.

A good classroom science program is built on a process approach to teaching. A process approach stimulates divergent thinking and provides a means for students to investigate their world based on what they know as well as on what they want to discover. It is your responsibility to generate situations and opportunities that enable scientific investigations to occur both in and out of the classroom.

Include the following processes into your classroom science program, and watch the magic happen:

◆ **Observing.** Observation involves all the primary senses: seeing, hearing, smelling, tasting, and touching. It is an immediate reaction to one's environment and is the source of knowledge that humans employ most.

How do your observations differ from (John's, Mary's)?

Have you ever seen or heard anything similar to this?

◆ **Classifying.** Classifying is the process of assigning basic elements to specific groups. All the items within a particular group share a basic relationship that may or may not be reflected in other groups. As new ideas are encountered, they are added to previously formulated groups on the basis of similar elements.

How are these items related?

How many different ways can you think of that these items could be grouped?

◆ **Measuring.** Scientists are constantly measuring. Measuring provides the hard data necessary to confirm hypotheses and make predictions. It provides accurate information for any discoveries.

Do you feel we need more data before we move on?

Do you think we should measure again?

◆ **Inferring.** Students often need to make conjectures on the basis of a minimum of data. Inferring is of two types: deductive (going from the general to the specific) and inductive (going from the specific to the general). Inferences are educated guesses about something happening in the present.

What reasons do you have for why this is happening?

What makes you think that way?

◆ **Communicating.** Communication is the means by which information is disseminated. It involves not only interacting with others but also organizing information so it can be effectively passed on to others.

Why is this easy (hard) to understand?

How can you share this with others?

◆ **Predicting.** Predicting is the process of extrapolating information based on a minimum of data or on information already known. The scientist then tries to confirm or refute the prediction based on the gathering of new data. Predictions differ from inferences in that they are educated guesses about future events—or what might happen.

How did you arrive at your prediction?

Do you have a reason for saying that?

◆ **Experimenting.** By definition, a true scientist is one who is constantly experimenting. Through experimenting, ideas are proven or disproved and hypotheses are confirmed or denied. Experimenting involves manipulating data and assessing the results. Students need to understand that they conduct experiments every day, from watching ice cream melt to deciding on what clothes to wear outside.

What else could we have done to arrive at this conclusion?

Do we need any more evidence before we can say that?

Worldly Wise: Teaching Social Studies

Social studies is a broad-based exploration of people, how they live, and how they get along with one another. Social studies also encompasses all the other disciplines of the elementary curriculum. For example, reading provides us with the tools to study and learn about people; science gives us opportunities to understand people and their interactions with the environment; language arts allows people to communicate with one another; and math provides us with the quantitative tools to measure and evaluate our world.

The scope and sequence of most social studies programs is based on tradition as well as suggestions from the National Council for the Social Studies (NCSS). Typically, most elementary programs are designed according to the following hierarchy:

◆ **Child/self.** At this stage, usually initiated at the kindergarten level, students are given opportunities to investigate topics most familiar to them, including understanding their persons, going to school, learning rules for safe living, and working together.

◆ **Families.** Here children are exposed to aspects of what families do, as well as the world beyond their own family. Topics at this level may include the relationship of the individual to the family, families and their needs, the way families work, and families in neighborhoods.

◆ **Communities/neighborhoods.** At this level, students are introduced to neighborhoods and communities. Typical topics include transportation and communication, community services, celebration of holidays, ways neighborhoods change, and rural and urban communities.

◆ **Cities/country.** At this stage, students are exposed to information on larger community concepts. Usually comparisons are made between communities and cities in terms of the parts of a city, life in early cities, local government, comparative cultures, and locations of cities.

♦ **States/regions.** This level of curriculum includes information on different sections of the United States as well as various geographical characteristics of selected states. Emphasis includes comparative studies on desert, mountain, plains, and forest regions of the United States and other selected areas within our country.

♦ **Nation/United States.** Here the primary emphasis is on the United States, although it may include reference to Canada and/or Latin America. Topics include the founding of our country, historical facts, geographical data, chronology, and our cultural and ethnic heritage.

♦ **World.** This level often includes a large number of topics dealing with either the Western or Eastern Hemispheres or both. Areas covered include ancient civilizations, Asia, Europe, Africa, and the Middle East. At this level, the curriculum is very crowded and diverse.

This curriculum is usually referred to as the *widening horizons* or *expanding environments* curriculum. It is based on the idea that children first need to deal with concepts relative to their immediate environment (self) and systematically progress to concepts that move in concentric circles out and beyond that environment.

Social studies is best taught when the emphasis is two-fold, first with a hands-on, minds-on focus, in which students obtain information from readings, discussions, AV, and teacher presentations (minds-on), and then get to create a product or participate in a tangible experience (hands-on).

The Least You Need to Know

♦ Teaching reading is a major emphasis for all elementary teachers.

♦ The language arts (reading, writing, listening, speaking) serve as a foundation for learning in all other subject areas.

♦ Good math instruction makes math relevant to students' lives.

♦ A process approach to science education will engage and stimulate all students.

♦ Social studies that is *hands-on, minds-on* is fun to teach and fun to learn.

21

Hormones and Nose Rings (Secondary Education)

In This Chapter

- ◆ Different types of secondary schools

- ◆ Nine or twelve months?

- ◆ A day in your life

- ◆ Block, block, who's there?

- ◆ Making the connection (the affective realm)

- ◆ Constructing knowledge; building lessons

When most people are asked to recall a significant year in their educational careers, many conjure up memories of a year in high school. For lots of folks, our high school years are the years filled with independence, social contacts, college preparation, sports memories, and extracurricular activities.

Teaching at the secondary level is no less memorable. Dealing with young adolescents (I sometimes referred to my teenage students as "hormones in tennis shoes") and all the social pressures and academic rigors of everyday life in a typical high school can be both demanding and fascinating. If you are about to become a high school teacher, congratulations. You're about to enter a field where no two days will be the same—ever!

It's an Amoeba!

Secondary schools are like amoebas (remember that microscopic creature you used to look at under the microscope in biology class?). They come in many shapes and sizes, and they keep changing all the time.

Three-Peat

Typically, secondary schools are organized in three different categories: high schools (grades 9 to 12 or 10 to 12), middle schools (grades 6 to 8 or 5 to 8), and junior high schools (grades 7 to 8 or 7 to 9).

Secondary Thoughts

A secondary school is any school that houses students in a combination of grades 7 through 12.

A *high school* is frequently built around a series of six or seven periods, each of which is about 50 minutes long. The school is often departmentalized, meaning there's a science department, a math department, a social studies department, and so on. There's usually a required set of courses for students to take as well as an offering of free electives. Teachers must have certification at the secondary level, as determined by their state.

A *middle school* is a relatively new and relatively amorphous entity. Middle schools usually have three of four grade levels, which may be organized by grade (as in an elementary school) or departmentalized. Periods may be up to 50 minutes long or arranged into blocks of basic subjects. Thematic instruction, where a group of teachers prepares a large unit of study, often predominates. Depending on the state, teachers may teach in a middle school with either elementary or secondary certification.

A *junior high school* will often have only two or three grade levels. Like a high school, it is often departmentalized into the major subject areas. A typical day will be built around a series of six or seven periods with opportunities for electives such as shop, art, and home economics. Teachers at the junior high school level must be certified secondary teachers in their state. Many school districts are moving away from a junior high school orientation toward the concept of middle school education.

Charters, Magnets, and Other Kinds of Secondary Schools

Secondary schools come in all shapes and sizes. We could say that there's something for everyone in the field of secondary education. Although we often think about the typical high school configuration (grades 9 through 12, a variety of subjects, sports teams, etc.) when we think about secondary schools, there is an increasing variety of educational experiences available at this level. You may be able to teach in one of these schools:

- ◆ **Charter school.** A school operated as a for-profit enterprise.

- ◆ **Magnet school.** A school that specializes in a specific subject area—science, for example.

- ◆ **Partnership school.** A school that has a formal relationship with an area business or industry to prepare students for the workplace.

- ◆ **Independent school.** A private school with no religious affiliation.

- ◆ **Prep school.** A college preparatory institution, typically private.

- ◆ **Agricultural school.** A secondary school that prepares students for careers in the agricultural fields.

- ◆ **Career academy.** A school that offers a specialized curriculum in one or more specific careers.

- ◆ **Residential school.** A school that houses students on-site and offers classes similar to those at local high schools.

- ◆ **Tech-prep school.** A school that is coordinated with the first two years of college and prepares students for an associate's degree.

- ◆ **Parochial school.** A religious-oriented school offering secondary courses in addition to religion classes.

180/2

In most school districts, the typical school year is composed of 180 days of instruction. This number may vary from school to school, district to district, and state to state. It may also be affected by severe weather (snow days), natural disasters, teacher work stoppages, or other unplanned events.

Most school districts begin their year in September and end the year in June. Schools are typically closed for several holiday periods, including Thanksgiving, Christmas or Hanukkah, New Year, and Easter.

However, some districts are moving to year-round education in which a school may be open for the entire year. In this operation, often called a 45/15 plan, teachers and students are in school for 45 days (9 weeks) and then are out of school for 15 days (3 weeks). This cycle repeats throughout the calendar year. There are usually several tracks of teachers and students (A track, B track, etc.). The starting and ending times of each track are staggered so that at any one time, one track is on vacation while the other tracks are in school. This method utilizes the high school's facilities more efficiently, rather than lying dormant for 3 months of the year.

It's a Daily Thing

Your instructional day as a secondary teacher is often clearly defined. Most schools divide the school day into seven or eight periods of instruction. Each period lasts for approximately 50 minutes each (with the possible exception of lunch period). Typically, the school day begins at about 8 A.M. and ends at about 3 P.M.

A Day in the Life ...

Here is a typical daily plan for most teachers:

- ◆ Teach seven or eight 50-minute periods of their assigned subject.

- ◆ Have one period for lunch (30 to 50 minutes).

- ◆ Have one period for *planning time* (usually 50 minutes).

Jabberwocky

Planning time is sometime referred to as conference time or a prep (preparation) period. This is a noninstructional time during the day when teachers grade papers, prepare lessons, meet with individual students, or tend to administrative duties.

It is not unusual for teachers to be assigned a variety of administrative tasks such as hall monitoring, bathroom duty, cafeteria duty, bus duty, and other similar duties. These are often rotated among teachers according to a set schedule.

Extracurricular = Extra Duties

Teachers will often take on the responsibility of supervising one or more extracurricular activities at the secondary level. These may include (but not be limited to) the following:

- ◆ Sports team coach

- ◆ Faculty adviser for a student publication (yearbook, newspaper, literary magazine)

- ◆ Technology coordinator

- ◆ Faculty adviser for a club (Chess Club, Math Club, Spanish Club, etc.)

- ◆ Adviser for a student service group

- ◆ Academic coach

Block and Roll

One of the current movements in secondary education is a move toward block scheduling. Simply stated, block scheduling is an expansion of the time available for instruction in each academic period. Typically, an academic period is 50 minutes long. In block scheduling, a period may last from 70 to 140 or more minutes.

Configure This!

The expansion of instructional time allows for a range of scheduling possibilities. Consider the following formats used by some schools:

- ◆ **5×7 Plan.** In this setup, the school year is divided into three trimesters, each one lasting for 12 weeks. The school day is divided into five 70-minute periods.

- ◆ **4×4 Plan.** In this arrangement, students take four 90-minute-long classes a day. The periods are sometimes referred to as macroperiods. Students may change their classes during the second semester of the school year.

- ◆ **A–B Plan.** In this plan, students take classes every other day for the entire school year. Periods are 90 minutes in length. This plan, a variation of the 4×4 Plan, is sometimes referred to as the *Alternating Day Plan*.

The Plus Side for Students

Block scheduling offers a variety of advantages for students. Chief among these is the fact that students can pursue a topic in greater depth. Because students take fewer classes during the day, the time they spend in any single class is more intense and often more productive.

Students also form close communities of learners. There is more social support for learning, and the development of mutual respect and group cohesiveness is enhanced considerably.

Researchers have discovered that students exhibit more academic satisfaction about their courses. Students demonstrate higher levels of course mastery and better retention of material. Because instruction is more sustained rather than fragmented, students tend to become more involved in a topic or concept.

The Plus Side for Teachers

Teachers also report several advantages of block scheduling. One of the most frequently mentioned is that teachers get to know their students better and can respond to individual issues or concerns. Instead of trying to learn the names and personalities of students in eight separate classes, teachers are able to develop closer relationships with students in the four or five periods they teach in a block schedule.

Another reported advantage is that discipline problems decrease in a block schedule plan. Students are not in the hallways as often, dropout rates are significantly reduced, and the school's climate is more positive.

Teachers also report that they are better able to challenge students in a block plan. They are able to pursue topics in greater depth, integrate more writing into a subject area, and assist students in achieving mastery of a topic through a wider variety of instructional methodologies (see Chapter 10).

Making the Connection

Success as a secondary teacher can often be based on one critical factor—your ability to connect with your students. That means you need to be aware of your students, not simply as students, but rather as human beings who have lives both in and out of the classroom.

Adolescents go through lots of questioning and lots of changes during this stage in their lives. According to teacher Phil Monteith, "We need to be culturally sensitive so we can make a human connection with kids." This doesn't mean being their friend; rather, it means being aware of their lives both in and out of school. It means knowing how their brains work (see Chapter 2); about their interests, hobbies, music, sports, and part-time jobs; their family lives; their friendships, cliques, and social groups; and their material world.

In essence, it means that we must be sensitive to a wide range of cultural issues— issues that may or may not have any direct connection with education but certainly do have a direct connection to learning.

It also means that as a secondary teacher, you need to consider the factors that either promote or hinder affective growth. The adolescent mind is in a state of turmoil and upheaval. This is a time when students wrestle with depression, suicide, psychological abuse, and substance abuse, among many issues.

 **Expert Opinion**

Some research suggests that up to 25 percent of a student's academic growth is determined by affective or emotional factors.

As a teacher, you must be aware of the indicators for these adolescent issues. You need to know what they look like, what they feel like and, most important, what to do about them.

That means taking advantage of the many services and resources available both inside and outside of the school, including guidance counselors, peer advising programs, community agencies, the police, and student assistance programs.

Many experienced teachers will tell you that if you're not sensitive to your students, you can't teach them. The personal connections need to be made first; then academic connections can happen.

A Change for the Better

One of the most exciting developments in secondary education is a shift away from a delivery system of teaching to a *constructivist* model of education. The traditional form of secondary teaching relies on a teacher giving or delivering instruction to students. You may recognize this as a teacher lecturing students and students dutifully recording the information in their notebooks. In short, an expert tells novices what they need to know.

Jabberwocky

Constructivism recognizes that knowledge is created in the mind of the learner. Teachers help students relate new content to the knowledge they already know. In addition, students have opportunities to process and apply that knowledge in meaningful situations (sometimes called hands-on, minds-on learning).

Psychologists have helped us look at the teaching-learning partnership in a new way. Through intensive research, we have learned that learning is not simply the accumulation of knowledge (which is often passive), but rather how we make sense of knowledge. This is referred to as a constructivist theory of learning.

We could say that constructivism is not the passive transfer of knowledge from a teacher to a student. Rather, it is how knowledge is constructed in the mind of each student. This is active learning and also active teaching.

Five Alive

Regardless of the subject you teach, the theory of constructivism will provide you with innumerable opportunities to "energize" your teaching and motivate your students. To do so, you need to include five elements in each lesson you present:

◆ Provide students with opportunities to tap into their prior knowledge (see Chapter 5). Assess what they know, and allow them to vocalize their past experiences, readings, or backgrounds of experience. Knowing what your students know and using that knowledge to construct a lesson is a powerful teaching tool.

◆ Provide students with opportunities to think about their own thinking (see Chapter 13). We call this *metacognition*. It can be accomplished through a systematic ordering of questions such as these:

   Is this idea similar to anything you may have read before?

   What were you thinking when you read this part of the chapter?

   What have we learned so far?

   Did you change your mind about anything after our discussion?

   Do you have any personal questions about this material that have not been answered so far?

   What did you do when you didn't understand something in the book?

What makes you feel your interpretation is most appropriate?

What new information are you learning?

How did you arrive at your interpretation?

◆ Remember that motivation is key to any successful lesson. Provide students with a wide range of methodologies (see Chapter 10), and allow them to make personal investments in their own learning. Use active experiences that tie the topic into students' everyday lives.

◆ Celebrate the diversity of students in your classroom. Provide individual learning opportunities geared toward the needs and abilities of every student (see Chapter 18). Don't teach all students in the same way. Provide a multiplicity of experiences geared for individual differences.

◆ Remember that learning happens best in a social context. The use of cooperative learning opportunities (see Chapter 12) allows students to process material and entertain a variety of viewpoints. Students see a host of perspectives on a topic, rather than a single, teacher-oriented view.

Caution!

A constructivist philosophy of teaching and learning can reinvigorate any secondary subject and promote learning as an active process. But if you are more familiar with traditional forms of teaching where the teacher delivers instruction, you may find this approach challenging.

There's a saying that's been around for a long time: we tend to teach as we were taught. If we have been taught with more traditional forms of instruction (such as lecture), we have a tendency to teach in roughly the same way. Yes, we are products of our environment or experiences.

Moving your philosophy to a more constructivist view may be a challenge. I suggest that you talk with colleagues, read current educational periodicals, and observe constructivist teaching (and learning) in action. Observe how students behave in a constructivist classroom; especially how they are actively engaged in the learning process. You may discover, as did I, that this shift in philosophy can result in some exciting and dynamic lessons, no matter what subject area you teach.

The Least You Need to Know

- ◆ Secondary schools come in an infinite variety of shapes, sizes, and forms.

- ◆ You can expect an array of experiences and tasks every day in your secondary school classroom.

- ◆ Block scheduling allows more time for teaching and more time for learning.

- ◆ Connect with your students' lives. You'll see the results.

- ◆ Constructivism involves and energizes students.

22

The Community of School

In This Chapter

+ Connecting with the school community

+ Two people you must befriend

+ The principal person

+ Some other school folks

+ Subs (not the underwater kind)

When you enter a school, you are entering a very special community—one that functions in much the same way as the community outside the school walls. People are in charge; people provide important services; and people need to work in harmony for the school to function effectively.

Your job as a classroom teacher is not to simply be an instructional leader for your students. You will also be asked to contribute to the greater good of the school community in which you live and work. The degree to which you are willing to do that will often determine the success you enjoy in your classroom. In this chapter, we take a look at the people you need to know to make that happen.

You Are Not Alone!

As a teacher, it is quite easy to walk into a school, enter your classroom, close the door, and not see any person over the age of 21 for the entire day—or even an entire week! The very nature of teaching often isolates us from the rest of our peer group, associates, co-workers, and colleagues. Contact with large intelligent beings may be minimal or nonexistent.

Teaching can be a very isolating profession. Most of your time will be spent alone in the classroom with students. But remember: your success as a classroom teacher is often determined not just by how well you are teaching a group of youngsters but also by how well you are connecting with the larger community.

It is equally important to take time to recognize that the community we call "school" would not exist or survive without the work and dedication of many individuals. Shouldn't we celebrate the work of all the members of our community? I think so.

Expert Opinion

Allow yourself time to interact informally with adults in your school community. Start a book club, talk over a cup of morning coffee, or meet for dinner. Get together with colleagues to see a movie, volunteer, or just talk about things other than school. Participate in the community choir, a theater group, a bowling league, a service organization, or a fund-raising walk. You'll be better for it!

Make Friends with School Staff (Two in Particular)

What if I told you that I have a piece of inside information that will virtually guarantee your success as a classroom teacher? Would you be interested? Of course, you would!

Then here it is: the two best friends you could ever have in a school are the school secretary and the custodian(s). These two people, more than anyone else, run a school. It doesn't matter whether you are teaching in a rural, suburban, or inner city school or whether you're teaching elementary school or high school; your friendship with the secretary and custodian(s) will virtually guarantee your success as a teacher!

Why is that? Just think about all the tasks and duties these people provide. How would the school be able to function, how would it exist from day to day, without the work and efforts of these individuals? The number of times the secretary saved my neck or the number of times the custodian got me something I really needed are more than the number of pages in this book. They were my lifesavers when I needed materials ordered, a lightbulb fixed, a report sent in on time, a bucket and mop for a classroom "accident," a call made to an irate parent, or a bunch of tables in my classroom for a special science experiment.

My friendship with the custodian and secretary paid more dividends than I could ever imagine. Notice that I used the word *friendship*. I depended on these people so I could do my job. I valued their support; I valued their input; but most important, I valued their camaraderie and friendship.

Establishing, fostering, and maintaining positive relationships with the secretary and custodian(s) is important both professionally and personally. Here are some guidelines:

- Don't assume that less education means less intelligence. One of my custodian friends can tear down and rebuild any computer hard drive faster (and better) than any technician at the local computer store.

- Learn the secretary's and custodian's names early on. Take time to find out about their families, hobbies, and pastimes. Learn about their lives away from the school.

- Always treat the secretary and custodian with respect and courtesy. Greet them every morning with a smile and a pleasant comment.

- As appropriate, send them a birthday card or note thanking them for their work.

- Talk positively about the secretary and custodian in your conversations with colleagues. Acknowledge and celebrate their contributions to the school community.

 Expert Opinion

Here's a neat idea. Make it a point to stop and converse with the secretary and custodian every day. Move beyond the simple "Hi, how are you?" greetings we often exchange with people as we rush through the day. Take 2 or 3 minutes for a brief conversation or a friendly talk. You may discover something interesting. You may discover a kindred spirit.

Obviously, the friendships you establish with the secretary and custodian are not simply for the purpose of getting something done later on. These people are valuable and critical elements in the overall functioning of the school and of the community in which you work.

The Principal Is Principle!

By definition, the school principal is the school's instructional leader. This individual makes almost every decision that affects the welfare and functioning of the school as a whole as well as of individuals within the school. The nature of your relationship with your building principal will have a major impact on your classroom performance—as well as your mental state.

Information, Please

Here's a tip that will almost guarantee a positive relationship with your principal: always keep her or him informed! The last thing any administrator needs or wants is a surprise. If you're inviting in a guest speaker, setting up a terrarium with a collection of snakes, or assigning a controversial book for your students to read, inform your principal!

Keeping your principal in the loop, information-wise, is always a good idea. If you have a problem student or are anticipating the storming of the office by an irate parent, be sure to let your principal know early on. A well-informed principal can assist you in working through a problem, particularly if she or he has information early in the process.

If you are planning to send any letters, messages, newsletters, or other types of communication home, it's always a good idea to run those by your principal first. That way, if a parent or community member has an issue or concern with one of those documents or the information in it, your principal will know how to respond in an appropriate manner.

It's Elementary

Invite your principal to be part of classroom celebrations, birthday parties, or other special events. Occasionally send homemade cupcakes, cookies, birthday cake slices, and other food items down to the principal's office. They may not get eaten, but they will let the principal know you are thinking about her or him, too. That's good public relations!

Thinking Positively

Often, teachers make the mistake of seeing the principal only when problems or crises crop up. However, it's vitally important that you share the positive events and celebrations that take place in your classroom, too. Here are some ideas:

- Invite your principal to be a guest reader.

- Share the academic accomplishments of the class as well as of individual students.

- Invite your principal to observe a particularly exciting lesson, guest speaker presentation, or science experiment.

- When sending out holiday greetings, don't forget your principal, too. As appropriate, send a birthday card or a vacation postcard.

- Send your principal outstanding examples of student work. Attach a brief note acknowledging and celebrating the progress of selected individuals or the entire class.

Office Time

One of the mistakes new teachers make is to send students to the office for every infraction or every misbehavior. But keep in mind that whenever you send a student to the office, you are also sending a message that you are not in control. As a result, your principal may get the impression that you cannot control your classroom or the behavior of your students and may form negative impressions about you.

That's not to say that a little office time might not be appropriate for some students. However, it's best to inform your principal early on about any potential problems or any potential situations. Constant and continual information is very important. Then, if it is necessary to send a student to the office, the principal will be well versed about the situation and can handle it appropriately.

Be sure you know the school's policy about sending students to the office. Have a conversation with your principal early in the school year to clarify any policies or expectations.

It's About Time!

Principals have a plethora of administrative tasks—all with due dates. He or she has reports to file with the district and the state, attendance forms to compile, financial matters to attend to, and various and sundry other tasks and assignments. Each must be reported according to a set schedule.

You can assist in this process enormously by getting in all your reports and paperwork in a timely fashion. Consider the following timely tips:

- Know when your lessons plans are due, and get them in on time.

- Send daily attendance lists to the office in a timely manner.

- Get any requisitions in on schedule.

- Order supplies and materials according to the established schedule.

Lean on Me: Paraprofessionals and Paid Aides

If you are fortunate, you may have paraprofessionals or paid aides to assist you in the classroom. These individuals can increase your effectiveness by taking over a variety of tasks and assignments that consume teaching time or need extra attention.

Fire Alarm _____

Paraprofessional and paid aides are a conduit from the school to the community at large. Whatever takes place in your classroom—your behavior and that of your students, as well as the goings-on of classroom life—will undoubtedly be reported to the general population at large. Use this fact to your advantage. Aides can be advocates for special programs or events. In addition, they can serve as valuable public relations spokespersons in their conversations with neighbors and friends.

Aides and paraprofessionals can assist in a wide variety of endeavors. Instead of assigning them to complete clerical and managerial tasks, take advantage of their involvement and expertise by assigning them to tasks such as the following:

- Monitoring computer work
- Tutoring individual students
- Reading to small groups of students
- Demonstrating an experiment
- Conversing or counseling with individual students
- Reviewing math skills
- Monitoring classroom learning centers
- Setting up displays and/or bulletin boards
- Correcting papers and exams
- Working with bilingual students
- Preparing and gathering materials for a lesson
- Helping returning students with makeup work
- Gathering, grading, and returning worksheets

- ◆ Assisting with club meetings

- ◆ Helping with seatwork

- ◆ Assisting special needs students

- ◆ Providing enrichment activities

- ◆ Assisting in lesson planning

The most effective use of aides and paraprofessionals hinges on several criteria. You must properly and thoroughly train both aides and paraprofessionals. Take several days or weeks to orient these individuals to the practices and procedures of your classroom. Be sure they are aware of their role(s) and responsibilities.

Take the time necessary to get to know your classroom assistants. Ask about their families, their education, their background, and their lives away from school. The most effective teacher/aide relationship is one based on mutual trust, interests, and concerns. Always keep the lines of communication open.

Provide a special place for an aide in your classroom, such as a desk, a file cabinet or drawer, or his or her own set of teacher manuals or other classroom materials. Remember that an aide is not a visitor to your classroom but rather a colleague who can help you teach more efficiently and effectively.

Regularly recognize and celebrate the contributions of your paraprofessionals and aides with a card, note, or special comment. An aide is also interested in the academic and social welfare of the students in your classroom. Be sure to reward her or his contributions appropriately.

Your Lifeline–Substitute Teachers

It's inevitable. You'll get sick, need to attend a conference, or have some kind of family obligation. Either you or the school will need to call in a substitute teacher to cover your class. Imagine the fear and trepidation of that person who walks into an unfamiliar classroom to teach an unfamiliar group of students with an unfamiliar lesson plan. It's pretty scary!

You can greatly assist any potential substitute teacher with a little preplanning. The preparations you do early in the school year will save you, your students, and especially the substitute teacher any unnecessary aggravation or concerns.

Prepare Your Students

When students know a substitute teacher is in for the day, their potential for mischief increases dramatically. Because their regular teacher is away, they feel they can "have a little fun" with the new person. I've always believed an ounce of prevention is worth a pound of cure, so here are some suggestions:

◆ Early in the school year, state your expectations for behavior when a substitute teacher is in the room. Post these expectations, include them in student notebooks, and put a copy in a substitute teacher's file.

◆ If you know you will be absent (attendance at a conference, for example), consider sending a letter home to parents several days in advance. Inform them about expected classroom behavior, and invite them to discuss those expectations with their children.

◆ Set up a buddy system with a nearby teacher. Whenever either of you is absent, the other will make frequent checks into the partner's classroom. Let students and any substitute know about this arrangement.

◆ Let your principal or supervisor know about the rules of conduct or expected classroom behavior when a substitute is in. Invite them to visit the classroom when you are absent, and let students know that there might be visitors whenever you're absent.

Prepare the Substitute

Most teachers have a special file folder or desk drawer in which they place materials that are useful for a substitute teacher. A substitute teacher will probably be unfamiliar with your class or your routines, so it's vitally important that you share information that is both practical and timely.

Include the following items in a folder, a notebook, or a file drawer for the substitute:

◆ A map of the school building.

◆ Daily schedule of activities.

◆ Class list.

◆ Attendance forms and procedures for filing them.

◆ Seating chart(s).

◆ A schedule of pull-outs. Students will come and go for music lessons, guidance office appointments, remedial reading classes, library time, and other responsibilities. Be sure these are clearly spelled out.

◆ Procedures for bathroom breaks, hall passes, early dismissals, lunch, and recess.

◆ Emergency procedures for natural disasters, terroristic threats, and unwanted school visitors.

◆ Student handbook.

◆ Administrative or school duties, including playground duty, bus duty, recess duty, or lunchroom duty. Be sure these are current.

◆ Discipline policy and/or classroom rules.

◆ Names and location of special teachers.

◆ Information about special needs students.

◆ Bus information.

◆ Location of textbook manuals.

◆ Location of supplies, materials, and equipment.

◆ Teacher handbook.

Expert Opinion

Instead of trying to cram all the information a substitute teacher needs into a single file folder, try using a plastic file crate (available at any office supply store). Put dividers into the crate, and use colored file folders for each of several categories (red—rules and procedures; green—schedules and routines; yellow—lesson plans; blue—maps and handbooks).

Plan Ahead with Plans

Whether you will know ahead of time you'll be absent or have to be out for an emergency for which you could not plan, you can still provide lessons for any potential substitute.

Some teachers write generic lesson plans that are included in any materials left for a substitute teacher. These open-ended lesson plans can cover basic concepts of a subject, an extension of a previously learned concept, or a series of cross-curricular extensions for any topic.

Include with one or more generic lessons some of the following for use by a substitute:

- A collection of puzzles, brain teasers, or creative-thinking activities

- A collection of joke books or poetry

- One or two videos related to a general topic

- Children's or adolescent literature to be read aloud to students

- Previously recorded audio tapes with directions for a scavenger hunt, listening activity, or mini-mystery

- A list of suggested art activities or hands-on projects

As part of the information you provide for a substitute teacher, invite anybody covering your class to leave you a note detailing the day's activities, the behavior of the students, and any unusual occurrences that took place. Plan some time immediately after your return to review this note and discuss it with your students. Be sure they know that you are intimately aware of everything and anything that took place while you were away.

Here's another tip: if you have had a particularly good substitute teacher in your classroom, let your principal know. You may be able to get that same substitute the next time you are out. Also, consider sending a substitute a card or note thanking her or him for their coverage of your classroom. That's good public relations—and good human relations, too.

A Word or Two of Wisdom

I wrote the following as part of a collection of reflective essays for classroom teachers. I wanted to convey the importance of celebrating the community we call school. As you read, think about whether or not you agree with my basic premise: that teaching is as much about people as it is about subject matter or lesson plans.

Often, we see people in stereotypical roles and we react to them in those roles. When I was growing up, I saw all school principals as males, with coats and ties, authoritative, unsmiling, and strict disciplinarians. Imagine my surprise when a new principal— a female—began working at a nearby school. It took me a long time to crack through my stereotypical vision of just what a principal should be or look like.

It's easy to create stereotypes. Principals are *supposed* to look a certain way; custodians are *supposed* to talk a certain way; and secretaries are *supposed* to work a certain way.

Often, we assign selected stereotypical roles to protect ourselves from getting to know a person better. When we put people in standardized roles, we may not discover their true selves. For example, we may fail to learn that the principal is a member of the local art association, the custodian is a black belt judo instructor at the YMCA, or the secretary plays guitar in a small band at the local Holiday Inn on weekends.

Perhaps the greatest reason for looking past the stereotypes we sometimes assign people is that it helps us to know the true person behind the job. We get to move past the occupation and into the real lives of the people we work with. A person is not a job description but an individual with skills, interests, and hobbies that may be far more interesting and conversational than what he does during his work day.

Looking beyond stereotypes helps us move past occupational labels to discover the real people behind those roles. One of my friends is a whiz at crossword puzzles, is a master at strategy games, and can solve almost any creative puzzle put before him. He's also a school bus driver for a local school district—and I've yet to beat him in a game of chess.

Here are three questions to ask yourself:

- ◆ Do you see people in terms of the roles they play rather than as real people with lives beyond the school environment?

- ◆ Do you have any stereotypes that might prevent you from communicating with people?

- ◆ Do you use stereotypes to insulate yourself from the community in which you work? Or live?

The Least You Need to Know

- ◆ Establish and maintain positive adult relationships throughout the school.

- ◆ Secretaries and custodians are the people who really run a school—treat them with respect.

- ◆ Always keep your building principal informed.

- ◆ Aides and paraprofessionals can be important assets in the well-run classroom.

- ◆ Prepare, prepare, prepare for substitute teachers.

Chapter 23

Reach Out and Touch Someone: Working With Parents

In This Chapter

- ◆ Open houses and back-to-school and meet-the-teacher nights
- ◆ Parent-teacher conferences
- ◆ Getting parents involved
- ◆ Maintaining parent involvement

It has often been said that parents are a child's first and best teachers. Without question, parents provide children with the basic foundations on which successful learning experiences can be built. The support, encouragement, patience, and understanding of parents have a profound effect on both the academic and social development of children.

When parents are involved in their children's academic affairs, students' scholastic achievement mushrooms significantly. This is equally true for elementary students, middle school students, *and* high school students.

This chapter provides you with tips, ideas, and suggestions on making the "parent connection" successful and pleasurable. Learn why parents are necessary allies and how to sincerely engage them in any classroom program.

The Universal After-School Question

By this point you may be thinking, "Hey, there seems to be a lot of stuff to juggle and manage as a teacher." Well, that's true. But here's a tip on how you can make that juggling a little easier and double your influence as a teacher: enlist parents as partners in your classroom instructional program.

But first, a story: in 1944, the nuclear physicist Isidor Isaac Rabi won the Nobel Prize for his work on atomic nuclei. After his acceptance speech, he was asked about some of the major influences in his life. He told the story about how he grew up in Brooklyn. When his friends all came home from school, their parents always asked them, "What did you learn in school today?" However, when Isidor came home from school each day, his mother always asked him, "Izzy, did you ask a good question today?" He told how that single question from his mother every day helped him develop the inquisitive mind necessary for academic success and his eventual scientific discoveries.

Expert Opinion

Here's a nifty idea I always share with parents: invite parents to change the typical question they ask their children every day. Instead of asking their children, "What did you learn in school today?" they should inquire, "What questions did you ask in school today?" By making this slight change, parents will be able to have more stimulating conversations with their youngsters instead of a series of painfully brief responses ("Nothing!"; "I dunno!").

Most teachers have discovered that parents can be very powerful allies in any child's education—from preschool up through twelfth grade. Keeping parents informed and inviting them to become part of the educational process can significantly influence any youngster's scholastic success. Teachers who take advantage of "parent power" are those who significantly multiply their teaching effectiveness.

Putting Out the Welcome Mat

Open houses—and their close cousins, the back-to-school night and the meet-the-teacher night—are one of the annual rites of passage for every classroom teacher.

Whether you are teaching elementary school or high school, you will undoubtedly be part of this event every year. Open houses occur sometime during the first few weeks of the school year and are an opportunity for parents to get to know you and their child's academic program.

Open houses, back-to-school night, and meet-the-teacher night provide parents with an "inside look" into the daily activities and occurrences of your classroom. It's also a wonderful opportunity for you to actively recruit parents as partners in the education of their children. Here are some tips and ideas that can help you make this annual event successful and purposeful:

- Send out personal invitations beforehand. You may want to invite your students to construct the invitations using art materials. Instead of asking students to take them home (where they may wind up in the washing machine), consider mailing the invitations. On the invitation, include the following information: name and address of the school, date and time of the event, your room number (and how to find the room), your name, and a brief outline of the evening's schedule.

- Plan your presentation and what you will be saying to parents beforehand. Be sure you share something about yourself (where you grew up, your education, your family, your educational philosophy) as well as some of your goals for the year. Your presentation should be no longer than 10 to 11 minutes tops! If your presentation is longer than 11 minutes, it will definitely fall on deaf ears (take it from me—this is an inviolable rule!). Here are some topics you might want to cover:

Elementary School	Middle School/High School
Daily schedule	Discipline policy
Homework	Homework
Grading	Grading
Classroom rules	Field trips
Remedial help	Report cards
Special programs	Fund-raisers
Reading curriculum	Extracurricular activities

- Dress professionally—remember, first impressions are often lasting impressions. Men should wear a coat and tie or at least a dress shirt and tie along with pressed slacks. Women should wear a pantsuit, blouse and skirt, or dress. Incidentally, go "light" on the perfume and aftershave.

Secondary Thoughts

Parent involvement is not just for elementary students. The success of students at the middle school or high school level is highly dependent upon the engagement parents as educational partners. Former high school teacher Phil Monteith says, "You better be in touch with parents, or you are missing a tremendous public relations opportunity. When middle school and high school teachers start a conversation with parents, then positive opinions about teachers in the community escalate."

◆ Prepare your room appropriately. Hang a "Welcome" sign outside the door, and be sure your name and the room number are prominently displayed. Have a sign-in sheet for parents as well as a handout listing the activities and presentations for the evening. Freshen up your bulletin boards, and print a daily schedule on the chalkboard. Set out sample textbooks, and be sure all desks and tables are clean. Be sure each child's desk has a folder with samples of the student's work. Post additional student work (be sure to have at least three samples for each student) on bulletin boards. Post photographs of students and activities throughout the room. Keep in mind that some parents may not have fond memories about *their* school experiences, so here's a great opportunity for you to win them over!

It's Elementary

A friend of mine shares this very important piece of advice:

When setting up your room for back-to-school night or open house, be sure to have plenty of adult chairs available. My first year of teaching first grade, I forgot this rule. As a result, I had many very large adults trying to sit in many very small chairs. It was quite embarrassing to watch people trying to stand up at the end of my presentation.

◆ Greet each and every parent at the door with a handshake and a smile. This is a wonderful opportunity for you to put your best foot forward. Be sure every parent has a name tag (remember that the last name of a student and the last name of her or his parents may be different—always, *always* check beforehand). Provide a tray of refreshments (ask for contributions, particularly if different cultures are represented in your classroom) and appropriate drinks.

◆ As parents arrive, direct them to a table on which you have a stack of index cards, pencils/pens, and an empty shoebox. Invite parents to write a question or two on a card and place it in the box. At the end of your presentation, quickly shuffle through the cards and respond to general questions or those most frequently asked ("How much homework do you give?" "How is reading taught?"). Inform parents that you will contact them personally to respond to more specific questions or ones that focus exclusively on their child's work or progress ("Why did Angela miss recess the other day?" "When will Peter be able to see the reading specialist?").

◆ Keep your presentation brief (remember K.I.S.S.—Keep It Short and Sweet!). Afterward, invite parents to stay and look at their child's work. Circulate around the room, try to meet all the parents again with another handshake and smile, and offer at least one positive remark about their child. This is not the time for personal conferences ("I'd really like to talk with you, Mrs. Smith. May I call you to set up a personal meeting at another time?").

Secondary Thoughts _____

For open houses at the middle school and high school levels, parents typically follow a much-abbreviated schedule of classes that their child participates in each day. It's important that you keep your presentation short and snappy because parents will need to move to several additional rooms throughout the evening.

Face to Face: Parent-Teacher Conferences

If there's one part of the school year that strikes fear into the heart of any teacher—it's *parent-teacher conference* time. Teachers who have been around a while will be more than willing to share some memorable stories about strange parents and even stranger conversations with those parents. Nevertheless, parent-teacher conferences are a wonderful opportunity to extend lines of communication between home and school, keep parents informed about their children's progress—both academic and social—and for developing cooperative strategies that can ultimately benefit every student.

You may be nervous about the thought of parent-teacher conferences. However, here's

Jabberwocky _____

A **parent-teacher conference** is a face-to-face meeting between one teacher and one or both parents (or guardians) of a student. It is an opportunity to discuss a student's academic progress and social behavior. Many schools schedule these in both the fall and spring.

something important to remember—most parents are just as nervous as you are. Your first and primary goal should be to help make them feel comfortable.

A friend of mine once said, "It's important to remember that children are ego extensions of their parents." If you tell a mother that her son is failing three subjects, you are, in effect, telling the parent that she, too, is a failure. On the other hand, if you tell Mr. Velasquez that his daughter is the most outstanding science student in the school, Mr. Velasquez will be mentally patting himself on the back all evening long.

Productive and successful conferences take careful planning. You should think about three stages: before, during, and after.

Before the Conference

Send a personal letter to each parent to confirm the day, time, and place of the conference. Inform parents ahead of time about the purpose of the conference. Gather file folders or portfolios of each student's work. Be sure your schedule is coordinated with other teachers in the school. Many parents will have more than one child in school and need sufficient time with each teacher.

If necessary, make arrangements for an interpreter for non-English-speaking parents. Review notes on each student's behavior, academic progress, and interactions with peers. Establish no more than two or three concerns or issues. More than that will discourage most parents. Clarify ahead of time who, exactly, will be attending each conference. Is it the child's biological parents, a relative, a guardian, a grandparent, a foster parent, or who? Check and double-check names.

Invite parents to bring a list of questions, issues, or concerns. Have sample textbooks readily available. Establish a waiting area outside your classroom. For reasons of confidentiality, you only want to meet with one set of parents at a time.

Don't conduct a parent-teacher conference from behind your desk. A teacher's desk is sometimes referred to as "power furniture," and it tends to inhibit conversation and makes many parents uncomfortable (perhaps a throwback to their days as a student). Instead, conduct your conferences at a table. Don't sit across from parents; instead, sit on the same side of the table as your guests. You will discover heightened levels of conversation and "comfortableness" on the part of parents this way.

During the Conference

Greet parents in a positive manner with a smile and a handshake. Keep in mind that a well-run parent-teacher conference focuses in on the following "must do's" every time:

◆ Provide parents with specific academic information.

◆ Invite and obtain additional information from parents.

◆ Listen carefully to parents. If you're nervous, you will tend to "take over" the conversation—by as much as 90 percent. Try for a 50-50 balance.

◆ Combine your perceptions and their observations into a workable plan of action. Ask for parent ideas, and use those ideas in addressing challenging situations.

◆ Let parents know that you are always available for follow-up (phone calls, personal meetings, etc.).

When talking to parents, always remember: show, don't tell. Provide specific examples of a student's work or behavior rather than labels or adjectives. Instead of saying, "Frankie is poor in math," paint a clear picture for Frankie's parents: "Last week Frankie struggled when we were learning to add two-digit numbers, and he didn't finish his assignment." Always provide parents with concrete examples rather than very broad generalities.

If you are sharing some negative information with parents, be sure you "sandwich" it. Begin with some positive information, then share the negative information, and conclude with another piece of positive information.

Always look for common solutions ("I understand your concern with Carmelita. Let's see if we can work on this together"). Have some duplicated resource sheets available for parents. These may include (but aren't limited to) the following: a list of community social service agencies, a homework help line, a list of private tutors in the community, websites for homework help, etc.

Always use "active listening" skills. If a parent says something about the child, try to use some of the parent's words in your response. For example, if Mr. Brown says, "Yeah, Tommie always seems to be shy whenever he's around other people." You say, "I understand that Tommie is hesitant to talk with other people—that sometimes happens in class. Perhaps I could put him in a smaller group so he will be less inhibited." By using active listening, you help build positive bridges of communication essential in any good conference.

Fire Alarm

Be careful of conversational traps. Experienced teachers will tell you that some topics should *never* be part of parent-teacher conferences, including the following:

- ◆ Comparing one child with another
- ◆ Psychoanalyzing a child
- ◆ Psychoanalyzing a parent
- ◆ Arguing with a parent
- ◆ Focusing on family problems
- ◆ Blaming the parent for the child's problems
- ◆ Talking about other teachers

Don't be afraid to ask for parent input or feedback ("By the way, Mr. Wilson, how have you handled Bobbie's silliness at home?"). By the same token, never give parents commands ("You should …" "You must …") Rather, offer concrete and specific suggestions in the form of an invitation ("Mrs. Harper, based on our conversation this evening, I'm wondering if you and Michelle could spend an additional 10 minutes a night on her spelling words?"). It is far better to "invite" parents to become part of the solution than "tell" them what they should or should not do.

Summarize some of the major points, and clarify any action that will be taken. Most important, always end a conference on a positive note! Don't just dismiss parents from the table. Stand up with them and personally escort them to the door with a smile, a handshake, and a "Thank you for coming."

After the Conference

Save a few minutes after each conference to jot down a couple notes. Don't take notes during the conference—it tends to inhibit many parents and makes eye-to-eye conversation difficult. Record your observations, perceptions, and suggestions on a 3×5 index card with the student's name at the top. File these in a recipe box for later reference.

Plan for some "decompression time" between conferences. You need time to gather your thoughts, regroup, and get ready for the next conference. A long string of back-to-back conferences will only add to your stress and increase your anxiety.

Be sure to follow up (as necessary) with phone calls, notes, messages, or letters to every parent, including those who didn't attend ("I'm sorry I missed you at the parent-teacher conferences last week. May I call you for a personal meeting?"). Immediate feedback is necessary to ensure parent cooperation and participation in any shared solutions.

"Hey, This Is Fun!": Getting Parents Involved

You can use a wide range of projects and activities to get—and keep—parents involved in the affairs of the classroom. Consider some of the following.

Reaching Out

Develop and design a series of orientation programs for parents new to the school or distract. It would be valuable to develop a slide program, a series of brochures, family guides, or other appropriate orientation materials to assist new families in learning as much as they can about your academic program.

Work with a group of parents to prepare a notebook of home or community activities for use during vacations. Include games, reading activities, places to visit, and sites to see in the community. Distribute these notebooks to all families prior to a vacation period, especially summer. Send parents a periodic newsletter updating them on classroom activities and projects.

Make a regular effort to communicate with parents through brief phone calls or short notes. Don't use the telephone to always relay bad news, but use it to celebrate academic accomplishments, too. Call one parent each week to relay some good news about what his or her child is doing.

It's Elementary

I used a technique I called "the 2-minute note." Each morning, I would write a short (two- to four-sentences) note about a positive event or accomplishment for a single student and invite the student to take the note home. I started alphabetically with a student at the top of my grade book and then, each day, selected the next student on my class list until I got to the bottom. Then, I would start again at the top. That way, every student would take home one two-minute note each month.

Sharing Resources

Periodically provide parents with lists of recommended children's literature. Work with the school librarian in distributing lists such as "The Principal's Top Ten Hits" throughout the year. Consider disseminating a list of books on child-rearing practices. If possible, plan a few share-and-discuss sessions with groups of parents to talk over selected books.

Provide parents with a calendar of upcoming classroom events. Many schools and districts send out a periodic newsletter; consider one specifically for your classroom. Include information on books you will read in the coming weeks, field trips, science projects, videos you will see, guest speakers, etc. Publish this on a frequent basis, and distribute it to all families.

Raise Your Hand: "Do I Have Any Volunteers?"

Recruit classroom volunteers. Use the telephone, informal surveys, questionnaires, and face-to-face contacts to solicit parent volunteers. Schedule a special orientation meeting providing potential volunteers with a set of responsibilities and expectations. Allow parents to observe the actual skills you would like them to perform, including marking papers, creating art materials, arranging field trips, supervising small-group work, carrying out remedial tasks, creating bulletin boards, or duplicating classroom materials.

> **Expert Opinion**
>
> Use the telephone as an instrument of good news. Often parents associate the telephone as something used to convey bad news (missed homework, tardiness, behavior problem). Call parents frequently to convey good news about a youngster's academic progress or to thank them for their help on a project.

Be sure to create a support system for parent volunteers. They need to feel that they are working under a trained professional. Plan frequent round-table conferences. Be sure all volunteers have an information packet of school schedules, school and classroom rules, a map of the school, procedures for student absences and tardiness, discipline procedures, dress code, etc.

The Final Word: Sustaining Involvement

Make some of these additional ideas part of your strategy to ensure sustained parent involvement:

◆ Encourage parents to participate continuously throughout the length of the school year.

◆ Be patient with parents. Some may be reluctant to get involved due to any number of extenuating circumstances. Keep trying, and never give up on *any* parent.

◆ Encourage parents to participate in the affairs of the unit through volunteering, observing, or sharing their hobbies, vocations, or vacations.

◆ Use your students as "recruiters" to get their own parents involved. Solicit their ideas as much as possible.

♦ Reward and/or recognize parents for their efforts, however small. Everyone likes to receive some form of recognition, and parents are no exception.

♦ It is vitally important that you be friendly, down to earth, and truly interested in parents and their children.

♦ *Most important:* communicate to parents the fact that their involvement is ultimately for the benefit of their children.

The bonds established between home and school can be powerful ones in terms of the effectiveness of any classroom program. When parents are employed as partners in the classroom, students are afforded a wealth of exciting educational possibilities.

The Least You Need to Know

♦ Parents are a powerful ally for any teacher.

♦ Successful open houses (back-to-school nights or meet-the-teacher nights) take planning and preparation.

♦ Parent-teacher conferences can open up positive lines of communication between home and school.

♦ You can get—and keep—parents involved in their children's academic life.

♦ Parent involvement must be a year-long effort for every teacher.

24

Taking Care of You: Stress Management 101

In This Chapter

◆ Defining stress

◆ The major stressors for teachers

◆ Stress reducers

◆ Self-improvement; self-renewal

Stress—it's a part of life! Ever since the first wholly mammoth began chasing the first caveman or cavewoman, stress has been a constant element of human life. Although we often think all stress is bad, believe it or not, there is also something known as good stress. Good stress is the anticipation of a first kiss, waiting for a loved one to come back from a long journey, or drawing to an inside straight in a game of poker. Good stress is often what propels us to satisfactorily complete a task.

But much of the stress we encounter as teachers is not good stress. It is the bad stuff—stuff that affects us physically, mentally, emotionally, spiritually, and professionally. It's the stress that has a negative impact on our attitudes, personality, and work performance. Defining the stressors of our lives is important; even more significant is how to deal with those inevitable events.

What Is Stress?

Interestingly, there's no universal agreement or exact definition for *stress*. For years, psychologists have disagreed on a precise definition, probably because stress appears in so many forms and is caused by so many factors—both good and bad.

Defining Stress

That said, here is a definition I find to be particularly appropriate for teachers: stress is what people experience when an event or situation challenges their ability to effectively cope with that event or situation. It is the difference between the demands of a situation and *your perception* of how well you will be able to deal with that situation.

Let's take that definition one step further. For the following three statements, put a number 1 in front of the situation that would cause you the most stress, a 2 in front of the situation that would cause you moderate stress, and a 3 in front of the statement that would cause you little or no stress:

_____   While you're driving, a cop pulls you over.

_____   The cop wants to sell you tickets to the upcoming local police ball.

_____   The cop gives you two all-expenses-paid tickets to Hawaii because of your outstanding driving record.

I think you might agree that these examples represent three differing levels of stress. One is severe, another is moderate, and the third is mild or minimal. Not surprising, each of us envisions stress in different ways. Throughout each and every day, many *stressors* impact our lives. As humans, we tend to automatically and arbitrarily categorize those stressors depending upon our perception of their severity.

Jabberwocky

A **stressor** is an event, circumstance, or situation that causes stress. Some stressors are mild, others are moderate, and still others are severe—just like the resulting stress.

If, for example, we categorize many events in our daily schedule as severe stressors, we have a very stressful day. On the other hand, if we group most of the events of our day as mild stressors, we tend to have a minimally stressful day. How we *perceive* stress will frequently determine how much that stress affects us—now and into the future.

A Model of Stress

Here's a good way of looking at stress. Proposed by the noted psychologist Albert Ellis, it's called the ABC model:

$$A \rightarrow B \rightarrow C$$

A is the **a**ctivating event or potentially stressful situation. B stands for your **b**eliefs, thoughts, or perceptions about A. C is the emotional **c**onsequence or stress that results from having these beliefs.

Here's another way of translating that equation:

A potentially stressful situation → your perceptions → your stress (or lack of stress)

Here's an example: you get a note from the principal for an after-school meeting to talk about the results your students got on the latest round of standardized tests.

A: Having to go to the principal's office → **B:** She's going to yell at me for some of the low scores → **C:** I have an upset stomach and a migraine headache, and I'm perspiring heavily.

The key part of this equation is **B**—your thoughts, views, ideas, and interpretations. Your perceptions are the key to determining how much stress you will feel.

Here's the important key: what you *think* about the stressor (or stressors) will either increase or decrease your level of "uncomfortableness." If we perceive an event or situation as beyond our control, our stress level goes up. If we perceive ourselves to have some degree of control over the event or situation, our stress levels go down.

Teacher Burnout

Here's a term you may have heard before: *teacher burnout*. It's that time in a teacher's career when she or he feels so overpowered by the demands or expectations of the job that she or he gives up—emotionally and professionally. Stress has overpowered them. Burned-out teachers often move on to other pursuits or other careers.

Jabberwocky

Teacher burnout is that time in a teacher's life when the demands and expectations of the job exceed one's *perceived* ability(ies) to accomplish them.

Although statistics on teacher burnout are hard to come by, estimates suggest that between 25 and 33 percent of all teachers experience high levels of work-related stress. Even more significant is the fact that new teachers appear to be more at risk than experienced teachers.

Expectations vs. Demands

When the demands of the profession become so overwhelming as to exceed the expectations, a teacher can experience burnout. The consequences often take the form of the following:

◆ High levels of anxiety

◆ Extreme exhaustion

◆ Increased frustration

◆ Depression

◆ Feelings of being overwhelmed

◆ Heightened irritability

◆ Withdrawal

◆ Nervousness

◆ Increased physical ailments

◆ Increased drug and alcohol consumption

Eventually, these factors (often in combination) lead to resignation, early retirement, or even dismissal. Surveys of new teachers indicate that 20 percent leave the profession within their first 3 years of teaching. The primary reason is often teacher burnout.

Gimmie Shelter! The Causes of Stress

With all teachers have to do, it might be easy to see the major causes of stress in a teacher's life. Teachers from around the country have reported the following as significant and frequent stressors:

◆ **Isolation.** Many teachers, particularly elementary teachers, point out that isolation (from other adults) is one of the major stress factors in their lives. Working with students all day long without significant adult conversation or interaction is a leading cause of teacher stress.

◆ **Low status of the teaching profession.** The public is often seen as uncaring or noncommittal toward teachers and the work they do. Many classroom teachers report that the public's negative attitudes or perceptions have a major impact on their stress levels.

◆ **Work overload.** Teachers are being asked to do more and more—often with less and less time available to do it. New materials, new regulations, new curricula, new regulations, and a host of other new stuff keep getting added to the pile, and there is often no relief in sight.

◆ **Standards.** The move to standards-based education, in which teachers often feel as though they are accountable for every tidbit of information presented in a classroom, is also seen as a burden. The pressure to have all kids perform well on all tests is frequently cited as a significant stressor.

Secondary Thoughts _____

In a recent survey, secondary teachers reported that the following factors (in ranked order of importance) contributed most to potential "burnout":

◆ Inadequate discipline policies of the school or district
◆ Poor administrator attitude
◆ Unmotivated students
◆ Lack of administrative support/encouragement
◆ Lack of decision-making power

◆ **Unruly, disruptive students.** Students who are undisciplined, disrespectful, and negative add a personal and professional burden to the lives of many teachers. Teachers frequently mention the increased numbers of children (elementary and secondary) who come to school with an "attitude."

◆ **Lack of parent support.** Parents who don't take (or who have never taken) an active role in the scholastic and academic lives of their children are another frustration for many teachers.

◆ **Unsupportive administrators.** Often principals and other administrators are often seen as the "enemy." Teachers mention that there sometimes seems to be little support (for discipline and curriculum change) from the front office and little encouragement for the daily grind.

◆ **Evaluations.** The annual or semi-annual evaluative process for teachers has been (and will always be) a source of stress, as it is for most workers.

Stress Relief

This assembly of techniques, ideas, and proposals can reinvigorate your life and help you more effectively deal with the stressors that are a normal and natural part of your everyday life. Some of these will be passive; some active. Use these, modify them to your own needs, and make them a part of who you are as an individual. You may discover heightened motivation, increased awareness, and a more even temperament.

- Accept your imperfections. Realize that you can't be all things to all people. Embrace your imperfections, and celebrate them.

- Every so often (once a week, for example) stop and give yourself a much-needed pat on the back.

- At the beginning of each week, take a few minutes to list five things you like about yourself. Put the list in your desk drawer, and peek at it every so often.

- Teachers spend a large part of their lives trying to make other people happy. It's equally important that you take time, each day, to recognize and celebrate the things that bring you joy and happiness.

- Take a course at the local college, enroll in a workshop, or participate in a conference or convention. Keep learning new stuff; keep your mind active and engaged.

- Take a daily walk or run. Use this time to get away from the pressures of your job or life. Use this time for self-reflection and self-renewal.

- Take a mini-vacation—frequently. Find someplace within an hour's drive of where you live, and spend some quality time there. Look for some of the following places:

airport	coffee shop	greenhouse	mountain
aquarium	country inn	hiking trail	museum
arena	county fair	historical area	nature park
ballpark	ethnic restaurant	hobby shop	ocean
beach	farm	home center	orchard
bicycle path	flea market	ice rink	planetarium
botanical garden	forest	lake	quarry
bus	gallery	library	river
cave	garden center	lumberyard	rock formation

small café	swamp	train station	winery
stable	theater	valley	zoo
state capital	tide pool		

Scout your local newspaper for more ideas. Plan a mini-vacation every week—explore the undiscovered, and learn about the unfamiliar.

- Play. No, seriously. When was the last time you played? Make regular time to do a crossword puzzle, play a game of cards, paint a picture, play pool, play a board game, or participate in any other frivolous activity.

- Each day, schedule time for yourself. Write down a time in your calendar to be spent on you. This may be a period of time when you read a chapter of a favorite novel, listen to your favorite music, engage in some mental imagery, or simply look out the window and enjoy the view.

Expert Opinion

Here are some ideas to think about:

Wonder like a child.

Ask questions without answers.

Imagine the improbable; dream the impossible.

Make love, not war (I'm a child of the '60s).

- Stretch it out. One of the ways we can recharge and re-energize ourselves is to take 5 or 10 minutes in the middle of the day to engage in simple stretching exercises. These will get you started:

    A leg up. Sit in your chair with your back straight and your feet firmly on the floor. Slowly lift both legs until your body forms an L shape. Hold that position for a count of 10. Lower your feet to the floor. Repeat 10 times.

    Necking. Reach up with your right hand, and place it on the left side of your head. Slowly pull your head down to your right shoulder. Straighten your head, and repeat 10 times. Repeat the procedure with your left hand and pull your head down to your left shoulder. Repeat 10 times.

    Chest stretch. Stand up straight. Bring your arms straight behind you, and clasp your hands together behind your back. Raise your shoulders slowly up and then slowly down. Repeat 10 times.

Twist and shout. Stand straight up. Touch your right shoulder with your right hand and your left shoulder with your left hand. Slowly turn your upper torso to the left. Return to the starting position, and slowly turn your upper torso to the right. Keep your feet in the same place each time. Repeat 10 times.

Push off. Stand approximately 2 feet away from a wall. Fall toward the wall with your hands firmly on the surface. Do a simulated push-up from the wall (let your head come close to the wall then push off with your hands). Repeat 10 times.

♦ Carve some time out of your day to tell someone how much you care. A phone call, a note, a letter, a message, a greeting card, or even a simple hug will bring something special into that person's life, as well as your own.

♦ Interact with adults away from the school. Foster relationships with adults who are not educators (you don't want to talk "shop" all the time). Participate, enroll, and contribute to volunteer organizations and service clubs. Join a church group, a community association, or a gym. Join the community choir, a theater group, a bowling league—anything you'd enjoy in the adult community outside school. It's important to participate in a variety of non-school–related functions.

Fire Alarm _____

Pace yourself. Don't try to implement every idea, strategy, or technique you've ever learned about teaching into the first week.

♦ Sometime, early in the day, engage in a period of time in which you close off the rest of the world to meditate, write in a journal, or simply daydream. Take some time each morning to create a positive image of your day.

Love Yourself

A former student of mine, who now teaches in a nearby school district, has this philosophy of life: "Love the kids, love the job, but take time to love yourself."

After 20 or 30 years in the classroom, how are some teachers able to approach each day with the same vigor and energy they had when they first started teaching? How are they able to continue to create exciting lesson plans and dynamic units that inspire their students week after week and month after month? How are they able to achieve balance in their personal and professional lives?

These are all good questions, and they all engender the same response. The key to success as classroom teachers lies in our ability to take care of ourselves. Devote time and energy to your own well-being, self-renewal, and personal objectives. Caring for yourself does not mean you become self-centered or selfish. Caring for yourself is a significant factor in the physical, emotional, and mental balance you need to maintain your stamina.

It all boils down to this: you cannot take care of others until you first take care of yourself. Teachers who give so much to others that they have little left for themselves begin to burn out. They lose touch with the core of their existence and with the magic of self-renewal that is within all of us. When you commit yourself to becoming the best you can be, you will discover a new energy, a new serenity, and a new spirit of giving that will empower you to help others. As you empower those around you, you will become a better teacher and a better human being!

Your Personal Stress Test

Are you able to manage the stress in your life? Here's a self-test to find out. Place a checkmark in front of each of the following statements that you sincerely believe about yourself. Remember, this is a self-test, so be true to *you!*

_____ I have limitations, and I accept them.

_____ I take time each day for myself—no one else, just me.

_____ I am grateful for the people in my life.

_____ I love, I am in love, and I am loved.

_____ I have made mistakes, but I have made peace with those mistakes.

_____ I have peace and serenity in my life.

_____ I take care of my needs.

_____ I have passion in my life.

_____ I regularly celebrate my achievements, large and small.

_____ I dream.

_____ I laugh at myself and with others.

_____ I share the real me with other people (both in and out of school).

_____ I embrace change—in myself and in the world in which I live.

_____ Students are my favorite teachers.

To score this self-test: the more checkmarks you have, the more you are able to manage the inevitable stressors in your life.

The Least You Need to Know

◆ Stress is the difference between the demands of a situation and your perception of how well you will be able to deal with that situation.

◆ A variety of stressors can affect your teaching and your life.

◆ Teacher burnout is a problem that can be controlled or reduced.

◆ You can reduce the stressors and the amount of stress in your personal and professional lives in several ways.

Chapter 25

Building Your Career

In This Chapter

- ◆ Your need to be reflective
- ◆ Your role as a teacher-researcher
- ◆ Talk to the pros
- ◆ Get out and discover
- ◆ Read and learn
- ◆ Lessons for life

I have always lived by a simple motto: the best teachers have as much to learn as they do to teach! No matter where I am in my teaching career, I can always learn something more, master something more, and improve something more. I have long realized that my teacher education did not end when I graduated from college. In fact, that's when it began.

As teachers, we have a multitude of responsibilities throughout our careers. One of the most important is our own education. While we may be committed to the educational advancement of our students, we should be no less committed to our own lifelong improvement as a teacher. Education is an ongoing process, rather than a final product.

You Need to Reflect

Throughout this book, I have tried to focus on the concept of *teacher as learner*. That means a teacher who *guides* rather than *leads*, *facilitates* rather than *assigns*, and *models* rather than *tells*. My 30+ years of teaching experience have taught me that the most successful teachers are those who are willing to learn alongside their students—providing students with the processes and the supportive arena in which they can begin to make their own discoveries and pursue their own self-initiated investigations.

Throughout this book, we have looked at all the attributes and the qualities of good teachers. But I've saved the best for last. That is, a good teacher is also a *reflective* teacher. A reflective teacher is one who thinks as much as acts and one who is constantly searching for self-improvement.

Mirror Image

Teachers who reflect are teachers who are open to change. Reflective teachers do lots of self-assessment, and in doing so, they help their students grow both as scholars and as individuals. Here are some reflective qualities essential to your success as a teacher:

- Be open-minded to new ideas and new possibilities.

- Think about the reason and rationale for every task and assignment.

- Be willing to take responsibility for your actions.

- Be open to improvement on both major and minor issues.

- Regularly assess your teaching philosophy.

- Make time for regular periods of self-questioning.

Take It Down

To think about what you do and why is critical to your success as an educator. It also sets the stage for self-discovery and self-improvement. But to do so, you need a record of your thoughts and your introspection. Teachers, at any stage of their careers, should be using some of these long-term suggestions:

- **Create your own teaching portfolio.** Continually add your best lesson plans, letters from students, annual evaluations, photos of special projects or displays, articles read, and notes from conferences or in-service programs. Occasionally review the portfolio for potential weak areas in addition to celebrating your ongoing accomplishments.

◆ **Maintain a reflective journal.** Keep an inexpensive notebook in your desk and write a comment, reflection, observation, or critique of your day or week. Do this on a regular basis, and review your notes periodically.

◆ **Keep a diary of your thoughts and ideas.** You might want to sit down with other teachers periodically to discuss those thoughts and share some mutually supportive responses.

Teacher as Researcher

One of the most important roles you can assume throughout your teaching career is that of a teacher-researcher. It's been my experience that the best teachers are those who continue to ask questions and continue to seek answers. For me, good teaching is an active search for new opportunities to make learning come alive for my students. I constantly ask questions and constantly search for answers to my own self-initiated queries.

It's important that you initiate some research in your own classroom—examining, exploring, and investigating the dynamics of learning and the potentialities of teaching. Many teachers (myself included) will tell you that an exploration of the *possibilities* of instruction, rather than the *absolutes*, is the surest way to keep your career fresh, motivating, and engaging. Here's another way to look at it: when you stop asking questions, you stop growing, learning, and teaching.

The first step in becoming a teacher-researcher is often the hardest. It begins with a question. Framing the question to guide your own classroom research is the key to successful discoveries. You might begin to frame your question by considering the answers to some other questions:

◆ What intrigues you in a classroom?

◆ What do you wonder about?

◆ What puzzles you?

◆ How can you provide for the learning needs of your students?

◆ What do you need to change?

Record your queries in a notebook, and use this document to direct some of your personal investigations, readings, Internet searches, and research. You can conduct this research during weekends, vacations, and over the summer months. Continuing to ask questions and continuing to seek answers is the surest path to a lifetime of teaching success that I know of.

We're All in This Together!

In many states and many districts *mentoring* or induction programs are in place for new teachers. New teachers are assigned to seasoned pros for guidance, support, and encouragement.

Mentoring is sometimes referred to as peer coaching. It allows you to take advantage of a fellow teacher's years of experience during your first and second year of teaching. While the duties and responsibilities of mentors vary from school to school, you can anticipate and look forward to the following:

- ◆ Help in designing lesson plans

- ◆ Assistance with school rules and regulations

- ◆ Advice on classroom setup and management

- ◆ Observation of a lesson

- ◆ Help finding your way around the school

- ◆ Introductions to the staff, including secretaries and custodians

- ◆ Guidance on how to operate the photocopy machine

- ◆ Suggestions for discipline problems

Jabberwocky

A **mentor** observes, coaches, and advises a new teacher. The mentor assists the new teacher in learning rules, procedures, and skills. A mentor is an experienced teacher who provides support, offers encouragement, and gives assistance.

But First ...

Being assigned a mentor for your all-important first year of teaching is a wonderful way to begin your teaching career. Here is a person to whom you can turn when you have an issue, a question, a worry, or when you just don't know where the teacher's lunchroom is located. Your mentor is your support system, your confidant, and often your friend. Take advantage of her or his wisdom and expertise.

You might need to take the first step. Don't wait for a suggestion or hint from your mentor. Ask lots of questions. Be proactive, and if you don't know something or don't understand something, ask your mentor. You are not demonstrating any incompetence by asking a question; rather, you are showing that you're trying to learn as much as you can about the real-world of teaching in a brand-new environment.

Let's Meet

One of the most invigorating ways to improve your teaching ability is to regularly attend a variety of professional meetings, workshops, and conferences. Local professional gatherings may be scheduled at a nearby hotel or banquet facility. Statewide or national conventions are typically scheduled at a convention center or other large facility.

Attendance at an education conference or convention can be a sound investment in your own career as well as in the success of your classroom program. Not only will you be able to hear fellow teachers from other parts of your region, state, or country, but also some leading experts in a specific field or discipline. Most important, attending a conference or convention provides you with numerous opportunities to rub elbows with and talk to teachers from around the country.

Conferences are a wonderful opportunity to gather the latest information about a topic, and they can be one of the most exciting resources you can use. The conference itself is not the resource; the information and other printed materials you gather at the conference can be exciting supplements to your overall classroom curriculum.

How can you find out about these professional gatherings? Try these suggestions:

- ◆ Check the bulletin board in the teacher's lounge. Announcements of conferences are frequently posted there.

- ◆ Access the website of a professional organization (see Appendix B). Most will have a Convention or Conference page. Check it frequently.

- ◆ Many educational groups and organizations have a newsletter or newspaper issued on a regular basis. Check them out in your school or local library.

- ◆ Several professional organizations have local or regional affiliates. They can provide you with information about upcoming conferences.

- ◆ Stay in touch with your fellow teachers. Talk to them about conferences they attend or meetings they go to on a regular basis. Their suggestions can be very helpful in your search.

Join the Club

Joining a professional association can provide you with a host of contacts and resources that can enhance your classroom teaching. Associations enable you to stay current in your field and provide a form of revitalization and renewal through professional contacts. Most of the organizations and associations offer a variety of printed materials (including a journal, books, pamphlets, brochures, and curriculum guides) that can add immeasurably to your competencies as a teacher.

Your level of participation in a professional organization can be minimal (paying your dues and reading one or more professional publications), or it can be considerable (serving in a leadership role or as an elected official). No matter how you choose to participate, you will discover a wealth of learning opportunities that can translate into improved levels of teaching competence in the classroom.

Here are just a few of the many professional organizations you can consider:

◆ International Reading Association (www.reading.org)

◆ National Science Teachers Association (www.nsta.org)

◆ National Council for the Social Studies (www.ncss.org)

◆ National Council of Teachers of Mathematics (www.nctm.org)

◆ National Council for Teachers of English (www.ncte.org)

Making the Connection: Networking

Throughout your career as a teacher, you will have numerous opportunities to meet and talk with many other teachers, not only within your own school or district but from other areas as well. Establishing and maintaining contacts with teachers can be a valuable resource for your classroom program. You will have a chance to share your successes and disappointments as well as new strategies, ideas, and techniques.

Jabberwocky

A **listserv** is an electronic list of e-mail addresses of individuals who belong to a specific group or organization. Individuals who belong to the list can e-mail (with a single message) all the people who are part of that list.

Your networking can start with the teachers in your own school and move outward from there. Attending local and state conferences can provide you with other opportunities to link up with teachers.

Attending a national convention will also allow you to network with educators from many different states, provinces, and perspectives.

Also, consider online chat rooms and *listservs* as a way of networking with teachers around the country. You can pose questions online or stay up to date with current issues and concerns in a specific discipline. These informal "conversations" provide a gold mine of information for any teacher.

Read All About It!

One of the most important ways you can stay current in your field, locate answers to your questions, and obtain some of the most creative and dynamic ideas is by reading professional books and articles.

Professionally Speaking

Joining a professional education association will often include a subscription to a journal or magazine. These offer some of the most current ideas and information available. You can read them at your convenience or file them away for future reference. Here are some tips for getting the most out of these resources:

- ◆ When you read a particularly interesting article, make two photocopies. Put one in a permanent file (that has been subdivided into specific topics or subjects). Send the other copy to a colleague.

- ◆ After reading a good article, place a Post-it on the side of the journal. You may want to color-code your notes, for example:

    Blue: can be used immediately

    Yellow: need to read it again

    Green: save and reflect on during the summer

    Purple: share with other teachers at my grade level

- ◆ After reading a particularly interesting article, summarize it on a 3×5 index card. Include bibliographic information, a brief summary of the article, classroom implications, and your personal evaluation of the article.

    File each card in a plastic recipe box and keep the box on your desk. Review the cards every so often.

Book It!

One of the best ways to gather information and discover exciting and dynamic new teaching strategies and techniques is through teacher resource books. These books, often available in trade bookstores as well as teacher supply stores, offer a convenient and easy-to-use resource for any classroom teacher.

You can also order these books through various publisher catalogs or websites. Other possibilities include online booksellers (Amazon.com, BarnesandNoble.com). In these books, you will discover advice from fellow educators that can have an immediate impact on your teaching expertise and your students' learning opportunities.

Scholars and Dollars

In many school districts, teachers are encouraged to pursue additional study—specifically at the graduate level. Graduate work is particularly meaningful because it provides you with opportunities to advance your education in a specific field of study. Additionally, you get the benefit of interacting with other teachers who are also discovering new ideas, new theories, and new information that can have an immediate impact on their teaching competence.

Graduate work also allows you to find answers to some classroom questions. You can enhance your teaching abilities, skills, and attitudes and become more confident in your professional goals.

 Fire Alarm _____

Don't begin any graduate work until after your second year of teaching. You need time after your undergraduate work for your brain to decompress and rejuvenate. Your first two years of teaching will take all your time and attention, and you don't need to be distracted with the academic requirements of one or more graduate courses. After your second year of teaching, you will be much better prepared to tackle graduate work and to see its direct implications in your classroom.

The other advantage of graduate work is that it is a way of advancing on your district's salary schedule. School districts will pay for all, most, or some of your graduate studies. Be sure to check with your administrator or the district office for the specifics of your district's policy on the financial aspects of graduate studies.

Obtaining a Master's degree can be both personally rewarding as well as a way to enhance your professional options. Check out the programs available at a nearby college or university.

Just a Few More Tips

In Chapter 3, I outlined some of the qualities and features of successful teachers. I wanted to illustrate the point that successful teachers are constantly in training. Or look at it this way: you never *become* a teacher, you are always *becoming* a teacher!

Here are a few more suggestions you may want to tuck into your memory file—ideas that can help you become the best you can be:

- Join or initiate a teacher discussion group. Meet regularly and talk about issues, concerns, or new teaching strategies.

- Once a month, set a personal goal for improvement. Do everything you can to accomplish that goal.

- Subscribe to a teaching magazine or professional journal. Read it regularly.

- Join a group or club that is not education-oriented. You need an emotional outlet such as an athletic club, literary group, theater group, or hobby-related activity.

- Socialize with the teachers in your building. Build camaraderie and group cohesiveness through social activities.

- Ask to observe veteran teachers in their classrooms. Watch what they do, and ask them why they do things in a particular way.

- Visit other schools. Ask permission to see what other teachers are doing in classrooms outside your school district. Request a professional day to conduct your observations.

A Final *Final* Thought

I have a friend who says, "Life is a do-it-yourself project." She believes that the best and most successful classrooms are places where teachers continuously learn and grow with their students.

I believe we do ourselves a great disservice when we fail to take the time to realize our own capacity for growth. Too often we think that because we have a college degree or we have been teaching for X number of years, we have our act together.

However, when we acknowledge the potential for growth in our lives, we can celebrate the possibilities for self-improvement and self-development. People who resist change and say, "That's the way I've always done it," frighten me. The implication is that if it worked in the past, it will surely work in the future. Coping with the world by clinging to the past makes life static, stagnant, and unrewarding.

There is real value in realizing our capacity for growth and development. Growing, changing, and becoming do not end with graduation and certification as a teacher. They are part of a lifelong process to be pursued and celebrated.

It is not the destination that is important but rather the journey.

The Least You Need to Know

- Reflective teachers build strong, long-lasting careers.
- Here's the key to success: ask lots of questions, and seek lots of answers.
- Tap into the experts to help you on this all-important journey.
- Get out and about, meet and greet, and expand your teaching horizons.
- Read to succeed!
- Life—and teaching—are do-it-yourself projects!

Glossary: Your Guide to Educationalese

ability grouping   Placing students into groups based solely on their achievement on a test.

academic standards   Statements that provide a clear description of the knowledge and skills students should be developing through instruction.

accommodation   A devise, material, or support process that will enable a student to accomplish a task more efficiently.

ADHD   Attention-deficit/hyperactivity disorder. This is a condition in which an individual has difficulty sustaining attention, focusing on information, and frequently demonstrates hyperactive behavior.

analysis   A level of questioning in which students break down something into its component parts.

anecdotal records   Narrative descriptions of student behavior or performance.

anticipation guide   A teaching strategy that encourages students to use their background knowledge about a topic before reading about that topic.

application   A level of questioning in which students take information and apply it to a new situation.

assessment   Gathering information about the level of performance of individual students.

attitudinal assessment   Determining the attitudinal or emotional growth of your students.

benchmarks   *See* performance standards.

bilingual   An individual's ability to speak his or her native language as well as an additional language fluently.

block scheduling   Longer academic periods (primarily at the high school level) that allow students to pursue a subject in more depth. Periods may range from 70 to 140 minutes in length.

bodily-kinesthetic intelligence   This intelligence focuses on physical activities; eye/hand coordination; and the ability to move around through dance, plays, or role-playing activities.

brainstorming   Generating lots of ideas from many individuals.

buzz session   A temporary group of students formed to discuss a specific topic.

CD-ROM   A computer disc of digitized sounds, activities, and/or pictures.

charter school   A school operated as a for-profit enterprise.

closure   The final instructional activity in a lesson plan.

comprehension   The way in which ideas are organized into categories.

constructivism   The way knowledge is created in the mind of a learner.

content courses   Teacher preparation courses that focus on the specific content of factual information about a subject (chemistry, social studies, algebra). College students in secondary teacher education programs most often take these courses.

cooperative learning   Placing students into small groups and having them work together toward a common goal.

copyright   The registration with the Library of Congress that protects a book or other printed material from unfair and/or unauthorized duplication.

creative thinking   Generating new ways of looking at a situation.

criterion check   A point in any lesson at which the teacher stops and checks to see if students understand the material up to that point.

critical thinking   The ability to analyze information.

deductive thinking   Going from the general to the specific. *See also* inductive thinking.

dehydration   A reduction of water content.

differentiated instruction   Providing instruction according to the different ability levels in a classroom.

dimensions of learning   The five basic elements of any teaching/learning situation: confidence and independence, knowledge and understanding, skills and strategies, use of prior and emerging experience, and critical reflection.

disruptive behavior   Any behavior that interferes with or impedes a teacher's ability to teach and students' abilities to learn.

educational technology   Any instructional aid or media teachers use to support the teaching and learning process.

elaboration   The expansion of an idea or thought.

elementary teachers   Teachers who teach preschool up through grade 6.

evaluation   A method of determining if students learned what they were taught. It is usually conducted at the end of a lesson.

extrinsic motivation   When an individual is motivated by outside factors or other people (as opposed to being motivated from within).

flexibility   The skill of drawing relationships between seemingly unrelated ideas (How are a brick and a book similar?).

fluency   The ability to create a lot of ideas.

formative evaluation   Evaluation that takes place between the introduction of material and its conclusion.

free lunch   A student's meal which is completely subsidized by government funds.

gifted students   Students who demonstrate high levels of imagination, curiosity, and intelligence.

graphic organizer   A chart, outline, or web of ideas or concepts visually organized into groups or categories.

heterogeneous groups   Groups of students of mixed abilities.

high-stakes testing   When students take standardized tests, the results of which are rewarded in some way (graduation, for example).

homeroom   The classroom a secondary student attends in the morning (or at the end of the day). Attendance is taken, announcements are made, and forms are completed in this room.

hypothesis   An assumption, interpretation, or guess based on currently available information.

IDEA   Individuals with Disabilities Education Act. This is the name given in 1990 to what was formerly known as Public Law 94-142 (the Education for All Handicapped Children Act).

IEP   A document that outlines specific learning objectives for a student and how those objectives will be carried out.

inclusion   Involving all students in the educational setting that best meets their needs.

inductive thinking   Going from the specific to the general. *See also* deductive thinking.

in-service teacher   An individual who has been hired by a district and is actively teaching.

INTASC   The Interstate New Teacher Assessment and Support Consortium. This a group of state education agencies and national educational organizations who work to reform the preparation, licensing, and professional development of teachers.

intelligence   The ability to use knowledge.

intermediate teachers   Teachers who teach forth, fifth, and sixth grade.

interpersonal intelligence   The ability to work effectively with other people.

intrapersonal intelligence   The ability to understand one's own emotions, goals, and intentions.

intrinsic motivation   Motivation that comes from within the individual.

knowledge   The facts and data of a subject.

laws of learning   Basic laws or rules by and through which learning occurs.

learning center   A self-contained section of the classroom in which students engage in independent activities.

learning disabled students   Those students who demonstrate a significant discrepancy between academic achievement and intellectual abilities in one or more areas.

lecture   Sharing information with students verbally.

lesson plan   An outline of goals and objectives, activities designed to help students achieve those goals, and objectives and ways to assess whether students have actually reached those goals and objectives.

listserv   A list of e-mail addresses maintained by a group or organization. E-mail can be sent electronically to everyone on the list by any member of the list.

locus of control   The degree to which individuals perceive they are in control. There are two types: external (people motivated by others) and internal (people motivated from within).

logical-mathematical intelligence   The ability to reason deductively or inductively and to recognize and manipulate abstract patterns and relationships.

magnet school   A school that specializes in a specific subject area.

manipulatives   Physical materials such as cubes, blocks, or balls that model mathematical concepts.

memory   The way we recall previously learned or previously experienced information.

mental imagery   Creating pictures or images in one's own mind.

mentor   An experienced teacher who assists a new colleague.

methodology   The way(s) in which information is shared with students.

methods courses   Teacher preparation courses that focus on the methods, ways, procedures, or strategies of teaching (the "how-to's" of teaching).

modification   Changes in the instruction, course content, or outcomes for special needs students.

motivation   An emotion or psychological need that incites a person to do something.

motivational opening   An initial activity or motivational devise in a lesson designed to get students' attention or tap into their background knowledge.

MP3   Moving Picture Experts Group Audio Layer 3. This is an audio compression technology that provides high-quality sound in a very limited space.

multimedia   A combination of technologies to create an instructional program or experience for students.

multiple intelligences   A theory that postulates that human beings have eight separate intelligences (rather than a single IQ score) that determine how they learn.

musical-rhythmic intelligence   Sensitivity to the pitch, timbre, and rhythm of sounds and the elements of music.

naturalistic intelligence   The ability of individuals to recognize plants and animal lives and to have an appreciation for nature.

neural forest   The connections that occur between brain cells. The more connections, the thicker the neural forest; the thicker the neural forest, the more we know about a specific topic.

neuron   A brain cell.

objective   A statement that describes what students will be able to do upon completion of an instructional experience.

originality   The creation of singular and unique ideas.

paraprofessional   An individual (usually uncertified) who works with a teacher in a classroom setting.

parent-teacher conference   A face-to-face meeting between a teacher and one or both parents (or guardians) of a student to discuss the student's academic performance and any concerns either party might have.

performance   The ability to effectively use new information in a productive manner.

performance assessment   When students demonstrate their mastery of material through a "hands-on activity" (assembling an electrical circuit, for example).

performance standards   Statements that describe what it will take for a student to demonstrate mastery of a standard.

phonemic awareness   A recognition that spoken words are composed of several individual sounds.

phonics   A recognition of sound-spelling relationships in printed words.

planning time   Time during the day when a teacher does not have students and can plan lessons and other activities.

portfolio assessment   A collection of materials designed to demonstrate progress over time.

praise   Verbal comments that recognize individual students.

prediction   An educated guess about something that may happen in the future.

prior knowledge   The knowledge a learner already has about a topic or subject. It is the past knowledge a learner brings to a new learning situation.

probing   A series of teacher statements or questions that encourage students to elaborate on their answers to previous questions.

problem-solving   The ability to identify and solve problems by applying appropriate skills systematically.

process evaluation   The way students go about learning. It may or may not be related to what they learned.

product evaluation   A formal test that occurs at the end of a lesson or lessons.

project assessment   When students design a project that illustrates a specific principle (science fair projects, for example).

prompting   Assisting students in thinking beyond their response to a question.

realia   Three-dimensional objects used for instruction.

reduced lunch   A meal that is partially subsidized by government funds.

remediation   A teacher comment that helps students reach a more accurate or higher-level response.

round robin   A small group setting in which each student shares information.

routines   Ways of managing the classroom; an established set of expectations.

rubric   A document that describes varying levels of performance (from high to low) for a specific assignment.

rule of two-thirds   In a traditional classroom, $\frac{2}{3}$ of class time is taken up by talking, $\frac{2}{3}$ of that time is taken up by teacher talk, and $\frac{2}{3}$ of the teacher talk is telling or disciplining.

search engine   A computer program designed to find websites based on keywords you enter.

second language learners   Students whose primary language is not English. They are learning English as their second language.

secondary teachers   Those teachers who teach in grades 7 through 12 (in most states).

section 504   A civil rights law that requires that institutions not discriminate against people with disabilities.

simulation   An activity in which students are given real-life problem-solving situations. The emphasis is on student decision-making.

specials   Classes usually designated as nonacademic. They typically include art class, P.E., library time, and music class.

standards   A description of what students should know or be able to do.

standards-based teaching   When teachers use activities and lessons to ensure that students master a predetermined set of requirements or standards.

stimulus   An event that causes something else to happen or take place.

stress   What people experience when a situation challenges their ability to effectively cope.

stressor   An event, circumstance, or situation that causes stress.

summative evaluation   Evaluation that occurs at the end of a unit of study.

synapse   The place where electrical and chemical connections are made between one brain cell and another.

synthesis   The combination of knowledge elements that form a new whole.

systems analysis   Analyzing the parts of a system and the manner in which they interact.

task orientation   The degree to which a teacher provides learning opportunities (as opposed to dealing with management issues) for students.

taxonomy   An orderly classification of items according to various levels (low to high, small to large).

teacher burnout   The time in a teacher's life when the demands and expectations of the job exceed one's perceived ability to accomplish them.

teacher's guide   A supplement to a textbook which includes a collection of teaching materials, lessons, ideas, and activities to help you teach the subject.

textbook   A collection of the knowledge, concepts, and principles of a selected topic or course.

verbal-linguistic intelligence   The ability to use and produce language effectively.

visual-spatial intelligence   The ability to create visual images in the form of drawings, designs, maps, puzzles, mazes, and other creative items.

wait time   The time between the asking of a question and the solicitation of a response.

Wow! Look at These Great Websites!

I could probably fill half this book (or more) with all the websites available to teachers. Suffice it to say, lots of resources and materials are available for you to use in your classroom. This appendix will provide you with a selection of the "best of the best."

As you know, the Internet is always evolving. Websites have a way of disappearing from sight (only to reappear later). They sometimes change into something new and different (surprise!). Or they may simply become extinct—all at the drop of a hat. The sites listed here were current and accurate as of the writing of this book. Most have been around for a while, and I suspect (and hope) they will continue to be available when you read this.

The volatility of the Internet also means you may find something different (or even unexpected) by the time you log on. Please be aware that some sites may change and others may be eliminated; new sites will be added to the various search engines you use at school or home. You may want to bookmark many of these or save them as favorites. You are sure to find a veritable plethora of possibilities online for you and your students.

Becoming a Teacher

If you're looking for some basic information about the teaching profession, you can't go wrong with this site. There's lots of stuff here for anyone considering teaching as a first or second career.

Teachers Count
www.teacherscount.org
This site provides basic information on why you should become a teacher, facts about teaching, salaries and benefits, how to become a teacher, and scholarships and funding options.

Lesson Plans

What if I told you that there are literally thousands of lesson plans already available for you to download and use right away? And what if I told you that those lesson plans were developed by real live classroom teachers and were classroom-tested and student-endorsed? Sounds good? You bet it does! Here they are.

Gateway to Educational Materials
www.thegateway.org/
This site provides educators with quick and easy access to thousands of educational resources found on various federal, state, university, nonprofit, and commercial Internet sites.

Kidz Online
www.kidzonline.org/LessonPlans/
This is a great source for secondary lesson plans. You can specify subject and grade level.

Learning Page
www.learningpage.com/
Look through the Learning Page's huge collection of lesson plans for your immediate use.

Lesson Planet
www.lessonplanet.com/
Search more than 30,000 lesson plans. Wow! What an incredible variety for any teacher.

The Lesson Plan Library
school.discovery.com/lessonplans/
Finds hundreds of lesson plans for teachers in elementary, middle, and high school.

Lesson Plans for Teachers

teacher.scholastic.com/lessonplans/

Get access to tons of lesson plans in all the grades from one of the biggest educational publishers.

The Lesson Plans Page

www.lessonplanspage.com/

If you're looking for more than 2,500 lesson plans in grades K–12, this is your place.

Lesson Plan Search

www.lessonplansearch.com/

Find hundreds of lesson plans in a variety of subjects and a host of topics.

LessonPlanZ.com

www.lessonplanz.com/

LessonPlanz.com is a searchable directory of free online lesson plans and lesson plan resources for all grades and subjects.

Teach Net

www.teachnet.com/

You can access lots of lesson plans and teaching resources on this site.

Teachers Net Lesson Exchange

www.teachers.net/lessons

Take a lesson, leave a lesson at the Teacher's Net Lesson Exchange. The lessons cover all subjects and grade levels and include links to the teachers who posted the lessons.

Online Experts

Wouldn't it be great if you and your students could have experts visit your classroom to offer their expertise on a subject? Well, they can! Experts are available online to answer questions posed by students and teachers and supply them with all the necessary information. Check out these sites:

AskA+ Locator

www.vrd.org/locator/subject.shtml

This is an all-inclusive expert site on a wide variety of topic areas.

Ask an Expert

www.askanexpert.com

Ask an Expert connects you and your students with hundreds of real-world experts, from astronauts to zookeepers. These experts have volunteered to answer your questions for free!

The Educator's Reference Desk
www.eduref.org/
The Educator's Reference Desk brings you 2,000+ lesson plans, 3,000+ links to online education information, and 200+ question archive responses.

First-Year Teaching

Your first year of teaching is always the scariest. Here's where you can lean on the shoulders of the experts. They'll hold your hand and give you all the support you need to make that all-important first year so successful.

Education World
www.education-world.com/a_curr/curr152.shtml
Here you'll find lots of resources and articles to help you survive and thrive.

ProTeacher
www.proteacher.com/010007.shtml
This site gives lots of information and lots of advice for beginning elementary teachers.

TeachersFirst
www.teachersfirst.com/new-tch.shtml
Here's some "real-world" advice from teachers who have been there and who can offer some practical advice.

Teaching Heart
www.teachingheart.net/newteacher.html
This site holds a wealth of resources and good suggestions for any first-year teacher.

What to Expect Your First Year of Teaching
www.ed.gov/pubs/FirstYear/index.html
This site has loads of archived documents to help you in your all-important first year.

Standards

Education in general, and each subject area specifically, has standards that are used to guide instruction and provide ways of assessing the quality of teaching. You need to know about these standards—no matter what grade or subject you teach. Here's where you can get the necessary information.

American Council on the Teaching of Foreign Languages
www.actfl.org
Foreign language standards.

Education World
www.educationworld.com/standards/
Here you can gain access to all the national and state standards for every curricular area. Check it out!

International Reading Association
www.reading.org
Reading standards.

International Technology Education Association
www.iteawww.org
Technology standards.

National Council for the Social Studies
www.ncss.org
Social studies standards.

National Council of Teachers of English
www.ncte.org
English standards.

National Council of Teachers of Mathematics
www.nctm.org
Math standards.

National Science Teachers Association
www.nsta.org
Science standards

State Standards.com
www.statestandards.com
State-by-state educational standards paired with lesson plans.

Classroom Management

It's the one question on the mind of every teacher: *How can I effectively manage a classroom (without losing my sanity)?* Here are some resources from the experts that can provide the answers you seek.

Kim's Korner
www.kimskorner4teachertalk.com/classmanagement/menu.html
This site has many ready-to-use ideas on classroom management.

Pacific.net

www.pacificnet.net/~mandel/ClassroomManagement.html

Find lots of great ideas and easy-to-read articles on classroom management here.

Pro Teacher

www.proteacher.com/

This site has a wealth of information, articles, and tips, especially for elementary teachers.

The Teacher's Guide

www.theteachersguide.com/ClassManagement.htm

This site has some resources on classroom management you'll want to check out.

Teacher Vision

www.teachervision.fen.com/

Check out this site for lots of ideas on classroom management as well as loads of resources for the busy teacher.

Connecting With Teachers

If you would like to communicate with teachers from around the world, check out the following site. Here you will be able to ask questions, pursue topics in depth, and get the latest information from your fellow educators. Conferencing, chat rooms, and e-mail opportunities allow you to get immediate answers to your concerns, issues, or questions.

Electric Schoolhouse

www.eschoolhouse.com

This site provides you with several opportunities to keep in touch with other teachers.

Miscellaneous Sites

Here, you will find a potpourri of sites that offer an array of resources, data, insights, and advice for any teacher—novice to expert.

A to Z Teacher Stuff

www.atozteacherstuff.com/

This site has more than 1,000 pages of free and downloadable lesson plans, units, activities, and printable worksheets.

About School
www.aboutschool.com/
This site has lots of resources for both teachers and students in grades K through 12.

Discovery School
school.discovery.com/
This is a far-reaching collection of lesson plans and teaching tools for any classroom teacher.

Eisenhower National Clearinghouse for Mathematics and Science
www.enc.org
This is a great site for all kinds of resources to teach science and math.

GEM: The Gateway to Educational Materials
www.thegateway.org/index.html
This government site will provide you with access to all sorts of Internet-based educational materials.

Kathy Schrock's Guide for Educators
school.discovery.com/schrockguide/
This site is a categorized list of sites useful for enhancing curriculum and professional growth. It is updated often to include the best sites for teaching and learning.

Middle Web
www.middleweb.com/
If you're planning to teach middle school, this is the site for you.

Teachers Network
www.teachersnetwork.org/
This is a site created by teachers for teachers. It has information for both new and experienced teachers.

And One More Site ...

Anthony D. Fredericks
www.afredericks.com
Don't forget my site. You'll discover some of the books I've written and information about my school visits. Check it out!

Resources for Teachers and Books for Kids

Over the years, I have been honored to write a variety of teacher resource materials and children's books. Unfortunately, I can't list them all here. So I've selected the ones I thought you might find most interesting. I am writing new ones all the time, so you may want to check out my website for the latest additions (www.afredericks.com).

Note: An easy way to locate many (though not all) of these books is to type my name in the *author* space of Amazon.com's or BarnesandNoble.com's search feature.

Teacher Resource Books by Anthony D. Fredericks

Here is a collection of how-to books on a wide variety of curricular interests, topics, and subjects. Check them out at your nearest bookstore, online store, or each publisher's website.

For Teachers of Students in Preschool Through Grade 2

The Complete Phonemic Awareness Handbook: More Than 300 Playful Activities for Early Reading Success (Harcourt Achieve, 2001). This book has more than 300 playful activities that help students focus on the sounds of language and their ability to manipulate that language.

Guided Reading in Grades K–2: Reading Strategies, Activities and Lesson Plans for Reading Success (Harcourt Achieve, 2003). This easy-to-use guide focuses on developing a classroom that supports, encourages, and motivates beginning readers to become successful in all their literary encounters.

Parent Letters for Early Learning (co-authored with Mary Brigham; Good Year Books, 1987). This time-saving resource offers more than 200 activities and projects that facilitate the academic and social development of preschoolers.

Teaching Comprehension in PreK–K (Harcourt Achieve, 2006). Specifically designed for teachers in preschool and kindergarten, this all-inclusive guide helps students achieve the basics of reading success through an easy-to-use series of literacy activities.

Teaching Comprehension in Grades 1 and 2 (Harcourt Achieve, 2006). Fostering good comprehension development is the focus of this book. First- and second-grade teachers will discover a plethora of practical guidelines and dynamic strategies that assure reading success for all students.

For Teachers of Students in Grades 1 Through 4

Tadpole Tales and Other Totally Terrific Treats for Readers Theatre (Teacher Ideas Press, 1997). This book is a collection of more than 25 readers theatre scripts that will motivate students and fill up any classroom with laughter and learning. Look for "Goldilocks and the Three Hamsters."

For Teachers of Students in Grades 1 Through 6

The Complete Guide to Thematic Units: Creating the Integrated Curriculum, Second Edition (co-authored with Anita Meinbach and Liz Rothlein; Christopher-Gordon Publishers, 2000). With 20 complete and thorough thematic units in science, social studies, language arts, and math, this resource provides busy classroom teachers with multidimensional units that will energize and motivate students in a wide range of learning opportunities.

The Integrated Curriculum: Books for Reluctant Readers, Grades 2–5, Second Edition (Teacher Ideas Press, 1998). This book offers engaging activities and exciting projects that stimulate reluctant readers into becoming eager learners in every dimension of the elementary curriculum.

Letters to Parents in Reading (co-authored with Elaine LeBlanc; Good Year Books, 1998). This guidebook provides more than 40 ready-to-duplicate letters to send home to parents weekly, with more than 200 easy-to-do reading activities especially created for family involvement.

MORE Social Studies Through Children's Literature: An Integrated Approach (Teacher Ideas Press, 2000). This book offers hundreds of activities designed to stimulate and engage students in positive learning adventures throughout the social studies curriculum. More than 30 complete units are included.

Science Adventures Through Children's Literature: A Thematic Approach (Teacher Ideas Press, 1998). Focusing on new national science standards, this activity-centered resource features the best in children's literature along with stimulating "hands-on, minds-on" activities, experiments, and projects.

For Teachers of Students in Grades 3 Through 6

Frantic Frogs and Other Frankly Fractured Folktales for Reader's Theatre (Teacher Ideas Press, 1993). This collection of more than 20 readers theatre scripts is guaranteed to bring snickers, chuckles, and belly laughs into the classroom and get everyone involved. Watch out for "Don't Kiss Sleeping Beauty, She's Got Really Bad Breath."

From Butterflies to Thunderbolts: Discovering Science with Books Kids Love (Fulcrum Publishing, 1997). Using award-winning children's literature, this teacher resource provides a world of discoveries for students in all the sciences—life, physical, earth, and space science.

The Gifted Reader Handbook (Good Year Books, 1988). This resource book is packed with reproducible sheets, independent projects, extended activities, and literature energizers that focus on five critical thinking skills for all gifted learners.

Guided Reading in Grades 3–6: 300+ Guided Reading Strategies, Activities and Lesson Plans for Reading Success (Harcourt Achieve, 2001). This classroom resource focuses on creating an invitational classroom in which students are empowered to become active participants in the reading process.

Investigating Natural Disasters Through Children's Literature (Teacher Ideas Press, 2001). Using high-quality children's literature as a springboard, this guide offers a participatory approach to the study of natural disasters, making even complex science concepts understandable to young readers.

Letters to Parents in Science (Good Year Books, 1993). This resource guide offers classroom teachers dozens of reproducible letters, calendars, and newsletters with fun-to-do activities that help develop students' science literacy and appreciation.

Silly Salamanders and Other Slightly Stupid Stuff for Readers Theatre (Teacher Ideas Press, 2000). Nurture students' language arts skills and the power of the imagination with more than two dozen reproducible scripts based on fractured fairy tales and twisted legends. Look for "Beauty and This Incredibly Ugly Guy."

For Teachers of Students in Grades 4 Through 8

Science Fair Handbook: The Complete Guide for Teachers and Parents (co-authored with Isaac Asimov; Good Year Books, 2005). Organization is the key to success when it comes to planning a science fair, and this book is packed with practical ideas, creative resources, judging guidelines, a planning guide, timetables, and hundreds of suggestions for student projects.

Geography Brainstretchers (Good Year Books, 1999). Filled with more than 70 critical-thinking activities, this resource will enable students to apply their problem-solving abilities to a wide variety of interesting problems in U.S. and world geography and map and globe skills.

Readers Theatre for American History (Teacher Ideas Press, 2001). Arranged chronologically, these 24 readers theatre scripts put students in the roles of selected historical figures, giving them a "you are there" perspective into American history.

Science Brainstretchers: Creative Problem Solving Activities in Science (Good Year Books, 1991). This book will foster critical-thinking and problem-solving skills with 70 challenging exercises for determining relationships, making inferences, and drawing conclusions.

Science Challenge (Good Year Books, 1998). More than 200 daily science investigations provide classroom teachers with a perfect reinforcement for any science program. These science activities challenge students to use higher-level thinking skills every day.

Science Fiction Readers Theatre (Teacher Ideas Press, 2002). This book has more than 20 scripts that will put students in the roles of explorers, discoverers, scientists—and, yes, a few aliens, too.

The Whole Earth Geography Book (Good Year Books, 1990). This book is a handy guide for any teacher, providing more than 200 reinforcement activities in all areas of geographic knowledge. Students are actively involved in a wide range of stimulating and creative projects.

For All Teachers (Grades Preschool Through 12)

Redefining the Three R's: Relax, Refocus, Recharge (Harcourt Achieve, 2003). This book helps teachers reduce stress and become more productive. It includes more than 6 dozen 2-page reflective essays on personal growth, relationship growth, professional growth, as well as opportunities for reflection and renewal.

Children's Books by Anthony D. Fredericks

This list is a collection of some of the children's books I have written over the years. Many are nonfiction books focusing on nature, environmental themes, and animals. Most are available in both hardback and paperback. Check them out at your local bookstore or online store. Watch for new ones, too!

For Children in Preschool Through Grade 2

Slugs (Lerner, 1999). Cited by the Children's Book Council and the National Science Teachers Association as one of the best science books in 2000, this book offers young readers all they ever wanted to know about these amazing creatures.

Zebras (Lerner, 2000). Colorful photographs and an easy-to-read text will supply young explorers with everything they need to know about these delightful animals.

For Children in Grades 1 Through 4

Around One Cactus: Owls, Bats and Leaping Rats (Dawn Publications, 2003). The saguaro cactus is a haven for a whole community of creatures—some cute, some creepy, all of them fascinating! The International Reading Association honored this book with the 2004 Teacher's Choice Award.

In One Tidepool: Crabs, Snails and Salty Tails (Dawn Publications, 2002). Life in a tide pool is delightfully and rhythmically presented in this engaging and captivating book that will inform and delight any reader.

Near One Cattail: Turtles, Logs and Leaping Frogs (Dawn Publications, 2005). A wetlands environment is never dull, always exciting. Young readers journey with a young girl as she explores this magical ecosystem. Hey, look at that frog!

Under One Rock: Slugs, Bugs and Other Ughs (Dawn Publications, 2001). This multiple award-winning rhyming story of underground critters will stimulate any reader to discover an unbelievable world of creepy, crawly things.

For Children in Grades 3 Through 6

Amazing Animals (co-authored with Sneed Collard; NorthWord, 2000). This amazing book profiles more than 60 different animals, lots of fantastic creatures and incredible critters.

Animal Sharpshooters (Watts, 1999). In this book, readers learn about animals that launch parts of their bodies or materials at other creatures. You won't believe the photos!

Bloodsucking Creatures (Watts, 2002). This book provides youngsters with an inside look into leeches, fleas, vampire bats, lampreys, and other creatures that live on a diet of blood. Yum yum!

Cannibal Animals: Animals That Eat Their Own Kind (Watts, 1999). This book shows how and why praying mantises, black widow spiders, lions, sharks, and even gerbils kill and eat their own kind. Gross!

Fearsome Fangs (Watts, 2002). Rattlesnakes, viper fish, piranhas, tiny shrews, and all sorts of fanged creatures slip and slide through the pages of this book. Watch out!

Moose (NorthWord, 2000). They're big, they're ugly, but they're never dull! Kids will discover all sorts of incredible information about these critters in the pages of this fascinating book.

No Sweat Science: Nature Experiments (Sterling, 2005). With more than 100 activities, experiments, and projects, this book will help youngsters learn about and enjoy the world in which they live.

Surprising Swimmers (NorthWord, 2000). Birds that "fly" underwater, snakes that live in the ocean, and fish with "wings" can all be found in the pages of this book.

Wild Animals (NorthWord, 2000). Readers will explore the fascinating world of pandas, cheetahs, elephants, and koalas in this photo-filled safari.

For Children in Grades 4 Through 8

Exploring the Oceans: Science Activities for Kids (Fulcrum Publishing, 1998). More than five dozen ocean-related activities, experiments, and projects provide young explorers with a host of learning opportunities in this award-winning book.

Exploring the Rainforest: Science Activities for Kids (Fulcrum Publishing, 1996). Young adventurers will be able to peek and poke through the various layers of the rainforest to discover much about this endangered ecosystem.

Exploring the Universe: Science Activities for Kids (Fulcrum Publishing, 2000). Stars, planets, and other celestial bodies fill the pages of this book and the minds of young scientists as they learn about the mysteries of the universe.

Tsunami Man: Learning About Killer Waves with Walter Dudley (University of Hawaii Press, 2002). Readers will be thrilled and awed by one of nature's most incredible natural disasters in this book of wonderful stories and fascinating facts!

Teacher Certification Tests: The Praxis Series

The Praxis Series is a set of exams designed to assess the content knowledge and academic skills of students who are entering or completing a teacher preparation program at a college or university. Most state education agencies also use this series as part of their teacher licensing and certification process. These assessments, administered by the Educational Testing Service (ETS), assess knowledge and skills at two levels of proficiency.

Praxis I: Academic Skills Assessments

This series of tests (often referred to as the Pre-Professional Skills Tests or PPST) measures your basic proficiencies in reading, mathematics, and writing. Many colleges and universities use the scores on these three tests as qualifiers for initial entrance into a teacher training program. The PPST is available in two versions: the Paper-Based Academic Skills Assessments and the Computerized PPST. Your state will determine which of the two versions (or either one) you may take. The qualifying or passing scores differ from state to state, too.

The Paper-Based Academic Skills Assessments

Test 1: Reading. This is a 60-minute test. You will be asked to read several 100- to 200-word passages and answer 40 multiple-choice questions based on those passages. The questions will be of two types: Literal Comprehension (vocabulary, main idea, details, organization) and Critical and Inferential Comprehension (generalizations, evaluation).

Test 2: Mathematics. This is a 60-minute test that has 40 multiple-choice questions. The questions are divided into five categories: Conceptual Knowledge (numbers, operations), Procedural Knowledge (estimation, probability, ratio, computation), Quantitative Information (graphs, data patterns, charts, tables), Measurement and Geometry (metric system, area, volume, shapes), and Mathematical Reasoning (logic, generalizations).

Test 3: Writing. This is a 60-minute test that is divided into two 30-minute sections. The first section consists of 38 multiple-choice questions. These questions are further divided into two topic areas: Usage (grammar, word choice, punctuation, capitalization) and Sentence Correction (sentence rephrasing, grammar errors). The second section is a single essay question on a specific topic.

The Computerized PPST

Test 1: Reading. This is a 75-minute test that includes 46 computer-generated multiple-choice questions. The questions are based on 200- to 400-word passages from a variety of subject areas (social studies, science, humanities, etc.). The questions are of two types: Comprehension (main idea, details, organization) and Analysis and Application (words in context, inferences, facts/opinions, arguments).

Test 2: Mathematics. This, too, is a 75-minute test that has 46 computer-generated multiple-choice questions. As in the paper test, the questions are divided among five separate areas: Number Sense and Operation (operations, problem-solving, number order), Mathematical Relationships (equations, probability, ratios, percents), Data Interpretation (relationships, charts, graphs, tables), Geometry and Measurement (volume, length, perimeter, systems of measurement), and Reasoning (drawing conclusions, logic).

Test 3: Writing. This 68-minute test is divided into 2 sections. The first is a 38-minute computer-generated series of 44 multiple-choice questions. These questions focus on structure, word choice, punctuation, and capitalization. The second portion of the test is a 30-minute single-essay exam. The essay is designed to determine your ability to state a position, formulate a thesis, organize ideas, vary sentence structure, and write effectively. You will type your essay into the computer.

Praxis II: Subject Assessments

This series of exams is designed to measure your content knowledge of the subjects you will teach. You will typically take these tests near the end of your teacher preparation program—often just prior to or during your student-teaching experience.

Principles of Learning and Teaching (PLT)

These tests are used to assess the beginning teacher's knowledge of pedagogy (teaching standards). Not every state requires these tests. These assessments are divided into four sets of grade levels: Early Childhood, Grades K–6, Grades 5–9, and Grades 7–12. You will take one of the four tests according to your area of certification. Each test includes four case histories, each followed by a series of three short-answer questions. You will be asked to analyze each case history and provide recommendations, teaching strategies, or interpretations. In addition, there are 24 multiple-choice questions that are also related to the case studies. These questions assess your knowledge of ...

- ◆ Student development and the learning process.
- ◆ Students as diverse learners.
- ◆ Student motivation and the learning environment.
- ◆ Instructional strategies.
- ◆ Planning instruction.
- ◆ Assessment strategies.
- ◆ Verbal and nonverbal communication technique.
- ◆ Cultural and gender differences on classroom communications.
- ◆ Types of questions that can stimulate classroom discussions.
- ◆ Reflective practices.
- ◆ Schools and communities.

Multiple Subject Assessment for Teachers (MSAT)

This series of tests (not required by every state) is designed to assess the knowledge and critical-thinking skills of prospective elementary school teachers. This test is offered in two sections.

The Content Knowledge Test is a 2-hour test that consists of 120 multiple-choice questions. This portion of the exam is comprised of the following subject areas: literature and language studies, mathematics, visual and performing arts, physical education, human development, history/social science, and science.

The Content Area Exercises is a 3-hour exam that consists of 18 short-essay questions. This text includes the following subject areas: literature and language studies, mathematics, visual and performing arts, physical education, human development, history/social science, and science.

Subject Assessments/Specialty Area Tests

These assessments are designed to measure your general and subject-specific teaching skills and knowledge. Typically, you will take these tests near the end of your teacher preparation program. The number of tests and the content of those tests are determined by the specific area of certification you are seeking (it is different for each level and each area of certification). Most tests range from 1 to 2 hours in length. The tests usually consist of a series of 75 to 150 multiple-choice questions as well as a number of short-answer questions based on case histories or individual reading passages.

The Specialty Area Tests and Subject Assessments include a variety of exams in each of the following subject areas:

- Arts
- Biology and General Science
- Business and Technology
- Education
- Education of Students with Disabilities
- English, Reading, and Communication
- Guidance, Administration, and School Services
- Languages
- Mathematics
- Physical Science
- Social Sciences

It is important to note that each state has its own individual requirements regarding the Specialty Area Tests you must take (and pass) for certification. For example, to be certified as an elementary teacher, you must achieve passing scores (which may change from year to year) on the following tests:

Colorado

10014—Elementary Education: Content Knowledge

Hawaii

10011—Elementary Education: Curriculum, Instruction, and Assessment

20012—Elementary Education: Content Area Exercises

Pennsylvania

30511—Fundamental Subjects: Content Knowledge

10011—Elementary Education: Curriculum, Instruction, and Assessment

South Carolina

30522—Principles of Learning and Teaching: Grades K–6

10011—Elementary Education: Curriculum, Instruction, and Assessment

20012—Elementary Education: Content Area Exercises

You can obtain information about all the required tests for your state as well as registration procedures by contacting the Educational Testing Service (ETS). A Registration Bulletin is available, or you can get information from the ETS website. You can register for all Praxis tests and find out individual state requirements (and passing scores for all tests) on the website. You can also find test center dates and locations, free practice materials, and answers to frequently asked questions on the web at www.ets.org/praxis.

Please note that every state has different requirements and the requirements are changing all the time. What you read here may have changed by the time you are ready for the Praxis tests. It's very important for you to check the ETS website on a regular basis so you can stay up to date on the latest requirements for the state(s) in which you wish to be certified.

For more information, contact The Praxis Series, Educational Testing Service, PO Box 6051, Princeton, NJ 08541-6051, 1-800-772-9476

Get Ready!

Taking the Praxis exams may be frightening. They don't have to be. A wide variety of resources can help you prepare for these tests. By taking time to check these out, you can provide yourself with some important information and practice that can lead to success on any exam.

Test-Preparation Books

You can obtain test-preparation books for the Praxis exams. These books, which include sample tests and sample questions so you can practice taking the exams, are often available at many large bookstores or online book distributors (such as www.amazon.com and www.b&n.com). Check out these suggested books:

Levy, J.U., and N. Levy. *Preparation for the Praxis II Exam*. Lawrenceville, NJ: Thomson/Peterson's (issued each year).

Palmer, Michael. *Kaplan Praxis*. New York: Kaplan (issued each year).

Postman, Robert. *How to Prepare for the Praxis*. New York: Barron's, 2001.

Websites

Some commercial websites offer instruction and preparation for the Praxis exams. You may want to check out the following:

Praxis Prep Info.
www.praxisprepinfo.com
At this site, you can obtain tips and hints for successfully passing the Praxis tests.

Praxis Secrets
www.praxis-secrets.com
This company offers study guides prepared by individuals who achieved high scores on the Praxis exams.

Praxis-Success.com

www.praxis-success.com

Here you can obtain a downloadable study guide that will help you prepare for all types of Praxis exams.

Teaching Solutions

www.praxis-test-coaching.com

This company offers strategies, skills, and study methods designed to help you achieve high scores on the Praxis exams.

Index